The Growth
of Competence

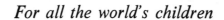

For all the world's children

The Growth
of Competence

Edited by

KEVIN CONNOLLY   and   JEROME BRUNER

Department of Psychology
University of Sheffield

Department of Experimental
Psychology
University of Oxford

Proceedings of a D.S.T. Study Group on
"The Growth of Competence" held jointly with
the Ciba Foundation, London, January 1972, being
the sixth study group in a programme on
"The Origins of Human Behaviour"

ACADEMIC
PRESS

1974

LONDON
NEW YORK

ACADEMIC PRESS INC. (LONDON) LTD.
24-28 Oval Road
London NW1 7DX

U.S. Edition published by
ACADEMIC PRESS INC.
111 Fifth Avenue,
New York, New York 10003

Library of Congress Catalog Card Number: 73-19003
ISBN: 0 12 185940 1

Printed by photolithography in Great Britain by
T. & A. Constable Ltd., Edinburgh

Contents

v

Language Acquisition and Development

Personality and Social Competence

Implications and Applications

Membership

M. S. AINSWORTH
Department of Psychology,
Johns Hopkins University,
Baltimore, Maryland, U.S.A.

J. BOWLBY
School of Family Psychiatry and
Community Mental Health,
Tavistock Centre, London, U.K.

W. BRONSON
Institute of Human Development,
University of California,
Berkeley, California, U.S.A.

J. S. BRUNER
(Chairman II)
Centre for Cognitive Studies,
Harvard University,
Cambridge, Massachusetts, U.S.A.
Now, Department of Experimental
Psychology,
Oxford University, U.K.

S. CAREY
Department of Psychology,
Harvard University,
Cambridge, Massachusetts, U.S.A.
Now, Department of Psychology,
Massachusetts Institute of
Technology

C. CAZDEN
Graduate School of Education,
Harvard University,
Cambridge, Massachusetts, U.S.A.

K. J. CONNOLLY
(Chairman I)
Department of Psychology,
University of Sheffield, U.K.

J. M. ELLIOTT
Department of Psychology,
University of Sheffield, U.K.

R. HESS
Department of Psychology,
Stanford University,
Palo Alto, California, U.S.A.

A. JOLLY
Lewes, Sussex, U.K.

W. McGREW
Gombe Stream Research Centre,
Kigoma, Tanzania

D. McNEILL
Department of Psychology,
University of Chicago,
Illinois, U.S.A.

M. P. M. RICHARDS
Department of Psychology,
University of Cambridge, U.K.

B. TIZARD
Institute of Education,
University of London, U.K.

D. WOOD
Center for Cognitive Studies,
Harvard University,
Cambridge, Massachusetts, U.S.A.
Now, Department of Psychology,
University of Nottingham, U.K.

Developmental Sciences Trust

The study group reported in this volume was organized under the auspices of the Developmental Sciences Trust in collaboration with the Ciba Foundation, which kindly accommodated the group, and the Carnegie Corporation, which made available a grant to cover the travel expenses of members.

The purpose of the Trust is to promote the growth of knowledge about the development of human behaviour and the factors that influence it. More specifically, the Trust aims, first, to stimulate and co-ordinate research in directions where it is most needed and to foster among scientists and teachers in these fields a developmental and multi-disciplinary perspective on human nature; second, to encourage the application of knowledge from the developmental sciences by those, in all sectors of society, engaged in coping with or preventing human problems.

Preface

In January 1972 a group of fifteen scientists, for the most part psychologists, met for five days at the Ciba Foundation in London to discuss the growth of competence in infancy and childhood. The concept of competence is less a scientific notion than it is a social and educational one, the brief which we gave ourselves was thus a wide one. What is competence and how do we use the notion? What of an evolutionary perspective on human growth, and what are the principal dimensions of competence? How does a child meet the demands of his environment, and how is he habilitated into a social world? How does the child acquire skills and make his way in our complex science-based technological society? Are certain skills more fundamental than others, and what common features do they share? What of educational and social implications, how shall a child be educated for life in a society which is undergoing massive and exceedingly rapid cultural change? These were some of the questions which concerned us though we were able only to touch upon some of them.

By far the greater proportion of our time was devoted to wide and free ranging discussions along our broad theme. Eight papers were prepared in advance of the meeting and these formed a scaffold for discussion but certainly not a constraint. From these discussions emerged a number of issues some of which were general in character whilst others were specific to the questions raised by the eight prepared papers. It was our original intention to produce for publication an edited version of the discussions. However, having examined transcripts we were doubtful of the utility of the discussions for a wider audience for whom they might well seem rather *cold* and perhaps disembodied. We decided therefore to encourage authors to modify the contributions as they saw fit in the light of the comments which were made and further to "commission" additional contributions. Almost all the original papers were modified, some quite extensively, and a further seven papers were written after the study group for inclusion in the volume. This accounts in large measure for the length of the period intervening between the meeting and the volume being submitted to our publishers.

This book is but a beginning and paradoxically a measure of its success will be how rapidly it is superseded by other books addressed to the same broad area. We believe that the growth and nurturance of the young to be of the utmost importance. Important that is; morally, socially, economically and scientifically. A child's wellbeing and wholeness as a person is of deep concern not only to parents but to each and every member of society. One service which historians perform for us is that of identifying the concerns of a people at a given point in time. A preoccupation of our age is a concern for social justice. The concern for others is born of a noble motive, compassion. Compassion, and its bedfellow passion, are valuable and desirable but in themselves they are not sufficient. The underlying problems demand all of our intellectual capacity in the search for solutions, they demand the sustained and serious attention of the biological and social sciences. We must aim to understand not only the child and his biological growth but also the effects of his social milieu on his psychological development.

All of the previous meetings under the aegis of the Developmental Sciences Trust have been interdisciplinary in character and the report of the Study Group on the growth of competence continues this custom. Our discussions ranged from primate evolution through the education of the young to the rights of women. As we stated above competence is not a clear scientific concept but rather a social and educational ideal. It follows therefore that a full appreciation of its logical and scientific "geography" demands that it be examined from the perspective of many different specialists each with their own conceptual and empirical tools. Perhaps more so than many themes this demands a broad trans-disciplinary examination. This book is addressed to a broad set of problems and it is our hope that in due course our concern will go from the *analysis* of social and biological scientists to the *synthesis* of the educationalist and the policy maker. Ultimately we believe our work should play a major part in shaping policy but for this to be effective our views must be based upon and firmly rooted in a detailed understanding which stems from a rigorous scientific analysis.

We are grateful for help and support to many people. The meeting itself was made possible by the generosity of the Ciba Foundation in London, who acted as our hosts, and the Carnegie Corporation in New York, a grant from which made it possible to assemble the group in London. Our particular thanks are due therefore to Dr. Gordon Wolstenholme and his staff at the Ciba Foundation, especially Dr. Ruth Porter and Miss Meave O'Connor, and to Mrs. Barbara Finberg of the Carnegie Corporation.

The organization of the meeting and the discussions owes much to Dr. Ann Harrison who unobtrusively and skilfully sorted out a large amount of rather messy paper. Colette Connolly helped greatly in sub-editing the papers and we are especially grateful for her attention to detail. Mrs. Audrey Rixham has typed and retyped quantities of complex material. Finally, we are grateful to Professor Brian Foss and the Trustees of the Developmental Sciences Trust for their support and encouragement.

May 1973   KEVIN CONNOLLY
                                              The Department of Psychology
                                                 University of Sheffield

                                                      JEROME BRUNER
                                    Department of Experimental Psychology
                                                 University of Oxford

Introduction

Competence: its Nature and Nurture

KEVIN CONNOLLY

University of Sheffield

JEROME BRUNER

University of Oxford

OUR TOPIC, COMPETENCE, is one that has many features. But our object is not only to examine the nature of competence, but also to explore how it is that one can cultivate competence in the young. We have much before us.

In one respect, when we talk about competence we are talking about intelligence in the broadest sense, operative intelligence *knowing how* rather than simply *knowing that*. For competence implies action, changing the environment as well as adapting to the environment. It seems in a sense to involve at least three things. First, being able to select features from the total environment that provide the relevant information for elaborating a course of action. This activity goes by several names; forming a schema, constructing a programme, etc. Secondly, having planned a course of action, the next task is to initiate the sequence of movements, or activities, in order to achieve the objective we have set for ourselves. And finally, we must utilize what we have learned from our successes and failures in the formulation of new plans. It is apparent that all three aspects of the problem are concerned with development, but it is the last of them that is most central to it.

Our concern is specifically with early competence and how its cultivation might effect the later functioning of the more mature organism. Traditionally the definition of childhood and the prescription of tasks suitable to it reflects the culture and the value it places upon the young. We need to know much more about the historical evolution of the concept of childhood. We need to know how varied educational enterprises (in or out of school) not only produce a child fitted for the society but also one capable of changing the society. Yet at the same time we must beware lest we become too pragmatic, too eager to "use" childhood well. Children need the opportunity to be themselves. For the years before maturity are not simply a training ground: childhood has, we believe, an intrinsic value for the individual. In the words of the Plowden Committee report (Central Advisory Council for Education, 1967), "Children need to be themselves, to live with other children and with grown-ups, to learn from their environment, to enjoy the present, to get ready for the future, to create and to love, to learn to face adversity ..." (para. 507, p. 188). The kind of development we are talking about cannot be spelled out in terms of monumental milestones, barriers over which children must climb in order to achieve adult status, whether they be moral, intellectual, or temperamental milestones.

In approaching our task it is plain that we shall have to go beyond description and analysis, to treat political issues and sensitive values. The problem before us has yet to be concisely formulated and in some ways we can well begin on a paradoxical note that "our problem is to find our problem". It will surely be as much a problem of how to intervene as it will be a problem of how to understand, for it is clear that it is not only the disadvantaged who are in need of help, but children at all levels in society.

Plainly, in any given society, there are a set of skills which are essential for coping with the existing realities. This is perhaps nowhere more clear than in the technological societies of the second half of this century. Some of the skills to which we refer are highly specific, and some are far more general, if equally essential. The general ones are the more interesting. One cannot manage a technology without some general sense of the forms of order that characterize nature, without ways of thought which are at least compatible with science and mathematics. "Middle-class education" with its emphasis on abstractness may not be universally admired in the developed world, yet it is quite apparent that it is a form of education created in response to demands for the management of a technological system. We would not wish to argue that technological adequacy is the major criteria by which the effectiveness of a modern educational system should be judged. In any case, the general skills of middle-class "technological" education include a capacity for combining information in a fashion that permits one to use it flexibly, to go beyond the information given, to draw inferences about things yet to be encountered, to connect and to probe for connections. This type of skill depends upon being able to develop constituent sub-routines which can then be recombined to fulfil the requirements of specific tasks. It is almost as with the learning of language where one learns an extensive lexicon, masters grammar, and is soon launched on a career as a generator of novel and useful utterances. We in modern technological settings took for granted that children learn this way. We know better now. Research over the last several years has taught us much. The slum, the ghetto, the sub-cultures of defeat do not equip their children with the easy abstract skills of the doctor's, lawyer's, or professor's children. We shall hear more of this matter in later discussion.

But if one can speak of non-specific intellectual skills, one should equally well note the importance of non-specific *emotional* skills: self-confidence is a good example of one such. One does not usually characterize it as a *skill* but rather as a trait or an attitude toward oneself. Yet it is a skill as well, for it involves learning that one can do things with a certain likelihood of success and moreover, with a fair likelihood of being able to run the course again should one fail. Work on conditioned helplessness in human beings and in animals alike indicated that when an organism comes to believe that his repertoire of reactions are no longer adequate to meet the challenges and tasks imposed upon him, he enters a passive phase in which he no longer tries, but simply learns to take the consequences of failure. We know from the work of Walter Mischel (1961) that the child who lacks confidence in his ability to cope begins to take rewards in the short run, and will no longer risk bigger rewards in the further future. Future orientation, then, is a skill that needs cultivating.

General skills, cognitive and emotional, appear to depend on what has properly been called a "hidden curriculum" in the home. But the issue is not to be resolved only by reference to the home and its atmosphere. We must go beyond the home of the individual child to the economic realities in which the child and his family find themselves. If it is not true that there are cultures of poverty, at least it can be said that there are sub-cultures of despair in which groups appear to have given up trying, appear to have given up the possibility that they may be able to achieve power over their own destiny. Unemployment, job discrimination, and evils of this order can, over generations, produce an official ideology of despair in a group. It was a study by Robert Hess and Virginia Shipman, published almost a decade ago (1965), that made us most aware of the reverberation of such a sense of defeat upon the mental development of the child. Despair transmits subtly to the young, and it was in the ingenious work of Hess and Shipman that we first began to recognize that parents could in fact instruct in such a fashion as to reduce effective functioning. We know also from the work of Schoggen (1967) that there often exists in homes with a long history of poverty an atmosphere that discourages the interrogative use of mind, where the family despairing about the future, gives up asking.

In such matters, individual development reflects the failure of a society to assure opportunity for the less favoured. Should one prepare a child to accept such a society? May it not be that the best intervention is to breed young revolutionaries, if only we knew how? In the United States, the privileged young are fond of criticizing middle-class education as producing the typical "hang-up of our times"—acceptance of a competitive and dehumanizing society that values technology above the individual and the community. But it is one thing to criticize such an alleged "hang-up" when one is free to reject it. For the poor, the hang-up is powerlessness and a feeling that there is no opportunity.

How indeed does one introduce institutions that can give better support to the growth of the young? A few generations ago this would have seemed a grotesque question. Yet today we must obviously develop institutions to support the family in raising the young. In the United States there are between five and six million women with children under the age of six who are in the labour force (U.S. Department of Labor, 1969). The lower the family income, the greater the likelihood that the mother of a young child will need to hold a job. What then may we say about the role of the mother in the raising of the very young? In the United States, the most advanced industrial nation in the world, the family is in deep trouble, not only because there is no ready facility whereby the mother can receive aid in raising her children, or in making it possible for her to be with her children herself. Just as a case in point, fifty years ago something of the order of slightly more than half of the families in the Commonwealth of Massachusetts had an older relative either living in the home or living within a mile. The figure today in Massachusetts is fewer than one in twenty families. In Britain Young and Willmott (1957) have contrasted the older style kinship patterns still to be found in Bethnal Green (where two-thirds of the married population have their parents living in the district) with those of the newer suburbs around London where in sharp contrast to Bethnal Green under one-twentieth of all parents and siblings living close enough for frequent visiting. We have created the isolated nuclear family with few forms of supplemental care accessible, neither kinsman nor service. The baby-sitting teenager and the commercial child minder are our principal inventions. Comprehensive child care assistance is needed, not in place of the family but as an aid to the family, and unfortunately, it is slow in making its appearance. It may well be that one of the most powerful ways in which we shall equip the young in the future, for taking their place in the larger society, is precisely to make supplemental care available so that the loneliness of the nuclear family in the urban setting, can once and for all be penetrated by the forces of a living community.

These are some of the problems that we shall have to face in our discussions over the days ahead. There are others relating to mass media, health care, and education. They are problems not only of individual psychology, but also of society and its values. We have a full agenda.

REFERENCES

CENTRAL ADVISORY COUNCIL FOR EDUCATION. 1967. *Children and their primary schools*, vol. 1. H.M.S.O., London.

HESS, R. D. and SHIPMAN, V. 1965. Early experience and the socialization of cognitive modes in children. *Child Dev.*, **36**, 869–886.

LABOR, U.S. DEPARTMENT OF. 1969. *Facts about day care*. Wage and Labor Standards Administration, Womens Bureau, Washington, D.C.

MISCHEL, W. 1961. Father-absence and delay of gratification: Cross cultural comparisons. *J. Abnorm. Soc. Psychol.*, **62**, 116–124.

SCHOGGEN, M. F. 1967. The imprint of low-income homes on young children. In Susan Gray and J. O. Miller (Eds), *Research, change, and social responsibility: An illustrative model from early education. DARCEE Papers and Reports* 2, No. 3. George Peabody College for Teachers, Nashville, Tenn.

YOUNG, M. and WILLMOTT, P. 1957. *Family and kinship in East London*. Routledge and Kegan Paul, London.

An Evolutionary Perspective

Nature and Uses of Immaturity[1]

JEROME S. BRUNER

To UNDERSTAND the nature of any species fully, we need to know more than the ways of its adults. We need to know how its young are brought from initial, infantile inadequacy to mature, species-typical functioning. Variation in the uses of immaturity tells much about how adaptation to habitat is accomplished, as well as what is likely to happen given a change in habitat. The nature and uses of immaturity are themselves subject to evolution, and their variations are subject to natural selection, much as any morphological or behavioural variant would be.

One of the major speculations about primate evolution is that it is based on the progressive selection of a distinctive pattern of immaturity. It is this pattern of progressive selection that has made possible the more flexible adaptation of our species. Too often this pattern is over-explained by noting that human immaturity is less dominated by instinct and more governed by learning.

Because our ultimate concern is with the emergence of human adaptation, our first concern must be the most distinctive feature of that adaptation. This feature is man's trait, typical of his species, of "culture using", with all of the intricate set of implications that follow. Man adapts (within limits) by changing the environment, by developing not only amplifiers and transformers for his sense organs, muscles, and reckoning powers, as well as banks for his memory, but also by changing literally the properties of his habitat. Man, so the truism goes, lives increasingly in a man-made environment. This circumstance places special burdens on human immaturity. For one thing, adaptation to such variable conditions depends heavily on opportunities for learning, in order to achieve knowledge and skills that are not stored in the gene pool. But not all that must be mastered can be learned by direct

[1] This chapter was prepared for the Study Group on Early Competence and presented later to a broader audience at the XXth International Congress of Psychology in Tokyo. In connection with its presentation at Tokyo, it was published for distribution there as a separate in the August 1972 issue of the *Am. Psychol.*

encounter. Much must be "read out" of the culture pool, things learned and remembered over several generations: knowledge about values and history, skills as varied as an obligatory natural language or an optional mathematical one, as mute as using levers or as articulate as myth telling. Yet, though there is the gene pool, and though there exist direct experience and the culture as means for shaping immaturity, none of these directly prepare for the novelty that results when man alters his environment. That flexibility depends on something else.

Yet, it would be a mistake to leap to the conclusion that because human immaturity makes possible high flexibility in later adjustment, anything is possible for the species. Human traits were selected for their survival value over a four–five-million-year period, with a great acceleration of the selection process during the last half of that period. There were crucial, irreversible changes during that final man-making period —recession of formidable dentition, doubling of brain volume, creation of what Washburn and Howell (1960) have called a "technical-social way of life", involving tool and symbol use. Note, however, that *hominidization* consisted principally of adaptations to conditions in the Pleistocene. These pre-adaptations, shaped in response to earlier demands of the habitat, are part of man's evolutionary inheritance. This is not to say that close beneath the skin of man is a naked ape, that "civilization" is only a "veneer". The technical-social way of life is a deep feature of the species adaptation.

But we would err if we assumed *a priori* that man's inheritance places no constraint on his power to adapt. Some of the pre-adaptations can be shown to be presently maladaptive. Man's inordinate fondness for fats and sweets no longer serves his individual survival well. And human obsession with sexuality is plainly not fitted for survival of the species now, however well it might have served to populate the upper Pliocene and the Pleistocene. But note that the species responds typically to these challenges by technical innovation rather than by morphological or behavioural change. This is not to say that man is not capable of controlling or, better, transforming behaviour. Whatever its origin, the incest taboo is a phenomenally successful technique for the control of certain aspects of sexuality—although its beginning among the great apes (Van Lawick-Goodall, 1968) suggests that it may have a base that is rooted partly in the biology of propinquity, a puzzling issue. The technical innovation is contraception, which dissociates sexuality from reproduction. What we do not know, of course, is what kinds and what range of stresses are produced by successive rounds of such technical innovation. Dissociating sexuality and reproduction, for example, may produce changes in the structure of the family by redefining the sexual role of women, which in turn may alter the authority pattern affecting the child, etc. Continuous, even accelerating, change may be inherent in such adaptation. If this is so, then there is an enormous added pressure on man's uses of immaturity for instruction. We must prepare the young for unforseeable change—a task made the more difficult if severe constraints imposed by human pre-adaptations to earlier conditions of life have created rigidities.

EVOLUTION OF EDUCABILITY

LeGros Clark's (1963) *echelle des etres* of the primates runs from tree shrews through the prosimian lorisiformes, lemuriformes, and related forms, through the New World and Old World monkeys, through the hylobates such as the gibbon, through the great apes, through the early hominids like Australopithecus and *Homo habilis* and other small-brained predecessors, terminating in the modern form of *Homo sapiens* with his 1 300 cm³ brain. Closing the gap between great apes and modern man is, of course, a complex and uncertain undertaking, particularly where behaviour is concerned, for all that remains are paleontological and archaeological fragments, and little by way of a behaviour record. But there are inferences that can be made from these fragments, as well as from the evolution of primate behaviour up to the great apes. Enough is known to suggest hypotheses, though no conclusions. Such an *echelle des etres* is bound to be only a metaphor since contemporary species are only approximations to those that existed in the evolutionary tree. But it can tell us something about change in the primate order. We propose to use it where we can to make inferences, not so much about pre-adaptations to earlier conditions that characterize our species, but rather more to assess crucial changes that have been recurring in immaturity. My interest is in the evolution of educability.

But you will know by my credentials that I am not primarily a student of prehuman primates. I have brought the materials of primate evolution together to understand better the course of human infancy and childhood, its distinctiveness or species typicality. I propose to go back and forth, so to speak, between primate phylogeny and human ontogeny, not to establish any shallow parallel between the two, but in the hope that certain contrasts will help us see more clearly. If indeed the fish will be the last to discover water, perhaps we can help ourselves by looking at some other species.

Specifically, I should like to look at several issues whose resolution might be of particular help. The first of these has to do with the nature and evolution of social organization within a species and how this may affect the behaviour of the immature. The second has to do with the structure of skill and how the evolution of primate skill almost inevitably leads to tool using. We must then pause to consider the nature of tool using and its consequences. That matter in turn leads us directly to the roles of both play and imitation in the evolution of educability. Inevitably, we shall deal with that distinctly human trait, language: what it is and how its emergence drastically alters the manner in which we induct young into the species.

My emphasis throughout is principally on the evolution of intellect—problem solving, adaptation to habitat, and the like. But it will soon be apparent that, to use the jargon (Bloom, 1956), one cannot easily separate the cognitive from the conative and the affective. I have been told that the Chinese character for *thinking* combines the character for *head* and the character for *heart*. It is a pity it does not also include the character for *others* as well, for then it would be appropriate to what will concern us. At the end of this paper, I try to deal with the question of what can be done to better equip the young for coping.

Any species depends, as we know from the work of the last half century (e.g. Mayr, 1963), on the development of a system of mutuality—a set of mechanisms for sharing a habitat or territory, a system of signalling that is effective against predators, dominance relations that are effective without being pre-empting (Chance, 1967), a system of courtship with matching mating releasers (Tinbergen, 1953), etc. There is, at the lower end of the primate line, a considerable amount of rather fixed or linear structure about such mutuality. Behaviour repertoires are limited in prosimians and in monkeys, and the combinatorial richness in their behaviour is not great (see Jolly, 1966), though one can make a case for their goodness of fit to habitat conditions (as Hinde, 1971, recently has). Even where there is, within a given species, an increased variety in behaviour produced by enriched or more challenging environments—as in the contrast between urban and forest-dwelling rhesus monkeys (Singh, 1969) or among Japanese macaques tempted by new foods introduced in their terrain (Itani, 1958)—the difference is not toward variability or loosening of social structure, but toward the incorporation of new patterns into the species-typical social pattern. Action patterns that are altogether fixed prevail; and *play*, that special form of violating fixity, is limited in variety, early and short lived, and irreversibly gone by adulthood—a matter to which I shall return.

There are notably fixed limits for the young of these species; and as the animal grows from infant to juvenile to adult—transitions usually marked by conspicuous changes in appearance and coat colour—social induction into the group is effected rapidly, usually by the quick response of a young animal to the threat of attack by an older animal in the troop. The sharply defined oestrous receptivity of the adult female almost assures that the young animal will be rejected and made virtually self-sufficient within a year. It is this sharply defined receptivity that also creates a scarcity economy in sexual access and leads to such a close link between male dominance and sexual access—perhaps the most notable source of linear, tight social structure virtually throughout the monkeys and prosimians. The comfort-contact system of mother and infant, involving not only initial nursing but also hair holding and grasping by the young for protection in flight and for sheer comfort, is obviously of great importance in prosimians, New World, and Old World monkeys. But as Dolhinow and Bishop (1970) have remarked, we must be careful about exaggerating it. Harlow's (e.g. 1959) pioneering studies do show that a macaque made solely dependent on a terry-cloth and wire-mesh mother surrogate is more backward than one dependent on a real mother. Yet, for all that, twenty minutes of play daily with peers in a play cage obliterates the difference between the three groups—another of Harlow's (Harlow and Harlow, 1962) findings. Note by way of contrast that a three-year-old chimpanzee deprived of a mother modelling the skilled act of fishing for termites seems not to be able to master the act later, even if among peers who are succeeding.

LOOSENING THE PRIMATE BOND

Probably the first step toward loosening the initially tight primate bond is the development of what Chance (1967) has referred to as an "attentional structure" within the group. Rather than behaviour patterns leading to constant interaction and mutual release of agonistic patterns, there is instead a deployment of attention in which the dominant animal is watched, his behaviour is anticipated, and confrontation is avoided. One of the major things that induction into a tightly organized Old World monkey group means, then, is an enormous investment in attention to the requirements of the troop—mating, dominance, food foraging, etc. There is, so to speak, little attentional capacity left for anything else.

The great apes represent a crucial break away from this pattern toward a far more relaxed one, and as we shall see in a moment, the effect on the young is striking. All three of the great ape species are virtually free of predators. None of them defends a territory. None of them has a troop structure nearly as well defined and rigidly maintained as, say, the least rigid Old World species, if such as phrase makes sense. In the gorilla, the orang-utan, and the chimpanzee, male dominance does not preclude copulation between a subdominant male and a female in the presence of the dominant male. It is even difficult, in fact, in the case of chimpanzee and orang-utan to define a dominant male in the monkey sense (cf. e.g. Goodall, 1965; Reynolds, 1965; Schaller, 1964). Indeed the route to dominance may even involve a superior technological skill. Note the increased deference paid to a male in the Gombe Stream Reserve who had learned to produce an intimidating din by banging two discarded tin cans together (Van Lawick-Goodall, 1968). Thus, too, while oestrus marks the period of maximum receptivity in which the female initiates sexual activity, her availability to a male may in fact continue even into the first two months of pregnancy (Reynolds, 1965). Doubtless the achievements of a 600–700 cm^3 brain in great apes also contributes to the further evolution of cerebral control of sexual behaviour of which Beach (1965) has written. The spacing of infants is over three years apart, on the average, and the bond between mother and infant, particularly in the chimpanzee, remains active for as long as five years (Van Lawick-Goodall, 1968).

One concomitant of the change is the decline in fixed patterns of induction into the group. There is much less of what might be called training by threat from adults or actual punishment by adults of a juvenile who has violated a species-typical pattern. The prolonged infant–mother interaction includes now a much larger element of play between them often initiated by the mother and often used to divert an infant from a frustration-arousing situation.

What appears to be happening is that, with the loosening of fixed bonds, a system of reciprocal exchange emerges, the structure of which is at first difficult to describe. In any case, the system makes it possible for chimpanzee and gorilla groups to encounter groups of conspecifics in their range without fighting; indeed in the case of the more flexibly organized chimpanzees, such encounters may even include sexual relations between groups and an exchange of members (Reynolds, 1965; Van Lawick-Goodall, 1968). There can be little doubt that primate evolution is strongly and increasingly characterized by such reciprocal exchange. The trend probably predates the emergence of hominids. In a recent article, Trivers (1971) said,

> During the Pleistocene, and probably before, a hominid species would have met the preconditions for the evolution of reciprocal altruism: long life span, low dispersal rate; life in small, mutually dependent, stable, social groups (Lee and DeVore, 1968; Campbell, 1966); and a long period of parental care. It is very likely that dominance relations were of the relaxed, less linear form characteristic of the baboon (Hall and DeVore, 1965) (p. 45).

As Gouldner (1960) reminded us a decade ago and as new studies on remaining hunter-gatherers reassert (Lee and DeVore, 1968), there is no known human culture that is not marked by reciprocal help in times of danger and trouble, by food sharing, by communal nurturance for the young or disabled, and by the sharing of knowledge and implements for expressing skill. Levi-Strauss (1963) posited such exchanges as the human watershed and classified them into three types: one involving the exchange of symbols and myths and knowledge; another involving the exchange of affectional and affiliative bonds, including the exchange of kin women in marriage to outside groups for political alliances, with this rare resource preserved by an incest taboo; and finally an exchange system for goods and service. The pressures in such primate groups would surely select traits consonant with reciprocity, leading to self-domestication by the selection of those capable of "fitting in". The incessant aggressiveness of the linear pattern would wane gradually.

What accompanies these changes is a marked transformation in ways of managing immaturity. The maternal buffering and protection of the young not only lengthens materially but undergoes qualitative changes. Several of these have been mentioned: a much prolonged period dominated by play; increased participation in play by adults, especially, though not exclusively, by the mother; decline in the use of punishment and threat as modes of inducting the young into the pattern of species-typical interactions. The most important, I believe, is the appearance of a pattern involving an enormous amount of observation of adult behaviour by the young, with incorporation of what has been learned into a pattern of play (Dolhinow and Bishop, 1970; Hamburg, 1968; Hayes and Hayes, 1952; Köhler, 1926; Reynolds, 1965; Rumbaugh, 1970; Van Lawick-Goodall, 1968; Yerkes and Yerkes, 1929)[2]. Though psychologists are chary about using the term imitation because of the difficulty of defining it, virtually all primatologists comment on the enormous increase in imitation found in chimpanzees in contrast to Old World monkeys (where there is genuine doubt whether imitation in any commonsense meaning of the term occurs at all). After its first appearance at about seventeen months of age, this pattern of observing and imitating takes up much of the time of infants and young juveniles —watching social interaction, watching the care of the young, watching copulation, watching agonistic displays, watching instrumental or tool behaviour. Such observation requires free attention on the part of the

[2] It should be noted carefully that in certain crucial ways, both mountain and lowland gorilla are exceptions to what is described here. For some interesting speculations about the lack of curiosity and imitativeness in the gorilla as related to his undemanding habitat and food supply as well as to his lack of need for cooperative efforts, see Yerkes and Yerkes (1929), Rumbaugh (1970), and particularly Reynolds (1965).

young; and, indeed, the incorporation of observed behaviour in play occurs most usually during the more relaxed periods in the life of the group. It was Köhler (1926), in his classic *The mentality of apes*, who commented initially on the intelligent rather than the mechanical or slavish nature of imitative behaviour in anthropoids—how the sight of another animal solving a problem is used not to mimic but as a basis for guiding the observer's own problem solving or goal striving. He used the term "serious play" (p. 157), and the literature since the early 1920s bears him out (e.g. Dolhinow and Bishop, 1970; Hamburg, 1968). In a word, the chimpanzee adult serves not only as a buffer or protector or "shaper" for the young but as a model—though there is no indication of any intentional modelling or of behaviour that is specifically "demonstrational".

To summarize briefly, the emergence of a more flexible form of social bonding in primate groups seems to be accompanied by the emergence of a new capacity for learning by observation. Such learning indeed may be necessary if not sufficient for transmission of culture. But that gets ahead of the argument still to be made; for there is still an enormous gap to be accounted for between the behaviour of a grouping of great apes, however flexible, and the mode of structuring of a human society, no matter how simple it may be.

OBSERVATIONAL LEARNING

There are many facets to observational learning (I cautiously continue to avoid the term *imitation*). There is ample evidence that many mammals considerably less evolved than primates can benefit from exposure to another animal carrying out a task; for example, the classic study of cats by Herbert and Harsh (1944) demonstrates improvement in escape from a puzzle box by cats who have seen other animals escape—and the more so if the cats observed were still inexpert at the task. Whether they are learning the possibility of getting out of the box, the means for doing so (by displacing a bar), or whatever, observation helps. So too with *Macaca fuscata*, the Japanese macaque, where the young animals learn to eat what the mother eats by eating what she leaves (Itani, 1958; Kawamura, 1959); or the naive, cage-reared *patas* monkey transported to a habitat and released in a natural troop, who learns from the group by following it in search of food.

But this is quite different from the sort of "serious play" to which Köhler (1926) referred. Consider an example:

I would call the following behavior of a chimpanzee imitation of the "serious play" type. On the playground a man has painted a wooden pole in white color. After the work is done he goes away leaving behind a pot of white paint and a beautiful brush. I observe the only chimpanzee who is present, hiding my face behind my hands, as if I were not paying attention to him. The ape for a while gives much attention to me before approaching the brush and the paint because he has learned that misuse of our things may have serious consequences. But very soon, encouraged by my attitude, he takes the brush, puts it into the pot of color and paints a big stone which happens to be in the place, beautifully white. The whole time the ape behaved completely seriously. So did others when imitating the washing of laundry or the use of a borer (pp. 156–157).

I consider such behaviour to be dependent on two important prerequisites, both amenable to experimental analysis:

The first is the ability to differentiate or abstract oneself from a task, to turn around on one's own performance and, so to speak, see oneself, one's own performance as differentiated from another. This involves self-recognition in which one, in some way, is able to model one's *own* performance on some selected feature of another's performance. This phenomenon in linguistics is known as *deixis*: as in learning that when I say *I*, it is not the same as when you say *I*, or that *in front* of me is not the same as *in front* of you or *in front* of the car (cf. Miller and Johnson-Laird[3]). It is a deep problem in language learning, and though it seems cumbersome and abstract in a discussion of hominid evolution, it may be amenable to demonstration. Indeed, I believe that the excellent study by Gallup (1970) indicates that there is a large gap between such Old World monkeys as the stump-tailed macaque and the chimpanzee: the latter can recognize his mirror image and guide self-directed behaviour by it (e.g. inspecting by touch a spot on the forehead seen in the mirror); the former cannot. The macaque, as a matter of fact, seems able only to attack or threaten its mirror image or to ignore it. These findings are surely not proof of the emergence of deictic capacities in the ape, but they do suggest a crucial trend for guiding one's own behaviour by feedback other than, so to speak, from action proper. Learning by observation is one instance of that class.

The second prerequisite for observation learning is a form of skill I now examine: *construction of an action pattern by the appropriate sequencing of a set of constituent subroutines to match a model* (Lashley, 1951). Observing the development of skilled, visually directed manipulatory activity in human infants and children, one is struck repeatedly by the extent to which such activity grows from the mastery of specific acts, the gradual perfecting of these acts into what may be called a modular form, and the combining of these into higher order, longer

[3] G. Miller and P. Johnson-Laird. *Presuppositions of language*. In preparation.

range sequences. Flexible skilled action may almost be conceived of as the construction of a sequence of constituent acts to achieve an objective (usually a change in the environment) while taking into account local conditions. As the Russian neurophysiologist Bernstein (1967) has put it, one can almost conceive of an initial skilled act as a motoric hypothesis concerning how to change the environment along a desired parameter. The flexibility of skill consists not only of this constructive feature but also of the rich range of "paraphrases" that are possible: for a skilled operator, there are many different ways of skinning a cat; and the word paraphrase is not amiss, for there is in this sense something language-like about skill, the kind of substitution rules that permit the achievement of the same objective (meaning) by alternative means.

If one compares the manipulatory activity of a child (or of a young chimpanzee) and a prosimian, such as a loris, the most striking difference is precisely the extent to which manual activity of human and chimpanzee is constructed of components to meet the properties of the task. The wide range of combinations in the use of the component gestures that go into the making of the final prehension—relatively independent movement of fingers, of hand, of wrist, etc.—is striking. But as Bishop (1964) pointed out, prosimians use virtually the same grip for a variety of activities: taking hold of a branch, grooming, taking a piece of fruit, etc. My own informal observation on slow loris confirms this. The grip is adapted to the task by changing the orientation of the whole hand, by altering speed or force, etc. Napier (1962) has noted how the development of flexibility is facilitated morphologically by the evolutionary selection of phalangeal flexibility, and change in the hamate and trapezium with emergence of power and precision grips, but I part company with Napier in that it is *not* so much a change of manual morphology that separates baboon from ape from man, but the nature of the *programme* that controls the use of the hands.

Imitation as "serious play"—incorporating what is observed into behaviour that is not mere mimicry but is directed intelligently to an end —must of course depend on "matching to model", on constructing behaviour in the manner we have just examined, and must be concerned with the kind of deictic anchoring that permits one to distinguish and relate what is analogous in my behaviour and in that of another member of the species.

EFFECT OF TOOLS

We must consider now the question of tools and their use, and what effect this evolutionary step may have had on the management of immaturity. We might begin with its first emergence in chimpanzees, but before we do, it is worth considering initially a speculation by DeVore (1965) on the emergence of bipedalism and the freeing of hands. According to this speculation, and it can be nothing more, two contradictory selection pressures operated on the emerging protohominid. The first was for bipedal locomotion and easy standing, freeing the hands. The second was for a larger brain to provide the more flexible programming for the hands (as discussed above). Bipedalism, involving stronger impact on the pelvic girdle, led to selection of a smaller bony aperture of the birth canal to assure greater structural strength of the pelvis. If a bigger brained creature is to get through a smaller canal, there is required, of course, a smaller initial brain size and, therefore, greater initial immaturity (the human brain grows from approximately 335 to 1 300 cm^3 during development)[4]. To assure the larger brain, the argument goes, there had also to be a recession in such apelike features as a heavy prognathous jaw as a base for effective dentition. *En route*, there is a critical point where the basic adaptation of the hominid must change.

So we may begin with the fact that tool using at its first appearance in apes comes before that point: it is an optional and not an obligatory adaptation. Chimpanzee survival does not depend on the use of sticks for fishing termites or on the use of crushed leaves as drinking or grooming sponges. As Jane Lancaster (1968) put it in a closely reasoned article on tool use, there is "a major change from the kind of tool use that is incidental to the life of a chimpanzee to the kind that is absolutely essential for survival of the human individual" (p. 62). Yet, in spite of the absence of "obligatory pressures", chimpanzees use tools optionally in an extraordinary variety of ways: for eating, drinking, self-cleaning, agonistic displays, constructing sleeping platforms, etc. Nor is it some accident of morphology: "the hands of monkeys and apes are equally suited to picking up a stick and making poking or scratching movements with it but differences in the brain make these much more likely behaviour patterns for the chimpanzee" (p. 61).

I would like to make the rather unorthodox suggestion that in order for tool using to develop, it was essential to have a long period of optional, pressure-free opportunity for combinatorial activity. By its very nature, tool using (or the incorporation of objects into skilled activity) required a chance to achieve the kind of wide variation upon which selection could operate.

[4] For an excellent account of the changes that occur during this enlargement, making possible greater flexibility of connection and possibly better memory storage, see Altman (1967). Some of the same changes during this period of expansion also occur as a result of challenging environments (Bennet *et al.*, 1964), and in the course of phylogeny (Altman, 1967).

Dolhinow and Bishop (1970) made the point most directly. Commenting first that "many special skills and behaviours important in the life of the individual are developed and practised in playful activity long before they are used in adult life" (p. 142); they then note that play "occurs only in an atmosphere of familiarity, emotional reassurance, and lack of tension or danger" (p. 142). Schiller (1952) reported, "with no incentive the chimpanzee displayed a higher variety of handling objects than under the pressure of a lure which they attempted to obtain" (p. 186). He reported, actually, that attempting to direct play by reinforcing chimpanzees for play behaviour had the effect of inhibiting play.

FUNCTIONS OF PLAY

Play appears to serve several centrally important functions. First, it is a means of minimizing the consequences of one's actions and of learning, therefore, in a less risky situation. This is particularly true of social play, where, by adopting a play face or a "galumphing gait" (Millar, 1968) or some other form of metacommunication (Dolhinow and Bishop, 1970), the young animal signals his intent to play. Now, so to speak, he can test limits with relative impunity: "There are many rules of what can and cannot be done in a troop, and most of these are learned early in life, when the consequences of violating them are less severe than later on" (Dolhinow and Bishop, 1970, p. 148).

Second, play provides an excellent opportunity to try combinations of behaviour that would, under functional pressure, never be tried.

> The tendency to manipulate sticks, to lick the ends, to poke them into any available hole are responses that occur over and over again in captive chimpanzees. These responses are not necessarily organized into the efficient use of sticks to probe for objects, but they probably form the basis of complex motor patterns such as termiting (Lancaster, 1969, p. 61).

Or in Van Lawick-Goodall's (1968) account:

> With the fruit, Figan devised a game of his own: lying on his back, he spins a *Strychnos* ball round and round, balancing it on his hands and kicking gently with his feet, like a circus bear ... Toys like this are not always at hand, but then the youngsters seem just as content to play with stones, leaves, or twigs. They may throw them, rub them over their bodies, pull leaves off stems, break and bend twigs, or poke them into holes in the ground. This form of play may be of tremendous importance in developing dexterity in manipulating objects. As the chimps grow older this skill becomes invaluable not only in routine activities such as nest-making and food-gathering, but also in the most specialized field of tool use (pp. 36–37).

And even in captivity, this same tendency to incorporate objects into manipulative pattern goes on undiminished, as one may judge from this report by Caroline Loizos (1967) of a young female chimpanzee habituating to and then "mastering in play" a tennis ball:

I bounce a tennis ball in front of the cage several times so that she hears as well as sees it and place it inside on the floor. She backs away, watching ball fixedly—approaches with pouted lips, pats it—it rolls. She backs hurriedly to the wall. Hair erection . . . J. pokes at it from a distance, arm maximally extended, watching intently; looks at me; pokes ball and immediately sniffs finger . . . She dabs at ball and misses; sniffs fingers; she backs away and circles ball from a distance of several feet, watching it intently. Sits and watches ball . . . (pause of several minutes) . . . walks around ball. J. walks past the ball again even closer but quite hurriedly. She lifts some of the woodwool in the cage to peer at the ball from a new angle, approaches ball by sliding forward on stomach with arms and legs tucked underneath her, so that protruded lips are very close to ball without actually touching it. Withdraws. Pokes a finger towards it and sniffs finger . . . returns to ball, again slides forward on stomach with protruded lips without actually connecting. Pokes with extended forefinger, connects and it moves; she scurries backwards; more dabs at it with forefinger and it moves again (but not far because of the woodwool in that area of the cage). J. dabs, ball rolls and she follows, but jumps back in a hurry as it hits the far wall. She rolls the ball on the spot with her finger resting on it, then rolls it forward, watching intently the whole time. She dabs again—arm movement now more exaggerated, flung upwards at end of movement. Tries to pick ball up between thumb and forefinger very gingerly . . . fails. Rolls it towards her, sniffs with lowered head. Picks it up and places it in front of her—*just* touches it with lips—pushes it into straw with right forefinger—touches it with lower lip pushed out, pokes, flicking up hand at end of movement, but backs away as it rolls towards her. Bites at own thumb. Dabs at it with lips, pulls it towards her and backs away. Examines own lip, squinting down, where it touched ball. Picks at it with forefinger and covers ball as it rolls (walking on all fours, with head down to watch ball as it rolls along at a point approximately under her belly). Pushes with outside knuckles. Stamps on it, dabbing at it with foot. Sits on it, rolls it with foot; carries it gingerly with hand and puts it on shelf, climbing up to sit beside it. It drops down—she holds it in one hand and pats it increasingly hard with the other. Holds it in right hand, picks at stripe on ball with her left. Rolls it between two hands. Rolls it between hand and shelf. Holds and pats; bangs it on shelf. Holds and *bites*, examining ball after each bite. Ball drops from shelf and she pats at it on ground with right hand. Lies on her back, balances ball on her feet, holding it there with hands; sits up, holds ball under chin and rolls it two or three times round back of neck and under chin. It rolls away and she chases it immediately and brings it back to shelf. Lies on back and holds it on feet. Presses it against teeth with her feet and bites—all fear appears to be gone—lies and bites at ball held in feet, hands. Rolls it in feet, hands. Climbs to ceiling, ball drops and she chases it at once, J. makes playface, rolls and tumbles with ball, around, over, under ball, bangs it; rolls it over her own body (pp. 194–195).

Various writers (Dolhinow and Bishop, 1970; Loizos, 1967; Van Lawick-Goodall, 1968) are convinced that the mastery of complex tool skills among subhuman anthropoids depends not only on observation learning but also on whether or not they take place in the close setting of the infant–mother interaction. Reference was made in passing to one of the infants in the Gombe Stream Reserve, Merlin, who lost his mother at age three and was "taken over" by older siblings. He mastered neither termiting nor nest building, skills that apparently require repeated observation.

Van Lawick-Goodall (1968) made it clear in her detailed reporting why such repeated opportunity to observe and play is necessary; mastery of a complex skill like termiting is a complex process of mastering *features* of the task—a non-mimicking approach—and then combining the mastered features. There is, for example, mastery of pushing a stick or grass into an opening, though initially this will be done without regard to appropriate rigidity of the probe or appropriate diameter, or appropriate length. It will be played with as a part skill once mastered— as Flint (2·8 years who had started at play termiting) pushing a grass stalk through the hairs of his leg. And sheer repetition will provide the familiar routinization that permits an act to be combined with other acts to meet the complex requirement of a stick of a particular diameter and rigidity, pushed in a particular way, withdrawn at a particular angle at a certain speed, etc. A comparable set of observations on human infants by Wood *et al.*[5] shows the importance of skill to three– five-year-olds in enabling them to benefit from demonstrations of how to put together an interlocking set of blocks to make a pyramid. Unless the child can master the subroutines, the demonstration of the whole task is about as helpful as a demonstration by an accomplished skier is to a beginner. As with the young chimps, so too with the young children: they take selectively from the demonstration those features of performance that are within the range of their capacity for constructing skilled acts. They are helped, but the process is slow.

One very crucial feature of tool skills in chimpanzees as in humans is the trying out of variants of the new skill in different contexts. Once Köhler's (1926) ape Sultan had "learned" to use a stick to draw in food,

[5] D. Wood, J. S. Bruner and G. Ross. *Modelling and mastery in construction task*. In preparation.

he tried using it very soon for poking other animals, for digging, and for dipping it through an opening in a cesspool. Once Rana had learned to climb up stacked boxes to get a suspended piece of fruit, she rapidly tried her new climbing routine on a ladder, a board, a keeper, and Köhler himself—most often forgetting the fruit in preference for the combinatory activity *per se*. Nor is this a response to the boredom of captivity, since the same variant exploration is to be found in the Gombe Stream animals studied by Van Lawick-Goodall (1968)—one of the most ingenious instances being the use of a twig as an olfactory probe by the juvenile female Fifi, an accomplished termiter:

> On three occasions (she) pushed a long grass stalk right into my trouser pocket, subsequently sniffing the end, when I prevented her feeling there with her hand for a banana. Each time there was in fact a banana there, and she followed me whimpering until I gave it to her (p. 206).

It is probably this "push to variation" (rather than fixation by positive reinforcement) that gives chimpanzee manipulation such widespread efficacy—such opportunism as dipping sticks into beehives for honey (Merfield and Miller, 1956), using sticks for clubbing lizards and rodents (Köhler, 1926), and using branches for striking at or throwing at big felines (Kortland and Koöij, 1963). The ecological significance of this wide potential repertory is attested to by observations of Kortland and his collaborators (Kortland, 1965; Kortland and Koöij, 1963; Kortland and van Zon, 1969). They have reported striking differences between forest-dwelling chimpanzees from the rain forest of the Congo and Guinea and those from the Guinea savanna. An animated, dummy leopard was placed in the path of the chimpanzees. Forest apes broke and brandished branches and swung them in horizontal orbit at the dummy. The only hit was by one animal, punching the dummy in the face from in front. Savanna apes warmed up with such sabre rattling, but then attacked the dummy *from the rear* with strong vertical blows with the heaviest available branch and scored violent hits—"showing both tactical cooperation between the actual assailants and vocal support by the onlookers" (Kortland and van Zon, 1969, p. 12). These authors suggest that open country prevents arboreal escape and thus poses for the animals a problem in tool manipulation that calls for great flexibility in adapting tools to local constraints.

The play aspect of tool use (and, indeed, complex problem solving in general) is underlined by the animal's loss of interest in the goal of the act being performed and by its preoccupation with means—also a characteristic of human children (Bruner and Koslowski, 1972).

Consider the following episode:

> Hebb recounted how a chimpanzee he tested solved problems for banana
> slice incentives. On one particular day, she arranged the banana slice
> rewards in a row instead of eating them! Apparently, she had solved the
> problems for their own sake. "I was out of bananas, but I offered her another
> problem . . . she solved the problem: opened the correct box and put a
> slice of banana into it. I took it out and then set the box again . . . I ended up
> with thirty slices of banana" (Rumbaugh, 1970, p. 56).

A far cry from reinforcement in any conventional sense!

Köhler's (1926) account contains an interesting happening. He gave a
handful of straw to one animal who tried to use it to draw in an out-of-
reach piece of fruit. Finding the straw too flexible, the animal doubled
it up, but it was too short, so he abandoned the effort. Modification is
systematic, most often directed to features relevant to the task, and is
combinatorial. It follows first constructions or first efforts at copying a
model. But it appears first in play, not in problem solving.

PLAY IN RELATION TO TOOL USE

I have described these play activities at great length because I believe
them to be crucial to the evolution of tool using—steps that help free the
organism from the immediate requirements of his task. Play, given its
concomitant freedom from reinforcement and its setting in a relatively
pressureless environment, can produce the flexibility that makes tool
using possible. At least two laboratory studies, one by Birch (1945)
and the other by Schiller (1952), indicate the necessity of initial play
with materials in order for them to be converted to instrumental ends.
They both used problems involving the raking in of food with sticks of
varying length—before and after an opportunity to play with sticks. Few
succeeded before play. Observed during play, Birch's animals were seen
to explore increasingly over three days the capacity of the sticks to
lengthen an arm. When put back into the test situation, all of these
animals solved the problem within half a minute. Perhaps, as Loizos
(1967) has suggested, it is the very exaggeration and lack of economy
of play that encourage extension of the limits.

Looked at logically, play has two crucial formal patterns: one
consists of a function and its arguments; the other, an argument and
the functions into which it can fit. A ball or a stick are fitted into as
many acts as possible; or an act, climbing, is performed on as many
objects to which it can be applied appropriately. This pattern, I would
speculate, is close to one of the universal structures of language,
predication, which is organized in terms of topic and comment:

John has a hat
John is a man
John jumps the fence, or

Brush the hat
Wear the hat
Toss the hat.

It is interesting that the language play after "lights out" of the three-year-old, reported by Ruth Weir (1962) in her remarkable book *Language in the crib*, takes precisely such a form. And I will not be the first to comment that the simultaneous appearance in man of language and tool using suggests that the two may derive from some common programming capacities of the enlarging hominid nervous system.

Another feature of play that is crucial to tool use is the feature referred to by Barsh (1972) as *dissociation*—"the ability to anticipate the potential component parts of an object" for use in a new arrangement. It is a question that occupied Köhler (1926) in terms of the ability of his animals to "dissolve visual wholes" of great visual firmness. A Russian investigator, Khroustov (1968), performed a most elegant experiment on tool using in a chimpanzee, showing to what degree these animals are capable of dissociation. Fruit was to be extracted from a narrow tube, and sticks of appropriate diameter were provided. The animal succeeded, and knowing the capability of the species, we are not surprised. The experimenter then provided a wood plaque too wide for the job. After inspecting it, the animal broke it along the grain to obtain a stick of appropriate size. Khroustov then painted a false set of grain lines on a plaque at right angles to the true grain. The animal, using them to guide a first splintering attempt and failing, looked more closely for the true grain and used it.

To summarize once again, the great ape possesses manipulative subroutines that are practised, perfected, and varied in play. These are then put together clumsily and selectively to meet the requirements of more extended tasks, very often in response to observing an adult in a stable and relaxed setting. The imitation observed is akin to imitation by a child of an adult speech model: the child's output is *not* a copy of the adult's; it has its own form even though it is designed to fill the same function. These initial acts are then modified in a systematic manner to fulfil further requirements of the task. The acts themselves have a self-rewarding character. They are varied systematically, almost as if in play to test the limits of a new skill. A baboon living in the same habitat as the chimpanzee is as eager to eat termites as is the latter; yet he shows none of these capacities even though he is seen to observe the chimpanzee exercising them often. He too is equipped with a good pair of hands. Note that there is an association between play and tool use, and that the natural selection of one, tools, led to the selection of the other as well, in the evolution of the hominids and man.

ADULTS AS MODELS

Neither among chimpanzees nor in the infinitely more evolved society of hunter–gatherers is there much direct intervention by adults in the learning of the young. They serve principally as models and as sources of the necessary affection (Bruner, 1965). Among the primates, there is very little intentional pedagogy of any kind. Hinde (1971) recently reviewed the literature and concluded as follows:

> On the whole, the mothers of nonhuman primates seem not to teach their infants. In a number of species, a mother has been seen to move a little away from her infant and then to wait while it crawled after her (e.g. Howler monkeys; Carpenter, 1934; rhesus, Hinde *et al.*, 1964; gorilla, Schaller, 1963; chimpanzees, van Lawick-Goodall, 1968): this has the effect of encouraging the infant to walk, but can hardly be called teaching. However, it is clear that infants learn a great deal from their mothers, especially in the context of avoidance and food-getting behavior. Even avoidance of snakes differs between laboratory and wild-reared monkeys and may depend in part on parental example (Joslin *et al.*, 1964). It has been shown in the laboratory that monkeys can learn to avoid situations or responses that are seen to cause pain to other individuals (Child, 1938; Hansen and Mason, 1962; Hall, 1968), and to accept food that other individuals are seen to take (Weiskrantz and Cowey, 1963). In nature, the infant's proximity to its mother ensures that it becomes rapidly conditioned by her fear responses (e.g. Baldwin, 1969) and that its feeding behavior is influenced by her (e.g. Baldwin, 1969). In the patas monkey (Hall and DeVore, 1965), Japanese macaque (*Macaca fuscata*) (Kwamura, 1969), and chimpanzee (van Lawick-Goodall, 1968), the young eat fragments that their mothers drop, as well as being especially likely to feed at the same food sources. Although by the time they are one year old, Japanese macaques are acquainted with all the types of food used by the troop, it is difficult to make them take new types of food in the laboratory. Apparently learning from the mother is normally important (Kawamura, 1959). Schaller (1963) records an infant gorilla removing food from its mother's mouth and eating it, and one case of a mother breaking off a stem for its infant to eat. Imitation, principally of the mother, is important for the development of tool-using behavior in wild-living chimpanzees (Goodall, 1964; van Lawick-Goodall, 1968); and the development of actions by imitation has also been recorded in hand-reared individuals (Hayes and Hayes, 1952;

Kellogg, 1968). In the latter case, the actions may be used for social communication (Gardner and Gardner, 1971).

In squirrel monkeys, food-catching skill is learned by younger juveniles from older ones, rather than from their mothers (Baldwin, 1969). However, it is by no means always the younger animals that learn food habits from older ones. Under natural conditions, young animals investigate new objects more than do older individuals, and this may lead to a transfer of feeding habits from younger to older animals. Thus, among the Japanese macaques, new foods tended to be accepted first by juveniles, and their use then diffused through the colony via their mothers and then the mothers' younger offspring and consorts (Itani, 1958). Although diffusion sometimes occurs in the opposite direction (Frisch, 1968), kinship ties are probably always important (Kawamura, 1959; Tsumori, 1967) (p. 32).

There may, however, be something like "tutor proneness" among the young—an increased eagerness to learn from adults. One study now in progress suggests how such tutor proneness may come about. Rumbaugh *et al.* (1972) are training chimpanzees and orang-utans under the following conditions. One group receives tutoring modelling on a variety of tasks; each task is presented on each new encounter in the form of a new embodiment of the problem. A second group gets the same problems, but each time in the same form, so that this group is essentially repeating. The third group is presented with the materials used by the others, but the human tutor model neither presents them as tasks nor models the solutions as in the first two instances. The tasks are mechanical puzzles, packing fitted containers within each other, searching for a hidden object, transporting an object to another part of the room, extracting candy from a container, etc. The reward is some combination of task completion and the tutor's approval. A preliminary finding of this work-in-progress is of particular interest. The apes in the more challenging first condition are the ones most likely to wait for the tutor to provide a clue before beginning on their own.

Does it then require a certain level of challenge and novelty to create tutor proneness in primates? Schaller (1964) remarked of the gorillas he observed in the Congo:

Why was the Australopithecus, with the brain capacity of a large gorilla, the maker of stone tools, a being with a culture in the human sense, while the free-living gorilla in no way reveals the marvellous potential of its brain? I suspect that the gorilla's failure to develop further is related to the ease with which it can satisfy its needs in the forest. In its lush realm there is no selective advantage for improvement . . . The need for tools . . . is more likely in a harsh and marginal habitat where a premium is placed on an alert mind . . . (p. 232).

And the same view was voiced by Yerkes and Yerkes (1929) in their classic work on the great apes, as well as by Vernon Reynolds (1965) who, in a penetrating article on the comparative analysis of selection pressures operating on chimpanzees and on gorilla, concluded:

> Finally, we may briefly consider the contrast in temperaments between these two anthropoid species. Comparative behavior studies in the past often stressed this difference. Tevis (1921), for instance, wrote, "In mental characteristics there is the widest difference between the two apes that we are considering. The chimpanzee is lively, and at least when young, teachable and tameable. The gorilla, on the other hand, is gloomy and ferocious, and quite untameable" (p. 122). It is possible to suggest an explanation for this contrast between the morose, sullen, placid gorilla, and the lively, exciteable chimpanzee. The difference seems to be most clearly related to the difference in social organization and foraging behavior. The herbivorous gorilla is surrounded by food: the more intensively it feeds, the slower it travels; its survival needs are easily met, and it is protected from predators by the presence of powerful males. Here there is no advantage to any form of hyper-activity except in threat displays and the charge of the big male, which is a hyper-aggressive behavior form. Chimpanzee survival, on the other hand, depends heavily on the fluidity of social groups and the ability to communicate the whereabouts of food by intense forms of activity (wild vocalizing and strong drumming). Moving rapidly about the forest, meeting up with new chimpanzees every day, vocalizing and drumming, and locating other chimpanzees by following their calls, are the basic facts of chimpanzee existence. Here an advantage may be seen in having a responsive, expressive, and adaptable temperament. Hyper-activity is the chimpanzee norm in the wild, and with it goes a volatile temperament (p. 704).

But here we encounter a seeming contradiction. The evolutionary trend we have been examining seems to have placed a major emphasis on a combination of developments: a relatively pressure-free environment with its concomitant increase in play, exploration, and observation; and at the same time, a certain challenge in the requirements of adaptation to a habitat. (Play in young gorillas and orang-utans in the wild, by the way, is not nearly as elaborate as in the chimpanzee (cf. Reynolds, 1965; Rodman, 1972; Schaller, 1963; Yerkes and Yerkes, 1929), and in neither of these species is there much challenge from the habitat.)

I believe that Desmond Morris (1964) has a resolution for this apparent dilemma—that, on the one hand, a non-pressureful habitat seems crucial and, on the other, challenge is significant. He made the distinction between two modes of adaptation to habitat, *specialist* and *opportunist*—the squirrel versus the rat, certain exclusively forest-dwelling monkeys like the vervet or green versus the adaptable rhesus (cf. Hinde, 1971). Non-specialists depend on high flexibility rather than on morphology or behavioural specialization. Aristarchus said it well and provided Isaiah Berlin (1953) with a famous book title: "The fox knows many things; the hedgehog knows one big thing".

One can only speculate that the evolution of intellectual processes in the primate stock from which man descended was in the direction of opportunism and away from specialism. It could be argued, indeed, that the original stock, as far as intellect goes, was closer to chimpanzee than to either of the contemporary pongids, though Rumbaugh (1970) believed that in certain forms of intellectual performance there are striking parallels between man and orang-utan. The argument for opportunism seems in fact essential to account for the rapid fanning out of the evolved species to such a variety of habitats.

INSTRUCTIONAL INTERACTION BETWEEN ADULTS AND YOUNG

What can be said of "instruction" of the young in the protohominids and early man? Alas, nothing definite. But contemporary "simple" societies, hunter–gatherers, provide certain clues. No matter how constraining the ecological conditions, there is among such people an expansion in adult–child instructional interaction, both quantitatively and qualitatively, of a major order. Although one cannot reconstruct the Pleistocene hunter–gatherer by reference to such isolated hunter–gatherers as the contemporary !Kung Bushmen, their practices do suggest something about the magnitude of the change. !Kung adults and children play and dance together, sit together, participate in minor hunting together, join in song and storytelling together. At frequent intervals, moreover, children are the objects of intense rituals presided over by adults—minor, as in the first haircutting, or major, as when a boy kills his first Kudu buck and undergoes the proud but painful process of scarification. Children also are playing constantly at the rituals, with the implements, tools, and weapons of the adult world. However, in tens of thousands of feet of !Kung film prepared by the Marshalls (see Bruner, 1966), one virtually never finds an instance of teaching taking place outside the situation where the behaviour to be learned is relevant. Nobody teaches away from the scene, as in a school setting. Indeed, there is nothing like a school.

Often the adult seems to play the role of inducting the young into novel situations that, without the presence of a protecting and familiar adult, would be frightening—as in extended trekking, in witchcraft ceremonials, and in many other spheres where the child comes along and participates to the limit that he is able. This induction to the margin of anxiety, I believe, starts very early. A study by Sroufe and Wunsch (1972) provides a hint of just how early that may be. The study sets out to explore what makes human infants laugh. From four months (when laughing first appears in reliable and recognizable form) into the second year of life, the sufficient stimulus for laughter becomes increasingly distal—at first being principally tactile and close visual (e.g. tickle plus looming), with incongruities following later, as when the mother adopts an unusual position such as crawling on all fours. Note, however, that at all ages, the capers most likely to produce laughter when performed by the mother are the ones most likely to produce tears when performed by a stranger. The mother seems able to bring the young, so to speak, to the edge of terror. King (1966) has suggested that this feature of mothering is universal; that among birds as well as mammals, the presence of the mother reduces fear of novel stimuli and provides the assurance necessary for exploratory behaviour. But it is only among humans that the adult *introduces* the novel, inducts the young into new, challenging, and frightening situations—sometimes in a highly ritualistic way, as with the *rites de passage*.

There is little question that the human young (and the young of the primates generally) are quite ready to be lured by the novel, given even the minimum adult reassurance. "Neophilia" is what Desmond Morris (1967) calls it. Such readiness for novelty may even be attested to by a superiority, at least among the great apes and man, of the young over the old in detecting or extracting the rules and regularities in new situations. At least one laboratory study, Rumbaugh and McCormack (1967), has even found a *negative* correlation between age and the ability to master learning-set problems—tasks that have a common principle but a new embodiment on each presentation, like "pick the odd one when two are alike and one is different"[6]. But note that it is in man only that adults arrange play and ritual for children that capitalize on this tendency.

It is obvious that the play and ritual in which young and adult humans are involved are saturated heavily with symbolism. Though the kind of mastery play I have been at some pains to describe in the preced-

---

[6] Rumbaugh (1970) commented in a recent review of the learning capacities of great apes: "It is frequently observed, however, that an animal that excels in learning when young remains excellent *if* frequently worked with as it grows to adulthood (at least eight years of age) and beyond. Might it be the case that early experience in some manner determines the avenues along which intelligent behavior will be manifest. If early experiences are with formal test and learning situations, will the animal's adaptability be maximally manifest as an adult in contexts of that order?" (p. 65).

ing discussion is still a feature of human play, there is added to it now an extraordinary range of play forms that have as their vehicle the use of *symbols* and *conventions*—two terms that will concern us in due course. Not only are sticks, so to speak, used as arrows or spears or even as novel and unusual tools, they may be used now in a symbolic way that transcends utility—as horses, for example when put between the legs (Vygotsky, 1967) or giant trees when propped up in the sand. The prop or "pivot" or toy (it is difficult to name the stick) is not used as a *utilitandum* (as, say, Khroustov's chimpanzee used a separated splinter to poke food out of a tube) but as a point of departure from the present perceptual situation. Though the stick must have some feature that is horselike (it must at least be "go-between-the-leggable"), it must now also fit into an imaginary situation. It is for this reason that the great Russian psychologist Vygotsky used the term pivot: the stick is a pivot between the real and the imagined.

Once the symbolic transformation of play has occurred, two consequences follow. Play can serve as a vehicle for teaching the nature of a society's conventions, and it can also teach about the nature of conventions *per se*. David Lewis (1969) defined a convention as an agreement about procedure, the procedure itself being trivial, but the agreement not. We drive to the right, or we exhibit a red light to port and a green to starboard. And it is evident immediately that a linguistic-cultural community depends on an easy and fluent grasp of convention on the part of its members. Symbolic play, whatever function it may serve for the individual child in working through his own problems or fulfilling his wishes at the fantasy level, has an even more crucial role in teaching that child fluency with rules and conventions.

As for pretraining in the particular system of conventions of the society, let me give an instance from an exotic culture. The reader can provide instances closer to home. This one is from Dolhinow and Bishop's (1970) review:

In New Guinea the Tangu engage in a ritual food exchange in which strict equivalence is maintained (Burridge, 1957). Equivalence is determined by mutual agreement between trading partners. The Tangu children play a game called taketak in which two lots of thirty spines of coconut palm fronds are stuck into the ground five yards apart. Individual spines within the lot are placed approximately six inches apart. The children have tops that are spun and let loose to try to touch the spines of the opponent's lot. The teams need not be equal, but the number of tops must be equal. The game proceeds as a series of bouts; within each bout, both teams must complete their turn. The game ends when, after any bout, both teams have an equivalent number of spines in and out, or, since this rarely occurs, when an end is mutually agreed upon. The object of the game is equivalence, just as in the food exchange ritual of the adults, and in both cases the outcome or equivalence is decided upon by mutual agreement. There is no winner or loser; the object is to tie (pp. 183–184).

USING SYMBOLIC MEANS: LANGUAGE

Having gone this far into symbolic play, I now turn to language in order to be more precise about what is involved when symbolic means are used for preparing the human young for culture. Higher primate skill, as I have described it, has about it certain languagelike properties. Skilled action, like language, has paraphrases and a kind of grammar. But there is also a communicative function of language; and it is this function, in all probability, that determines many of its design features (cf. Hockett, 1960). I have emphasized the similarity between action and the structure of language in order to propose a critical hypothesis: the initial use of language is probably in support of and closely linked to action. The initial structure of language and, indeed, the universal structure of its syntax are extensions of the structure of action. Syntax is not arbitrary; its cases mirror the requirements of signalling about action and representing action: agent, action, object, location, attribution, and direction are among its cases. Whatever the language, the agent–action–object structure is the form soon realized by the young speaker. Propositions about the evolution of language are justly suspect. I offer this hypothesis not on the basis of evolutionary evidence but on developmental grounds. For what the child himself shows us is that initial development of language follows and does not lead his development of skill in action and thought. It is only *after* a distinction has been mastered in action that it appears in initial language; and when it first does so, it is referenced by paraphrase of previously learned words or phrases (cf. Slobin, 1971). Piaget (1967) put it succinctly: "language is not enough to explain thought, because the structures that characterize thought have their roots in action and in sensorimotor mechanisms that are deeper than linguistics" (p. 98).[7] And, to use Cromer's (1968) words: "once certain cognitive abilities have developed, we find an active search . . . for new forms. Suddenly, forms (and words!) which the child has been exposed to for years become a part of his own speech" (p. 219).

At the onset of speech, then, language is virtually an outgrowth of the mastery of skilled action and perceptual discrimination. These

---

[7] This is not to say that once a language has been mastered to a certain level (unfortunately, not easily specifiable), it cannot then be used to signal properties of action and events that up to then had *not* been mastered by the child. It is in this sense that language can in fact be used as a medium for instruction (see Bruner *et al.*, 1966).

abilities sensitize and almost drive the child to linguistic development. De Laguna (1963, orig. publ. 1927) remarked that the most likely evolutionary explanation of language lies in the human need for help, crucial to the "social–technical way of life" that is distinctly human (cf. Washburn and Howell, 1960). De Laguna went on:

> Once we deliberately ask the question: What does speech do? What objective function does it perform in human life—the answer is not far to seek. Speech is the great medium through which human cooperation is brought about. It is the means by which the diverse activities of men are coordinated and correlated with each other for the attainment of common and reciprocal ends (p. 19).

Having said that much, we must next note that with further growth, the major trend is a steadfast march *away* from the use of language as an adjunct of action or as a marker for representing the immediate experience. If in the beginning it is true (Block, p. 107, cited in De Laguna, 1963, orig. publ. 1927, pp. 89–90) that "a substantive does not denote simply an object, but all the actions with which it is in relation in the experience of the child", it is soon the case that language in the human comes increasingly to be free of the context of action. Whereas "to understand what a baby is saying, you must see what the baby is doing", nothing of the sort is true for the adult. This brings us to the famous De Laguna dictum, the implications of which will concern us for the remainder of this article[8]:

> The evolution of language is characterized by a progressive freeing of speech from dependence on the perceived conditions under which it is uttered and heard, and from the behavior which accompanies it. The extreme limit of this freedom is reached in language which is written (or printed) and read. For example, it is quite indifferent to the reader of these words, under what physical conditions they have been penned or typed. This represents, we repeat, the extreme limit of the process by which language comes to be increasingly independent of the conditions of its use (p. 107).

We need not pause long on a comparison of language as it is acquired and used by man and by the chimpanzee—notably by the chimpanzee Washoe (Gardner and Gardner, 1971; Ploog and Melnechuk, 1971). For one thing, Washoe's language acquisition is not spontaneous, and she can be seen from the film record to be both reluctant and bored as a language learner. There is neither the play nor the drive of the human

---

[8] For excellent accounts of the process of decontextualization in language, see Werner and Kaplan (1963) and Luria and Yudovich (1956). Both of these volumes provide rich documentation and interesting commentary on the point.

child, the *Funktionslust* (Bühler, 1934), that keeps the child exploring and playing with language. The young chimpanzee's grammar is tied perpetually to action. The nominatives and the attributives of early childhood speech, naming objects and attributing properties to them, are lacking and never seem to appear in Washoe. The evident delight of Matthew (Greenfield *et al.*, 1972) in the use of such nominatives as "airplane", "apple", "piece", and "cow" is quite as important as the fact that these holophrases were used in a context of action. Roger Brown (1970, 1971) has commented that virtually all of the two-sign and three-sign "utterances" in Washoe's use of American sign language were either "emphasizers" of action (*Hurry open*), "specifiers" of action (*Listen dog*, at sound of barking), or indicated agents for action (*You eat, Roger Washoe tickle*). David McNeill (1973) put it concisely: Washoe's grammar can be characterized by the single proposition:

$$s \ldots p^n$$

or, "statement that raises a predicated action to a higher level", a grammatical form not spontaneously present in human adult speech[9]. In a word, chimpanzee use of a taught form of human speech is strongly tied to action, beyond which it tends not to go, either spontaneously or by dint of teaching effort.

On the other hand, the development of language in humans not only moves in the direction of becoming itself free of context and accompanying action, it also frees the attention of the user from his immediate surroundings, directing attention to what is being said rather than to what is being done or seen. In the process, language becomes a powerful instrument in selectively directing attention to features of the environment represented by it.

With respect to the first of these, language processing goes on in its very nature at different levels. We process the phonological output of a speaker, interpret his syntax, hold the head words of imbedding phrases until the imbedded phrase is completed and the tail is located to match the head word, etc. At the same time, we direct attention to meanings and to references. The acts of language, argue Miller and Johnson-Laird (see footnote 3, p. 15), by their very performance free attention from control by immediate stimulation in the environment. One might even argue that the requirement of organizing what one experiences into

---

[9] McNeill also made the cogent point that perhaps (as with Premack, 1971) chimpanzees can be taught a human-like syntax, a not uninteresting point; but they seem not to acquire it as children do, by a process not so much of detailed learning or imitation as of spontaneous constructions of grammatical utterances most often exhibiting initial grammatical rules not present in the adult speech to which they are exposed.

sentence form may impose upon experience itself a certain cast—the classic arguments of Humbolt (1836) and Benjamin Lee Whorf (1956). Once language captures control of attention, the swiftness and subtlety of attention change come to match the swiftness and subtlety of linguistic manoeuvring. Language permits search specifications to be set in such a fashion as to fulfil any question that may be asked. The eye-movement records collected by Yarbus (1967) provide stunning illustration of the tactics of the language user: how, while guiding his eye movements by physical features of a picture of scene, he manages at the same time to pick up the features that answer questions he is entertaining—looking now to pick up the ages of people, now to judge their furniture, now to see what they are doing, etc.

To summarize, then, though language springs from and aids action, it quickly becomes self-contained and free of the context of action. It is a device, moreover, that frees its possessor from the immediacy of the environment not only by pre-emption of attention during language use but by its capacity to direct attention toward those aspects of the environment that are singled out by language.

I have gone into this much detail regarding early language because it is a necessary preliminary to a crucial point about the management of immaturity in human culture. I have commented already on the fact that in simple, hunter–gatherer societies, there is very little formal teaching outside the sphere of action. The child is not drawn aside and told how to do it: he is shown while the action is going on, with language as an auxiliary and as a marker of action—an aid in calling attention to what is going on that is relevant. Over and beyond that, the principal use of language was probably some mix of guiding group action and giving shape to a believe system through myths and incantations, as Susanne Langer (1969) has long proposed. I rather suspect that increasing technology imposed an increasing demand on language to represent and store knowledge in a fashion to be helpful outside the immediate context of original use. L. S. B. Leaky[10] suggested that once stone instruments came to be made to match a pattern rather than by spontaneous breaking, as in fabricating an Acheulan pebble tool with a single-face edge, *models* could be fashioned and kept. He has found excellent, obsidian-grained hand axes at Olduvai that appear never to have been used; he speculates that they were "models for copy", with a religious significance as well.

But an inert model is a poor thing; it is, in effect, an end state, something to be attained with no intervening instruction concerning means. Language does better than that, and it is interesting to see the extent

[10] L. S. B. Leaky, personal communication, April 1966.

to which magic becomes mixed with practice and imitation in a primitive technology. A good example is afforded by the boat building and inter-island navigation of the pre-literate Puluwat Islanders in the Marshalls, recently described in rich detail by Gladwin (1970) in a book entitled *East is a big bird*. Theirs is a system in which East is marked by Altair at horizon elevation, distance by a commonsense speed-estimating method, with distance "logged" by noting the supposed parallax of islands at different distances over the horizon. Final homing on an island is accomplished by noting the direction of end-of-day nesting flights of boobies and frigate birds. And the lot is peppered with sundry omens given by weeds and sea turtles and the feel of things. I happen to be a navigator myself. I am impressed not only that the system works but that it is genuinely a *system*; it ties together means and ends. The framework of the system can be *told*; however, without language it would be impossible, for the ingredients of the system involve reference to the absent or invisible, to the possible, to the conditional, and even (I suspect) to the knowingly false (the white lies all navigators must tell to keep the trustful sailors trusting). There must have been hunting systems and seasonal marking systems of this sort, representable outside the setting of action, in use by very early man—probably much earlier than heretofore suspected (cf. Marshack, 1972).

Increasingly, then, language in its decontextualized form becomes among human beings the medium for passing on knowledge. And, of course, the emergence of written language—a very recent innovation from an evolutionary point of view—gives this tendency still further amplification. Once this mode of transmitting knowledge has become established, the conditions for the invention of school—a place where teaching occurs—are present. School is a very recent development in evolutionary terms, even in historical terms. I explore now some of the consequences of these developments for our mode of dealing with, informing, and shaping the immature.

FROM "KNOWING HOW" TO "KNOWING THAT"

As soon as schools, pedagogues, and the storing of decontextualized information received legitimacy—and it was probably the written word that accomplished this legitimization—the emphasis shifted from *knowing how* to *knowing that*. Even growth becomes redefined in accordance with the shift—the adult "having" more knowledge, that is, "knowing about" more things. We have even come to define the needs of infancy in these terms, as "the need for experience" (rather than, as Bowlby, 1969, noted, in terms of the need for love and for predictability). Knowledge in some way becomes a central desideratum. And when, as in the United States, attention turns to the children of the underprivileged and the exploited, their difficulty is likely to be, and indeed in this case was, attributed to "cultural deprivation". Hence, an "enriched environment" was prescribed much as if the issue were avitaminosis[11]. Dewey (1916) referred early to this diagnosis as the "cold-storage" ideal of knowledge and, of course, attacked it vigorously.

But this is too simple, for in fact there is great power inherent in decontextualized knowledge—knowledge represented in a form that is relatively free from the uses to which it is to be put or to which it has been put in the past[12]. It is not too serious an oversimplification to say that it is precisely such a process of reorganizing knowledge into formal systems that frees it of functional fixedness. By using a system of notation that redefines functional requirements in formal terms, far greater flexibility can be achieved. Rather than thinking in terms of "hammers", with all of their associated conventionalized imagery, one thinks instead in terms of force to be applied in excess of a certain level of resistance to be overcome. It is, in effect, the way of science to render the problem into this form in order to make the solving of *particular* problems mere instances of much simpler general problems and thereby to increase the range of applicability of knowledge. Why should the Puluwatan navigator struggle with such a set of complexities as I have described, when all it gets him is competence over a few hundred miles of ocean, and a shaky competence at that! He would be more accurate and more general, as well as more flexible, if he learned to take the elevation of a heavenly body, note the time, and reduce the sight to the easily solved spherical triangle of the western navigator. Such a system would serve him anywhere.

But there are two problems (at least!) in this ideal of efficient formal knowledge rather than implicit knowledge, to use Polanyi's (1958) phrase. The first grows out of the point already made about skill and its de-emphasis. That de-emphasis comes out of what I believe to be a misplaced confidence in the ease with which we go from *knowing that* to *knowing how*. It is not easy; it is a deep and perplexing problem. Let me call it the effectiveness problem. Just as deep is a second problem: it may well be that the message of decontextualization and formal structure is implicitly antifantasy and antiplay: call this the engagement

---

[11] For a discussion of these problems in childhood as reflecting the growth of skills for surviving under hopeless conditions, see Bruner (1970), Cole and Bruner (1971), and Denenberg (1970).

[12] For a fuller discussion of the nature of thought processes employing formal and functional modes of organizing knowledge, the reader is referred to Bruner *et al.* (1956); Polanyi (1958); Popper (1954); Bartlett (1958); and Piaget's (1971) striking little volume on structuralism.

problem. The two together—effectiveness and engagement—bring us to the heart of the matter.

With respect to effectiveness, it is probably a reasonable hypothesis that as technology advances, the effector and the energy components of industrial activity become increasingly remote from human empathy; neither the arm nor the hand any longer give the models for energy or for artificing. Energy and the tool kit become, for planning purposes, black boxes, and the major human functions are *control* and the *organization* of work. There is a spiral. It becomes possible to talk about the conduct of work almost without reference to skill or vocation—wheat production and steel production and gross national product and energy production and balance of payments. With work and competence presented in that mode, the young become more and more remote from the nature of the effort involved in running a society. Vocation, competence, skill, a sense of place in the system—these become more and more difficult for the young to fathom—or, for that matter, for the adult. It is difficult for the child to say what he will do or what he will "be" as an adult. Effectiveness becomes elusive.

For while the new technological complexity produces an enormous increase in production processes and distribution processes, it produces no increase either in the number or in the clarity of comprehensible vocations. Production and distribution, in high technology, do not provide an operator with an opportunity to carry through from the initiation of a recognizable problem to its completion, or to see plainly how his task relates to the cycle from task initiation to task completion. Intrinsic structure and reward are removed. The result is what Norbert Wiener (1950) long ago called "work unfit for human production". The industrial revolution removed the worker from the home. Its technological elaboration made the worker's work away from home incomprehensible to the young and the uninitiated—the latter, often a worker himself. The greatest tribute to technique decontextualized from vocation, carried to an extreme where it becomes fascinating, is the *Whole earth catalogue*. Even the counterculture reaches a point where it is without vocations but offers only spontaneity as a contrast to over-rationalized "vocationless" work.

School, separated from work which itself has grown difficult to understand, becomes its own world. As McLuhan (1964) insists, it becomes a medium and has its own message, regardless of what is taught. The message is its irrelevance to work, to adult life. For those who wish to pursue knowledge for its own sake, this is not upsetting. But for those who do not or cannot, school provides no guide—only knowledge, the relevance of which is clear neither to students nor to teachers. These are the conditions for alienation and confusion. I would urge that when adult models become incomprehensible, they lose the power either to guide or to inspire. I do not mean to settle the question here as to whether present adult models are in fact totally relevant to the problems of those entering society now. I will, however, return to it later.

Bronfenbrenner (1970) in his book on child rearing commented on the accelerating trend toward generational separation in technical cultures. The self-sealing peer culture, the denigration of adult ideal figures, the counter-culture committed to protest and romanticized ideals—these are by now familiar instruments of separation. But I believe them to be symptoms of the struggle to adjust to a social–technical order that changes at a rate faster than comprehension of it can be achieved and widely transmitted. This, you recall, is the problem with which we started: how can a system for preparing the immature for entry into the society deal with a future that is increasingly difficult to predict within a single lifetime? Many of the means for inducting the young into the social group, a heritage of the evolution of man's capacity for culture, appear to become ineffective under such conditions when such rapid change becomes the rule. Observation and imitative play, demonstration in context of skilled problem solving, induced tutor proneness, an effective microcosm in the form of an extended family or a habitat group, and the concept of vocation—are all seemingly threatened. Yet, I wonder.

I do not propose to become gloomy. Surely human culture and our species are in deep trouble, not the least of which is loss of heart. But much of the trouble is real: we are degrading the biosphere, failing to cope with population, permitting technology to degrade individuality, and failing to plan. Many of the experimental and often radical efforts of the young represent, I believe, new variants of ancient, biologically rooted modes by which the young characteristically work through to maturity. And a great many of these efforts are in response to the new conditions we have been at such pains to describe—a rate of change faster than can be transmitted intergenerationally with concomitant likelihood of disastrous consequences. Let me conclude with a closer analysis of this point and, in so doing, come to what was referred to above as the problem of engagement.

PROBLEM OF ENGAGEMENT

A great many of the world's schools are conventional and dull places. They do not foster much productive play and little of what Jeremy

Bentham (1840), in his *Theory of legislation*, called "deep play" and condemned as irrational and in violation of the utilitarian ideal. By deep play, Bentham meant play in which the stakes are so high that it is irrational for men to engage in it at all—a situation in which the marginal utility of what one stands to win is clearly less than the marginal disutility of what one stands to lose. Bentham proposed, good utilitarian that he was, that such play should be outlawed. But as the anthropologist Geertz (1972) commented in his close analysis of cockfighting in Bali, "despite the logical force of Bentham's analysis men engage in such play, both passionately and often, and even in the face of law's revenge" (p. 15). Deep play is playing with fire. It is the kind of serious play that tidy and even permissive institutions for educating the young cannot live with happily, for their mandate from the society requires them to carry out their work with due regard for minimizing chagrin concerning outcomes achieved. And deep play is a poor vehicle for that.

What strikes me about the decade just past is the enormous increase in the depth of play in adolescence and, by reflection downward into lower age groups, among the young. Willingness to risk future preferment by dropping out of the system that is designed to qualify one for the future, in return for a season of communcal mutuality—surely the balance of utility to disutility is not Benthamite. Such wagers are highly dangerous for the lives of the individuals involved in them. (Note that Russian roulette is the worst bargain to be had in deep play.) When one finds deep play, the inference must be that there are deep and unresolved problems in the culture. There always are, but that does not mean that one should not look carefully at what these are and what they signify for the future. There is ample reason to believe that the present forms of deep play point to a thwarted, backed-up need for defining competence, both individually and socially, to oneself and to others. Recall that in most previous cultural eras, adults provided challenge and excitement and a certain sense of muted terror for the young by induction into rituals and skills that had momentous consequences. Engagement was built into the system. One knew the steps to growing up, both ritually and in terms of skill.

If adult life ceases to be comprehensible, or begins to be less a challenge than a drag, then engagement is lost—but only for a while. I have the impression of something new emerging. What takes the place of the deposed, incomprehensible, or worn-out competence figure, the classical adult image of skill? At first, of course, protest–withdrawal figures will—the pop figures of rock and the Timothy Leary prophets who offer an intravenous version of competence via subjectivity. I believe that gradually there is emerging a new form of role bearer—the *intermediate generation*—adolescents and young adults who take over the role of acting as models. They exist visibly in context. Their skills and vocation are proclaimed, miniaturized to appropriate size, and personalized. I should like to propose that such an intermediate generation is a response to the crisis of a change rate that goes faster than we can transmit from generation to generation.

Lest we go too rapidly, consider the pointlessness of an intergeneration in a society *with* continuity. Turnbull's (1961) account of a Pygmy group in Africa serves well:

> When a hunting party goes off there are always people left in the camp—usually some of the older men and women, some children, and perhaps one or two younger men and women. The children always have their own playground, called bopi, a few yards off from the main camp. . . .
>
> There were always trees for the youngsters to climb, and this is one of the main sports even for those not yet old enough to walk properly. The great game is for half a dozen or more children to climb to the top of a young tree, bending it down until its top touches the ground. They then all leap off at once, and if anyone is too slow he goes flying back upward as the tree springs upright, to the jeers and laughter of his friends.
>
> Like children everywhere, Pygmy children love to imitate their adult idols. This is the beginning of their schooling, for the adults will always encourage and help them. What else is there for them to learn except to grow into good adults? So a fond father will make a tiny bow for his son, and arrows of soft wood with blunt points. He may also give him a strip of a hunting net. A mother will delight herself and her daughter by weaving a miniature carrying basket. At an early age, boys and girls are "playing house" . . .
>
> They will also play at hunting, the boys stretching out their little bits of net while the girls beat the ground with bunches of leaves and drive some poor tired old frog in toward the boys . . . And one day they find that the games they have been playing are not games any longer, but the real thing, for they have become adults. Their hunting is now real hunting; their tree climbing is in earnest search of inaccessible honey; their acrobatics on the swings are repeated almost daily, in other forms, in the pursuit of elusive game, or in avoiding malicious forest buffalo. It happens so gradually that they hardly notice the change at first, for even when they are proud and famous hunters their life is still full of fun and laughter (pp. 128–129).

The transition is gradual, its excitement increased from time to time by rituals. But technological societies move away from such gradualism as they become increasingly developed. Indeed, the Protestant ethic made very early a sharp separation between what one does when young and what one does later, with the transition very sharply defined. In the western tradition there grew a puritan separation of the "works of the

adult" and "the play of the babes". But it was clear to both sides what
the two were about. Now "the play of the babes" has become separate
from, dissociated from, the adult community and not understood by that
community any better than the young comprehend or accept the ideals
of the adult community.

A place is made automatically, perhaps for the first time in our cultural
tradition, for an intermediate generation, with power to model new
forms of behaviour. Their power comes precisely, I think, from the
fact that they offer deep play, that irresistible charisma that so disturbed
the tidy Jeremy Bentham. They are modelling new life styles to fit better
what is perceived as the new and changing conditions, new changes that
they claim to be able to see—perhaps rightly, perhaps not—more
clearly than those who had adapted to something still earlier. The great
question is whether the intermediate generation can reduce the uncertainty of growing up under conditions of unpredictable change, can serve
as mentors as well as charismatic vendors of deep play, and as purveyors
of effectiveness as well as of engagement.

I do not think that intermediate models are a transitory phenomenon.
I believe that we would do well to recognize the new phenomenon and
to incorporate it, even make it easier for the young adult and later
juvenile to get more expert at it. Nobody can offer a blueprint on how
an intermediate generation can help ready the less mature for life in an
unforeseeably changing world. It is not altogether a comfortable problem
either, for the way of cultural revolutions and Red Guards (both
composed of intermediates) can only inspire caution. But letting the
young have more of a hand in the teaching of the younger, letting them
have a better sense of the dilemmas of society as a whole, all of these
may be part of the way in which a new community can be helped to
emerge. What may be in order is a mode of inducting the young by the
use of a more communal system of education in which each takes
responsibility for teaching or aiding or abetting or provoking those less
able, less knowledgeable, and less provoked than he.

It was in the universities that these current matters first surfaced—
a long way from the high savannas of East Africa where we began our
quest for an understanding of immaturity and its uses. One becomes
increasingly shaky the closer one comes to man in his contemporary
technological society. I would only urge that in considering these deep
issues of educability we keep our perspective broad and remember that
the human race has a biological past from which we can read lessons
for the culture of the present. We cannot adapt to everything, and in
designing a way to the future we would do well to examine again what
we are and what our limits are. Such a course does not mean opposition

to change but, rather, using man's natural modes of adapting to render change both as intelligent and as stable as possible.

REFERENCES

ALTMAN, J. 1967. Postnatal growth and differentiation of the mammalian brain, with implications for a morphological theory of memory. In G. C. Quarton, T. Melnechuk and F. O. Schmitt (Eds.), *The neurosciences: a study program*, Vol. 1. Rockefeller University Press, New York.

BARSH, R. 1972. The evolution of tool use. Unpublished research paper. Center for Cognitive Studies, Harvard University.

BARTLETT, F. C. 1958. *Thinking: an experimental and social study*. Basic Books, New York.

BEACH, F. 1965. *Sex and behavior*. Wiley, New York, London and Sydney.

BENNETT, E. L., DIAMOND, M. C., KRECH, D. and ROSENZWEIG, M. R. 1964. Chemical and anatomical plasticity of the brain. *Science, N.Y.*, **146**, 610–619.

BENTHAM, J. 1840. *The theory of legislation*. Weeks, Jordan, Boston.

BERLIN, I. 1953. *The hedgehog and the fox*. Simon and Schuster, New York.

BERNSTEIN, N. 1967. *The coordination and regulation of movements*. Pergamon Press, Oxford.

BIRCH, H. G. 1945. The relation of previous experience to insightful problem-solving. *J. comp. physiol. Psychol.*, **38**, 367–383.

BISHOP, A. 1964. Use of the hand in lower primates. In J. Buettner-Janusch (Ed.), *Evolutionary and genetic biology of primates*, Vol. 2. Academic Press, London and New York.

BLOCK, S. C. 1974. Early competence in problem-solving. In K. J. Connolly and J. S. Bruner (Eds.), *Growth of Competence*. Academic Press, New York and London.

BLOOM, B. (Ed.). 1956. *Taxonomy of educational objectives*. McKay, New York.

BOWLBY, J. 1969. *Attachment and loss*, Vol. 1. Basic Books, New York.

BRONFENBRENNER, U. 1970. *Two worlds of childhood, U.S. and U.S.S.R.* Russell Sage Foundation, New York.

BROWN, R. W. 1970. The first sentence of child chimpanzee. In *Psycholinguistics: selected papers by Roger Brown*. Free Press, New York.

BROWN, R. W. 1971. Are apes capable of language? *Neurosci. Res. Prog. Bull.*, **9** (5).

BRUNER, J. S. 1965. The growth of mind. *Amer. Psychol.*, **20**, 1007–1017.

BRUNER, J. S. 1966. *Toward a theory of instruction*. Harvard University Press, Cambridge.

BRUNER, J. S. 1970. *Poverty and childhood*. Merrill-Palmer Institute, Detroit.

BRUNER, J. S., GOODNOW, J. J. and AUSTIN, G. A. 1956. *A study of thinking*. Wiley, New York.

BRUNER, J. S., GREENFIELD, P. M. and OLVER, R. R. 1966. *Studies in cognitive growth*. Wiley, New York.

BRUNER, J. S. and KOSLOWSKI, B. 1972. Preadaptation in initial visually guided reaching. *Perception*, **1**, 3–14.

BÜHLER, K. 1934. *Sprachtheorie*. Jena.

CHANCE, M. R. A. 1967. Attention structure as the basis of primate rank orders. *Man*, **2**, 503–518.

CLARK, W. E. LE GROS. 1963. *The antecedents of man: an introduction to the evolution of the primates*. Harper and Row, New York.

COLE, M. and BRUNER, J. S. 1971. Cultural differences and inferences about psychological processes. *Amer. Psychol.*, **26**, 867–876.

CROMER, R. F. 1968. The development of temporal reference during the acquisition of language. Unpublished doctoral dissertation. Department of Social Relations, Harvard University.

DENENBERG, V. H. (Ed.). 1970. *Education of the infant and the young child.* Academic Press, New York and London.

DEVORE, I. 1965. *The primates.* Time-Life Books, New York.

DEWEY, J. 1916. *Democracy and education.* Macmillan, New York.

DOLHINOW, P. J. and BISHOP, N. 1970. The development of motor skills and social relationships among primates through play. *Minnesota Symposium on Child Psychology*, vol 4.

GALLUP, G. G., JR. 1970. Chimpanzees: self-recognition. *Science, N.Y.*, **167**, 86–87.

GARDNER, B. J. and GARDNER, R. A. 1971. Two-way communication with an infant chimpanzee. In A. M. Schrier and F. Stollnitz (Eds.), *Behavior of nonhuman primates*, Vol. 4. Academic Press, New York and London.

GEERTZ, C. 1972. Deep play: notes on the Balinese cockfight. *Daedalus*, **101**, 1–38.

GLADWIN, T. 1970. *East is a big bird.* Harvard University Press, Cambridge.

GOODALL, J. 1965. Chimpanzees of the Gombe Stream Reserve. In I. DeVore (Ed.), *Primate behavior: field studies of monkeys and apes.* Holt, Rinehart and Winston, New York.

GOULDNER, A. 1960. The norm of reciprocity: A preliminary statement. *Amer. Sociol. Rev.*, **25**, 161–178.

GREENFIELD, P., MAY, A. A. and BRUNER, J. S. 1972. *Early words* (a film). Wiley, New York.

HALL, K. R. L. and DEVORE, I. 1965. Baboon social behavior. In I. DeVore (Ed.), *Primate behavior: field studies of monkeys and apes.* Holt, Rinehart and Winston, New York.

HAMBURG, D. 1968. Evolution of emotional responses: Evidence from recent research on nonhuman primates. *Science and Psychoanalysis*, **12**, 39–54.

HARLOW, H. F. 1959. Love in infant monkeys. *Scientific American*, **200**, 68–74.

HARLOW, H. F. and HARLOW, M. K. 1962. The effect of rearing conditions on behavior. *Bull. Menninger Clinic*, **26**, 213–224.

HAYES, K. J. and HAYES, C. 1952. Imitation in a home-raised chimpanzee. *J. comp. physiol. Psychol.*, **45**, 450–459.

HERBERT, M. J. and HARSH, C. M. 1944. Observational learning in cats. *J. comp. physiol. Psychol.*, **37**, 81–95.

HINDE, R. A. 1971. Development of social behavior. In A. M. Schrier and F. Stollnitz (Eds.), *Behavior of nonhuman primates*. Academic Press, New York and London.

HOCKETT, C. D. 1960. The origins of speech. *Scientific American*, **203**, 88–96.

HUMBOLDT, W., VON. 1836. *Ueber die Verschiedenheit des menschlichen Sprachbaues.* Berlin (facsimile ed., Bonn, 1960).

ITANI, J. 1958. On the acquisition and propagation of a new food habit in the natural group of the Japanese monkey at Takasakiyama. *Primates*, **1**, 84–98.

JOLLY, A. 1966. *Lemur behavior: a Madagascar field study.* University of Chicago Press, Chicago.

KAWAMURA, S. 1959. The process of subculture propagation among Japanese macaques. *Primates*, **2**, 43–54.

KHROUSTOV, G. F. 1968. Formation and highest frontier of the implemental activity of anthropoids. In *Seventh International Congress of Anthropological and Ethnological Sciences*, Moscow, 503–509.

KING, D. L. 1966. A review and interpretation of some aspects of the infant-mother relationship in mammals and birds. *Psychol. Bull.*, **65**, 143–155.

KÖHLER, W. 1926. *The mentality of apes*. Harcourt, Brace, New York.

KORTLAND, A. 1965. How do chimpanzees use weapons when fighting leopards? *Yearbook of the American Philosophical Society*, 327–332.

KORTLAND, A. and KOÖIJ, M. 1963. Protohominid behaviour in primates. In J. Napier and N. A. Barnicot (Eds.), *The primates*. Symposia Zoological Society of London, **10**, 61–88.

KORTLAND, A. and VAN ZON, J. C. J. 1969. The present state of research on the dehumanization hypothesis of African ape evolution. *Proceedings of the International Congress of Primatology*, **3**, 10–13.

LAGUNA, G. A., DE. 1963. *Speech: its function and development* (orig. publ. 1927). Indiana University Press, Bloomington, Illinois.

LANCASTER, J. B. 1968. On the evolution of tool-using behavior. *Amer. Anthrop.*, **70**, 56–66.

LANGER, S. 1969. *Philosophy in a new key* (rev. ed.; orig. publ. 1942). Harvard University Press, Cambridge.

LASHLEY, K. S. 1951. The problem of serial order in behavior. In L. A. Jeffress (Ed.), *Cerebral mechanisms in behavior: the Hixon symposium*. Wiley, New York.

LEE, R. B. and DEVORE, I. (Eds.). 1968. *Man the hunter*. Aldine, Chicago.

LEVI-STRAUSS, C. 1963. *Structural anthropology*. Basic Books, New York.

LEWIS, D. 1969. *Convention*. Harvard University Press, Cambridge.

LOIZOS, C. 1967. Play behavior in higher primates: a review. In D. Morris (Ed.), *Primate ethology*. Aldine, Chicago.

LURIA, A. R. and YUDOVICH, F. Y. 1959. *Speech and the development of mental processes in the child*. Moscow, 1956. Staples Press, London.

MARSHACK, H. 1972. *The roots of civilization*. McGraw-Hill, New York.

MAYR, E. 1963. *Animal species and evolution*. Harvard University Press, Cambridge.

McLUHAN, M. 1964. *Understanding media*. McGraw-Hill, New York.

McNEILL, D. 1972. Sentence Structure in Chimpanzee Communication. K. J. Connolly and J. S. Bruner (Eds.), *Growth of Competence*, Academic Press, New York and London.

MERFIELD, F. G. and MILLER, H. 1956. *Gorilla hunter*. Farrar, Strauss, New York.

MILLAR, S. 1968. *The psychology of play*. Penguin Books, Baltimore, Md.

MORRIS, D. 1964. The response of animals to a restricted environment. *Symposium of the Zoological Society of London*, **13**, 99–118.

MORRIS, D. (Ed.). 1967. *Primate ethology*. Weidenfeld and Nicolson, London.

NAPIER, J. R. 1962. The evolution of the hand. *Scientific American*, **207**, 56–62.

PIAGET, J. 1967. *Six psychological studies* (Ed. by D. Elkind). Random House, New York.

PIAGET, J. 1971. *Structuralism*. Routledge and Kegan Paul, London.

PLOOG, D. and MELNECHUK, T. 1971. Are apes capable of language? *Neurosci. Res. Prog. Bull.*, **9**, 600–700.

POLANYI, I. 1958. *Personal knowledge*. University of Chicago Press, Chicago.

POPPER, K. 1954. *Nature, mind and modern science*. Hutchinson, London.

PREMACK, D. 1971. On the assessment of language competence in the chimpanzee. In A. M. Schrier and F. Stollnitz (Eds.), *Behavior of nonhuman primates*, Vol. 4. Academic Press, New York and London.

REYNOLDS, V. 1965. Behavioral comparisons between the chimpanzee and the mountain gorilla in the wild. *American Anthropologist*, **67**, 691–706.

RODMAN, P. 1972. Observations of free-ranging orangutans in Borneo. Colloquium talk at the Center for Cognitive Studies, Harvard University.

RUMBAUGH, D. M. 1970. Learning skills of anthropoids. In, *Primate behavior*, Vol. 1. Academic Press, New York.

RUMBAUGH, D. M. and MCCORMACK, C. 1967. The learning skills of primates: A comparative study of apes and monkeys. In D. Stark, R. Schneider and H. J. Kuhn (Eds.), *Progress in primatology*. Fischer, Stuttgart.

RUMBAUGH, D. M., RIESEN, A. H. and WRIGHT, S. C. 1972. Creative responsiveness to objects: A report of a pilot study with young apes. Privately distributed paper from Yerkes Laboratory of Psychobiology, Atlanta, Georgia.

SCHALLER, G. 1963. *Mountain gorilla*. University of Chicago Press, Chicago.

SCHALLER, G. 1964. *The year of the gorilla*. University of Chicago Press, Chicago.

SCHILLER, P. H. 1952. Innate constituents of complex responses in primates. *Psychol. Rev.*, **59**, 177–191.

SINGH, S. D. 1969. Urban monkeys. *Scientific American*, **221**, 108–115.

SLOBIN, D. 1971. Cognitive prerequisites of language. In W. O. Dingwall (Ed.), *Developmental psycholinguistics: a survey of linguistic science*. University of Maryland Linguistics Program, College Park.

SROUFE, A. and WUNSCH, J. P. The development of laughter in the first year of life. *Child. Dev.*, **43**, 1326–1344.

TINBERGEN, N. 1953. *The herring gull's world: A study of the social behavior of birds*. Collins, London.

TRIVERS, R. 1971. The evolution of reciprocal altruism. *Quart. Rev. Biol.*, **46**, 35–57.

TURNBULL, C. 1961. *The forest people*. Simon and Schuster, New York.

VAN LAWICK-GOODALL, J. 1968. The behavior of free living chimpanzees in the Gombe Stream Reserve. *Anim. Behav. Monogr.*, **1**, 165–301.

VYGOTSKY, L. S. 1967. Play and its role in the mental development of the child (1933). *Soviet Psychology*, **5**, 6–18.

WASHBURN, S. L. and HOWELL, F. C. 1960. Human evolution and culture. In S. Tax (Ed.), *The evolution of man*. University of Chicago Press, Chicago.

WEIR, R. H. 1962. *Language in the crib*. Mouton, The Hague.

WERNER, H. and KAPLAN, B. 1963. *Symbol formation*. Wiley, New York.

WHORF, B. L. 1956. *Language, thought and reality: selected writings* (Ed. by J. B. Carroll). M.I.T. Press, Cambridge; Wiley, New York.

WIENER, N. 1950. *The human use of human beings; cybernetics and society*. Houghton Mifflin, Boston.

YARBUS, A. L. 1967. *Eye movements and vision*. Plenum Press, New York.

YERKES, R. M. and YERKES, A. W. 1929. *The great apes: a study of anthropoid life*. Yale University Press, New Haven.

The Study of Primate Infancy

ALISON JOLLY
Lewes, Sussex

LET ME BEGIN with the conclusions. There are only two: simple, and I hope, very obvious. First, that a detailed comparison between human infants and infant primates is feasible. Second, that this comparison should be enlightening.

This paper is in the nature of a research proposal, not a report on work already done. I think that such research will be carried out fairly soon, though not primarily by me—some is already under way. I am particularly glad to be talking to this study group because you may be able to suggest guidelines and priorities for primate research which will be most useful to your own fields of interest.

The paper falls into three parts. First, why detailed cross-species comparisons of infant behaviour have not yet been made. Second, two attempts to relate human infant behaviour to primate studies: neonatal reflexes as part of an adaptive complex of clinging or being carried, and primates' object manipulation as it might relate to Piagetian stages of sensorimotor intelligence. Third, a section on relative rates of development in social, motor, and cognitive (or "adaptive") spheres— not to give any answers, but to show the kind of comparative table I hope the next five years of research will fill in.

When we do identify similar behavioural elements, and describe their functional relations among the primates, I think this will have important repercussions on developmental theory. We will then be able to arrange the elements of behaviour into many different sets of adaptive wholes: the cross-sectional complex that allows an infant of any one age to relate effectively to its environment, or the longitudinal complex which is appropriate to its own species. There will obviously be great differences in the mixes which make up the behavioural complexes of different species at different ages, if only because other primates' motor development is relatively more rapid than humans'. If there turn out to be finer-grained differences between species in social development and in the solving of cognitive tasks (differences that within a species might be called decalages), the other primates could add a new dimension to developmental studies. We would then want to know why capacities which seem logically connected, that compose one age-complex in humans, were not so connected in a monkey species. Or, if the primates achieve emotional and cognitive stages in the same order, and with much the same degree of consistency as human infants, this could enormously reinforce the current logic of developmental psychology.

BACKGROUND: WHY DETAILED COMPARISONS ARE ONLY NOW BECOMING POSSIBLE

In human psychology, you have now a far-reaching set of descriptions of a child's mental development in the first year of life. On the social side there is the sequence of non-specific smiling, specific attachment, and wariness or fear of strangers. On the perceptual side, there is the work of Bower (1969), Fantz (1967), Kagan (1959) and White (1970). On the cognitive side there are both the observations and the theoretical formulations of Piaget (1954) and Bruner (1968). Although Piaget's work dates from the thirties, and study of social smiling from Spitz and Woolf (1946), it is only recently becoming possible to put together the perceptual, cognitive and social aspects into one coherent description (e.g. Schaffer, 1971). Thus, psychologists are arriving at a theoretically powerful, and observationally detailed account of early infant development.

Primatologists are also arriving at a far deeper understanding of primate behaviour, chiefly as a result of field studies over the past ten years. For the present discussion, two aspects are most important: the adaptive complex of a primate species' behaviour in relation to its environment, and the sophistication we can now recognize in primate social relations.

Evolutionary theory explains how an animal's behaviour is adapted to its physical and social environment. We can expect most aspects of behaviour to function as a coherent whole, the so-called adaptive complex. To take an example almost at random, black-and-white colobus monkeys (*Colobus guereza*) eat mature leaves, while the congeneric red colobus (*Colobus badius*) largely eat new shoots. This ecological difference presumably influences manipulative patterns, and perhaps thereby such mental attributes as attention span. It also leads to striking social differences. The black-and-white colobus can sit virtually in one place throughout the year, for wet tropical forest provides mature leaves nearly everywhere in all seasons. One troop has been known to sleep in the same tree for five years. In contrast, the red colobus must range widely, semi-nomadically, as different trees put out new shoots. This in turn means that the black-and-whites can live in small, sedentary groups of 5–10 animals, defending their patches of territory. Troops bellow at each other to keep away, or males display at males of other troops, bouncing about in the tree-tops. Although the forest may support many red colobus, the reds must all feed together in the same tree at the same season, so their troops are large, with 40–80 animals together. Male black-and-whites may be autocratic, with an obvious alpha leader of the harem, and only one or two subordinates. We know less of the social behaviour of the reds, but there the males must associate with many potential rivals. Black-and-white infants grow up among adults, or with at most one or two peers of their own age, while red infants may share a communal playgroup. Vocal communication differs: black colobus have a series of discrete calls, which can communicate information between troops, whose animals are out of visual contact. Red colobus have a continuously intergrading series of calls, used in intra-troop communication (Clutton-Brock, 1971; Marler, 1969, 1970). These two species will become even more interesting when we learn something more about the olive colobus (*Procolobus verus*) an elusive swamp-living monkey which, alone of all the higher primates, has been seen carrying its baby in its mouth like a kitten or a bushbaby, not clinging to the fur (Booth, 1957).

The various aspects of a species' behaviour form an adaptive complex which allow animals to survive in and exploit their environment. However, it is only the field studies of the past decade which have begun to make clear how different primate societies do relate to their environment.

A second break-through in these field studies revealed the sophistication of primate (or mammalian) social behaviour. Long-term observation of the Gombe Stream Chimpanzees (van Lawick-Goodall, 1968, 1971) and Japanese macaques (Itani, 1963; Kawamura, 1958; Miyadi, 1967) in particular have revealed the network of kinship groupings, the mother's effect on an infant's social rank, mother–son incest barriers, individual personalities, and transmitted culture. We have moved from a reductionist view of a caged rhesus as "the" monkey, to an understanding that higher primates have the rudiments of most human interpersonal relationships. We can therefore legitimately look for the ontogeny of these relationships in the infant and juvenile primate.

Thus, it is only relatively recently that primatology has shown we can study primate juvenile behaviour in such relevant detail, and that child psychology has shown what details to look for. There is, however, a "technical" difficulty which has delayed the comparison—that higher

Fig. 1. Black and white colobus (*C. polykomos kikuyensis*) mother and 12 day old infant. Many primate species have a natal colouring which distinguishes the young infants. The thumbless colobus hand is adapted for hooking round branches. (Courtesy of the Zoological Society of San Diego.)

primate babies spend the first weeks or months of life clinging to their mothers (Figs 1 and 2), this means that the baby really has no signal that we can use, like human social smiling, as an index of attachment. Therefore to study the onset of differential attachment, one would need to compare multiple measures, as Ainsworth (1967) did for Ganda babies particularly direction of gaze, and quickness or strength of clinging.

There are only passing remarks in the literature about any non-human primate's ability to recognize, or to recall its own mother. Rowell (1963) described an eight-day-old rhesus following its mother's movements visually, though it was being carried by another female.

FIG. 2. Red colobus (*Colobus badius*) mother, in the wild. The head of an all-black. newly born infant can be seen on her chest, with its tail protruding above her thigh. The mother is rather doubtfully "presenting" to a male some feet behind her. (Courtesy of T. Clutton-Brock.)

Ploog (1969) believes that squirrel monkeys treat their mother as a succession of stimuli, not a social partner, through the first two weeks of life. Woolridge (1971) has recently described black-and-white colobus development in captivity. She says that "aunts" are allowed to take the infant from the first day of life, but specific attachment to the mother, shown by the infant's struggle to return to its own mother appears at three weeks. Hayes (1951) noted that Viki, her home-raised chimpanzee, went through a period of fear of strangers at six months, rather like human "eight months anxiety".

Mason *et al.* (1971) have begun to study systematically the relative roles of touch and vision in infant attachment. They found that at two weeks, rhesus infants were only slightly more reassured by contact with a familiar than with a visually unfamiliar surrogate mother, while at six weeks there were significant differences. When the infant rhesus could see but not touch the surrogate mothers, the familiar mother was slightly more reassuring at both ages. It must be said that though this study asks interesting questions, the methods might appal child psychologists. The "mothers" are fur-covered blocks of wood, 7 in. × 4 in. × ½ in. Testing takes place first at two weeks and monthly thereafter, and the measures used (at least in their preliminary report) are easily quantifiable scores, such as heart rate and distress calls. Whatever changes take place more quickly (more easily recorded with multiple observational criteria) or what might happen with more optimal mothers, appears to have been neglected.

Lemmon (1971) in an equally preliminary report suggests that human mothering rapidly produces the distance social signals, even in chimpanzee infants. "Obvious positive social responses have been recorded within the first three days in all chimpanzee infants removed from their mothers at birth. The most obvious of these is the smiling response, most effectively elicited by the human face about 12 in. away, accompanied by soft vocalization. Infants left with chimpanzee mothers have not been observed to regard the mother's face within the first three months or smile within the first six. By two weeks of age, human-reared infants track a light in the dark, although chimpanzee-reared infants show no such response until ten weeks of age." It may be that Lemmon's "social smile" is what other observers call a "fear grin", and it may be that the smile is highly ambivalent in chimpanzees between fear and greeting. However, the accelerated rate of development seems incontestable.

Some perceptual experiments (Fantz, 1968) and some cognitive ones (Zimmermann and Torrey, 1965) have been done with very young monkeys. In view of Lemmon's results, there may be great differences in the development of hand-reared and normal mother-reared infants. Perhaps most information could be gained from the offspring of wholly tame mothers that let you handle their children. This rapidly becomes research on pets, a procedure both theoretically and emotionally at odds with the Harlow school of primate psychology (e.g. Gluck and Harlow's, 1971, scathing comments on Hebb, Scott and others for studying home-reared animals). Thus, few American primate psychologists have examined infants with the necessary detail, while most field workers have thought it more important to observe their animals' behaviour in the natural environment than to hand-tame them for experimental manipulation. However, Struhsaker's (1971) quantitative analysis of maternal behaviour in wild vervets (*Cercopithecus aethiops*) shows how much can be done with wild, undisturbed troops, given good observation conditions and appropriate statistical techniques. This leads one soon to expect field descriptions like Hinde's analysis of the infant and maternal roles in promoting contact (Hinde and Spencer-Booth, 1971), and in fact Owen has such data on the Gombe Stream baboons (Hinde, personal communication).

One body of research has tried to be directly comparable, the study of infant separation from the mother. This has, of course, contributed a great deal: Harlow's (1965) initial demonstration of the sexual and maternal incompetence of isolation-reared rhesus; Hinde's (1971b) analysis of the role of maternal rejections, and differences between removing the mother or the infant; Rosenblum's (1971) comparison of multi-mothered bonnet macaques with the coercive mothering of pigtailed macaques. However, these studies have not as yet calibrated the ages and duration of separation. Harlow's group worked with a minimum isolation period of three months, Rosenblum 2–8 weeks. Hinde studied separation of 18–32 week old infants, Rosenblum 2–6 month old infants. Spencer-Booth and Hinde (1971a, b) find little or no difference in the effects of maternal separation between 18–32 weeks of age. However, separating the infant for two weeks depressed its activity after reunion with the mother, more than separation for one week. They have normative data for time on and off the mother, frequency of maternal and infant approaches and so forth, but they do not complicate their analysis with extrapolations to the stages of independence of the human child. It seems likely that initial attachment occurs much earlier than the separation tests, perhaps in the first week or two of life.

Hinde, in fact, is careful even in lectures not to hazard a guess as to the approximate ages of his rhesus in human terms, for no single answer could be correct. The basic cross-species calibration, which would permit one to relate primate separation studies to similar observations made on humans, such as those of Schaffer and Emerson (1964), has yet to be done.

Of course, these ideas are not new, they underlie the classical attempts to raise chimpanzees in human homes—Nadia Kohts' (1923), the Kelloggs' (1933), the Hayes' (1951). What is new is our more detailed and powerful understanding of children's development, which gives a much better idea of what to look for among the primates. Furthermore, after reading Warren's (in press) account of the loose comparisons between African neonates and published European norms, by workers who have not tested a European sample for themselves, one realizes the difficulties and outright mistakes that have characterized comparative studies even within our own species. Developmental testing does not seem to be a mechanical science, but a craft learned by practice and apprenticeship. It is not surprising that the older published primate data is largely incommensurable with the published human norms, quite aside from the fact that most primate research has aimed to answer other questions.

THE FEASIBILITY OF COMPARISON

Two examples may illustrate the feasibility of detailed comparison. The first is a look at a single adaptive age-complex, that of the normal human neonate, with some questions about how single reflexes or perceptual characteristics might be derived from a clinging primate ancestor. This illustrates how such comparisons make sense at the single reflex level, even though the reflexes add up to different behavioural complexes in humans and various other primates. Second, is a longitudinal list of the Piagetian stages of sensorimotor intelligence, with experiments that represent the human child's achievements at different ages. This may indicate that child psychology can indeed provide a new theoretical orientation for studies of primate intelligence.

A. The Neonatal Adaptive Complex

All higher primate infants, except our own and perhaps the olive colobus, cling to their mothers' fur for the first days or weeks of life. Most newborn primates can support themselves on their mothers' fur from birth, and may climb unassisted to the nipple. The record for precocity seems to be infant squirrel monkeys, which may begin climbing with the hands before the hindquarters are delivered, and thus assist their own birth (Takeshita, 1961–62). However, most mothers hold their infants at some time, and even squirrel monkeys carry an incapacitated infant (Rosenblum, 1968). Chimpanzee and gorilla mothers generally support their young with a hand, especially when moving, for the first month or two of life. Our closest primate relatives thus have more helpless neonates than do the true monkeys (Fossey, 1971; van Lawick-Goodall, 1971; Schaller, 1963).

Among the lemurs, three species of one genus differ sharply in their maternal behaviour. Ringtailed lemurs are relatively precocious, climbing actively on to "aunts" in the first week of life; brown lemurs are more helpless, leaving the mother only in the second month, while variegated lemurs are born hairless and helpless in a nest, where they are left for the first 3–4 weeks (Klopfer and Klopfer, 1970; Klopfer, in press). The lemurs indicate to us how widely development may differ even between closely related species. It is conceivable that our own infants became nest young at a fairly early stage in our evolution, differing from gorilla and chimpanzee as the variegated lemur differs from other lemurs.

Gorilla, chimpanzee and orang-utan all build sleeping nests. Van Lawick-Goodall describes sick chimpanzees, either incapacitated by polio or simply under the weather with bad colds, remaining in their nests for much of the day. Thus, although the apes do not use their nests to give birth, or as places to recuperate after childbirth, this could have been a fairly easy transition for early hominids. On the other hand, it seems unlikely, looking at our infants, that early human mothers left their babies behind in a nest, until the advent of blankets, safe anti-predator homes, and possibly bottle-feeding.

Much of the human neonate's behaviour instead fits into the pattern of clinging or being carried by a mother: for us as for other newborn primates the mother is most of the environment. The traction reflex ensures that an infant's hand will close, or close tighter, when its own weight pulls its arm muscles (Twitchell, 1970). Prechtl (1965) points out that the Moro reflex, given when the baby is holding on to something, would tighten the baby's grasp when it is startled by a sudden jerk from its mother's movement. In general, the neonate is able to move more coherently when prone than supine, but perhaps "prone" should be read "in ventral contact", and means largely on the mother as opposed to on the ground. Many of the pushing, crawling, and head lifting movements of the neonate work as well when he is tipped at an angle on the mother as when prone. However, the chimpanzee neonate, who is carried underneath the mother's belly, can lift its own head in supine position from four weeks, as compared with six months in the human.

The action of the hand itself, which is very similar in all baby primates, splays the fingers apart in extension, then brings them close and parallel in flexion, as a whole hand movement. This is not so much a "grasp" reflex as a "tangling" reflex—hair is caught quite firmly between the proximal ends of the fingers and under the knuckles, although the infant may have less strength in grasping a dowell or branch that lies across the palm. Hair which is long and straight enough to stick between the fingers is more easily grasped—were our ancestors shaggy rather than woolly? (Fig. 3a and b).

On the perceptual side, if an infant's eyes only focus at $7\frac{1}{2}$ in. (White, 1970) this would mean that nearby parts of its mother are in focus, while tracking moving objects at 2–3 ft possibly allows the infant to follow some movements of her head or hands. The "doll's-eye reflex", in which the eyes remain fixed in one direction while the body is turned,

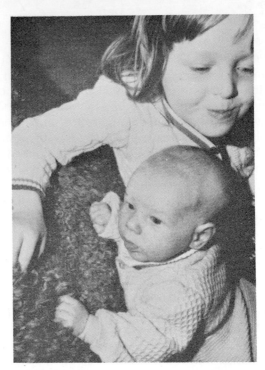

FIG. 3(a). Six-week infant propping himself on a sheepskin coat, which is at a 45° angle. The infant's hands are typically clenched, but have little purchase on the short fur. Ventral contact allows the "prone" reflexes of pushing and head-lifting, while semi-erect posture allows maximum alertness.

FIG. 3(b). Six-week infant lifting a goatskin coat, while being lifted himself. The long fur caught between fingers and under the knuckles gives him maximum purchase.

perhaps provides moments of perceptual constancy. (Do all young mammals have a doll's-eye reflex? Or mainly the primates who are carried? Or only the altricial human?) Of course, vision probably plays a very minor role in the infant's first week or so. It may be that newborn infants have tactile preferences for skin over fur (in our case) or fur over skin (in infra-human primates). It also seems likely that newborns can smell not just anise or asafoetida (Lipsitt, 1967) but the compound odour of a post-parturient mother, since it would be more adaptive to find the way to the callostrum than the Pernod.

The list could be lengthened, with physiological adaptations, etc., but enough has been said to show how one age-level might be described, with many behavioural elements each fitting into a single adaptive complex. The point is, that to compare humans usefully with other primates, we must break down each complex into single components or reflexes, to see what part they play in each species.

B. Cognitive Stages

The Piagetian account of infant development provides a *natural* ordering of experiments—the order in which they would be solved by a growing child, whether or not one accepts Piagetian mechanisms of mental progress from stage to stage. This is treated more fully in Jolly (1972) so the possible correspondences are only listed here. In referring to Piagetian stages, I am not trying to imply that any primate develops step by step like climbing a staircase—rather, I am using these stages as convenient reference points (see Hinde, 1971a, on uses and abuses of developmental stages).

1 and 2. Stages of reflex and primary circular reactions

Diagnosis: Stage 2 ends with co-ordinated reaching.
Human 0–4 months, rhesus 0–15 days, chimpanzee 0–8 weeks.
Newborn chimpanzees differentially watch patterns and follow contours (Fantz, 1968).
Twelve-day rhesus can recognize and generalize form, brightness and colour discriminations (Zimmermann and Torrey, 1965).

3. Stage of secondary circular reactions

Diagnosis: co-ordinated reaching and grasping, but does not uncover hidden objects.
Human 4–8 months. No developmental data so far on primates' search for hidden objects.
Adult slender loris (*Loris tardigradus*) are said not to uncover a hidden

object, or push open a cage door left ajar, or reach around a transparent barrier, unless intensively trained (Jolly, 1964; Subramoniam, 1957).

Adult lemurs (*Lemur fulvus*) repeat an oriented reach with little attention to the connection of objects; upward on a box or its hinged lid, downward in or beside a bottlemouth, or bring a hand to their mouth whether or not they have dropped a raisin (Jolly, 1964).

4. Stage of co-ordination of secondary schemas

Diagnosis: child finds object hidden in one place, but does not find it in a second place, instead returning to the first. This, in primate terms, is a delayed response test.

Human 8–12 months, rhesus? to five months.

Strong position habits affect the responses of young rhesus monkeys, chimpanzees, and adult lemurs. Although there are great differences in speed and efficiency on delayed response tests, all species of primates seem to solve such tests as adults (Fletcher, 1965; Harlow *et al.*, 1971; Zimmermann and Torrey, 1965).

5. Stage of tertiary circular reactions

Diagnosis: solves delayed response, combines objects, does not use delayed imitation or symbols.

Human 12–18 months. Chimpanzee 11–18 months (hand-raised) or eleven months to several years (wild).

Piaget compares performance at this level to Kohler's "insight" tests solved by juvenile chimpanzees: pulling in food with sticks or on strings, piling boxes, etc. (Kohler, 1927; Schiller, 1957).

Wild chimpanzees begin termite fishing with inadequate sticks and straws at two years and achieve an adult technique by five years. Wild chimpanzees do not combine more than one tool, except in one possible case where a juvenile (Fifi) fished for a dropped leaf-sponge with a short stick. They do use sticks as clubs, levers, probes and missiles, and leaf-sponges for drinking water or for cleaning themselves (van Lawick-Goodall, 1968, 1971). Some populations use sticks or rocks to hammer hard nuts (Struhsaker and Hunkeler, 1971).

6. Stage of mental representation

Diagnosis: internal representation of actions, delayed imitation, pretence, words.

Human eighteen months on. Trained chimpanzee eighteen months on.

Washoe soaped and bathed and dried her doll, Viki mixed cakes, etc. (Gardner and Gardner, 1972; Hayes, 1951).

Washoe and Sarah used symbols, whether or not one calls it language (Gardner and Gardner, 1972; Premack, 1970).

Julia could trace a complex maze backwards from goal to start, before making first move, or a five-step series of tools opening locked boxes before making one first choice of tool (Dohl, 1968; Rensch and Dohl, 1968).

Figan pretended to leave banana boxes, leading away more dominant males, then doubled back to feed alone (van Lawick-Goodall, 1971). It is worth noting that the human-trained chimpanzees reached stage 6 in dealing with objects at eighteen months or two years, while the wild chimpanzee achieved social pretence at adolescence. Perhaps Figan should be credited not with pretence, but with deceit.

7. Stage of preoperational thought

Learning sets and repeated reversal learning. Rhesus monkeys do not solve these problems at four months, and do not reach an adult level even at one year (Harlow et al., 1971).

Oddity problems. Rhesus, chimpanzees and nursery-school children all solve these, and data exists on non-verbal oddity learning in nursery-school children (Brown and Lloyd, 1971; Davis et al., 1968). Rhesus and chimpanzees solve Weigl-type oddity problems, in which a stimulus tray of one colour requires the choice of the odd stimulus, while another colour requires the subject to choose the end one of two similar stimuli. This is similar to Premack's symbols for "same" and "different" (Meyer et al., 1965).

Classification. Rhesus monkeys can choose a class of "all blue objects" or "all flower pictures" out of mixed groups of red and blue, or flowers and insects. Viki, the chimpanzee, sorted objects into two, but not more categories, and could choose different categories, such as form or colour, for sorting the same set of objects (Hayes and Nissen, 1971; Lehr, 1967; Weinstein, 1945).

Seriation. Adult rhesus monkeys and chimpanzees can choose a series of symbols for food, in order, from the symbol for the largest to the smallest piece. This seems close to true seriation, and compares with human non-verbal seriation (Braine, 1959; Kapunè, 1966; Menzel, 1969).

So far as I am aware conservation and intersecting class experiments have not been carried out with primates.

TABLE I. *Summary of data on behavioural development from Hinde (1971b). Reprinted with permission of the auth*

Species	Authority	Type of study	Releases grip for tactile exploration	Coordinated reaching	Eye-hand coordina
Marmoset (*Callithrix jacchus*)	Epple, 1967	Lab. group			
Tamarin, Pinché (*Saguinus geoffroyi, S. oedipus*)	Epple, 1967	Lab. group			
Howler (*Alouatta villosa*)	Carpenter, 1934, 1965 Altmann, 1959	Field Field		10 days	
Cebus (*Cebus apella*)	Nolte and Dücker, 1959	Lab. *N* = 1	2nd week	2–3 weeks	16 da
Squirrel monkey (*Saimiri sciureus*)	Hopf, 1967 Vandenbergh, 1966 Rosenblum, 1968 Baldwin, 1969	Lab. Lab. group *N* = 1 Lab. *N* = 6 Field	2nd week	*c.* 2 weeks 1st week *c.* 2 weeks 3rd week	
Rhesus (*Macaca mulatta*)	Hinde *et al.*, 1964 Hinde and Spencer-Booth, 1967a Southwick *et al.*, 1965	Lab. groups Field *N* = 1	5(3–6) days	9(6–10) days	18(16–24
Stumptail (*Macaca arctoides*)	Bertrand, 1969 and personal communication	Lab. and zoo *N* = 1–5	Day 3–6	*c.* 2 weeks	*c.* 16 d
Mangabey (*Cercocebus albigena*)	Chalmers, 1967 Chalmers, personal communication	Field *N* = 1–2 Lab. group *N* = 4		36(34–40) days	2½–3½ v 44(34–51
Baboon (*Papio ursinus, P. anubis*)	De Vore, 1963 Hall and De Vore, 1965 Rowell *et al.*, 1968 Rowell, personal communication	Field ⎱ Field ⎰ Lab. colony *N* = *c.* 6	3 days	3 days	8 da
Vervet (*Cercopithecus aethiops*)	Chalmers, personal communication	Lab. group *N* = 5		20(8–44) days	39(26–54
Vervet (*Cercopithecus sabaeus*)	Schlott, 1956 ⎱ Moog, 1957 ⎰	Zoo	15 days		
Sykes' monkey (*Cercopithecus mitis*)	Chalmers, personal communication	Lab. group *N* = 2		29, 34 days	34, 44
Talapoin (*Cercopithecus talapoin*)	Hill, 1966	Lab. *N* = 1	2 days	4 days	4 da
Allen's swamp monkey (*Cercopithecus nigroviridis*)	Pournelle, 1962				
Patas monkey (*Erythrocebus patas*)	Goswell and Gartlan, 1965	Lab. *N* = 1	Day 2	Day 5	Day
Hanuman Langur (*Presbytis entellus*)	Jay, 1963, 1965 Sugiyama, 1965a Yoshiba, 1968	Field Field Field		7 days	17 d
Chimpanzee (*Pan troglodytes*)	Van Lawick-Goodall, Mason, 1965b	Field Lab.		6–10 weeks	
Gorilla (*Gorilla gorilla*)	Schaller, 1963	Field, zoo		7–11 weeks	

[1] The figures in the body of the table refer to first ages at which criteria were seen to be re

mic Press.[1]

g solid ood	Off mother	More than 2 ft from mother	Steady walking	Competent climbing off mother	Sexual or pseudo-sexual behavior	Weaning
5 days	17–21 days (all adults)					60 days
days	23 days (all adults)					
weeks days	15 days (all adults)		c. 1 month	15–20 days		1¼–2 years
s 4 days	c. 5 weeks			6–7 weeks		
veeks nonth	c. 3 weeks 14 days c. 3 weeks 5 weeks		6 weeks	2 weeks 6 weeks	4–5 months 8–10 weeks	c. 9 months 8–11 months
31) days	9(4–15) days	1–2 weeks	2–3 weeks	3–4 weeks	Mounting: ♂ 12th–46th week Presenting: ♂ 25th–30th week ♀ 13th–18th week	Variable 3–13 months
	4 days	7 days				By 12 months
8 days	c. 15 days	20–21 days	3–4 weeks		Mounting: ♂ 9–11 weeks Presenting: ♂ 7–12 weeks ♀ 7 weeks	Variable c. 1 year
51) days	2–9 days 4–11 days 14(9–36) days	6 weeks	3–4 weeks 44(35–51) days	c. 6 weeks 22(12–36) days		
onths	c. 4 weeks					11–15 months
weeks	<1 week		c. 21 days	c. 20–35 days		
8) days	6(3–8) days		31(26–49) days	15(8–29) days	Mounting 81, 89 days	
days	21 days			27–30 days		60 days
days	4, 14 days		34, 34 days	14, 26 days		
days	6 days		c. 8 days	17 days	54 days	50 days
days	14 days					75 days
y 12	Day 8					
onths	1–2 weeks (all adults)	c. 2 weeks	c. 3 weeks			11–15 months
day	9 days (all adults)	c. 4 weeks	8th week	c. 2 months	c. 10 months	Up to 20 months
onths	14–22 weeks	7–9 months	c. 12 months		9 months	11–15 months 2–5 years
onths onths	c. 3 months		4–6 months 5–6 months	c. 6 months		

s are indicated in brackets and medians precede the brackets. For reservations, see text.

TABLE II. *Comparison of rates of development of rhesus and stumptailed macaques with human infants. After Hinde (1971b), Illingworth (1971), Jensen (1961), Mowbray and Cadell (1962) and Rowell (1963). m, months; w, weeks; d, days*

Age	Rhesus and stumptailed Macaques	Humans
0 w	Visual localization of sound,	Hunger cry, pain cry
1–7 d	discomfort cry, whoo cry	
1 w	Off mother, follows mother	
7–14 d	with eyes	
2 w	Grasps object, eats solid food,	
15–21 d	more than 2 ft from mother	
3 w	Loses Moro reflex, incipient	
22–28 d	reaching, steady walking	
4 w	Primitive squeeze raisin,	Stares at face
29–36 d	competent climbing off	
1 m	mother	
5 w	Palmar grasp of raisin,	
37–42 d	rough and tumble play,	
	peer play	
6 w	Scissors grasp on raisin,	
	greeting growl	
7 w	Pincer grasp on raisin	
8 w		Turns head to sound,
2 m		incipient reach
9 w	Allogrooms, lipsmack	
10 w	Social fear calls	Loses Moro reflex
11 w		
3 m		Follows mother with eyes, smiles to face not just a spot
4 m		Reaches for large object, swipes small object
5 m	Social threat calls (this occurs *c.* 18 m in human), delayed response tests	
6 m		Primitive squeeze pellet
7 m		Palmar grasp pellet
8 m		Scissors grasp of pellet, fear of strangers
9 m		
10 m		
11 m		
12 m		Pincer grasp of pellet, peer play, rough and tumble play, delayed response

RELATIVE RATES OF DEVELOPMENT

Hinde (1971b) has given a very useful summary of the quantitative data on primate behavioural development, Table I. His main conclusion is that, despite the inadequacies of the data, the various species of primate clearly develop at widely differing rates. Ideally, one would like to follow Hinde's table with a description of even one species' development in the motor, social, and cognitive spheres. Table II provides some information on the development of macaque monkeys. Jensen's account of prehension in a single stumptailed macaque is all there is to compare with the rhesus, bonnet or pigtail macaque data on the development of social behaviour.

Within each study, the order of appearance of the different characteristics is similar for macaque and human. The swipe is followed by palmar grasp, scissors grasp, and pincer grasp in that order (Connolly and Elliott, 1972). Visual attention to faces is followed by greeting gestures, later fear gestures and much later threat. The Moro and the "forced" grasping reflexes persist up to or after the infant monkey can walk steadily, while the human has several months gap between the loss of these ancestral clinging reflexes and the emergence of crawling. The monkeys are climbing at 3–4 weeks, before developing the species' greeting noise at six weeks and before any fine prehension of small objects.

The information in Table II suggests that, in man, as compared to the macaque, social responses appear earlier than fine prehension. However, since the two sets of macaque data are from different studies of different species this suggestion must be viewed cautiously. A more valuable comparison might at this stage be drawn between the growth of the rhesus' attention to faces and greetings and Wolff's (1963) natural history of the smile: or the development of fear and Schaffer's (1971) "perceptual" of expressed fear of strangers.

Similar comparisons are equally necessary on the cognitive side. Zimmermann and Torrey's (1965) estimate of five months as the age at which rhesus monkeys can solve delayed response tests is included but perhaps a rhesus given a Piaget type test would locate a doll hidden under one of two blankets a month or so before it could work to the assembly line criteria of the Wisconsin General Test Apparatus.

Comparisons between gorilla, chimpanzee and human infants are given in Tables III and IV. Here it is possible to see differences in greater detail. In the nonhuman species the motor control necessary to lift the head when supine or while being pulled into a sitting position comes relatively early—chimpanzee infants are carried upside down on their

TABLE III. *Comparison of rates of development between chimpanzee and human infants. After Hayes (1951), Hinde (1971b), Knobloch and Pasamanick (1959a and b), v. Lawick-Goodall (1968) and Lemmon (1971). m, months*

Age	Chimpanzee	Human
0 m	No head lag, when pulled to sit, sustains head in zone III when prone, smiles to human face, tracks light in dark (human-reared)	
1 m	Incipient reach, stands holding mother, lifts head supine, head bobs when sitting, tracks objects past midline when supine, brings object to mouth	Smiles to human face
2 m	Coordinated reach and grasp, play face when tickled, head set forward when sitting, rolls from supine to prone, reach to chimps, tracks light in dark (chimp-reared)	Incipient reach, tracks objects past midline when supine, head bobs when sitting
3 m	Obtains Gesell ring by string, lifts head when pulled to sit, pivots when prone, crawls on stomach, regards chimpanzee faces, off mother, sit to prone	Object to mouth, head set forward when sitting, sustains head in zone III when prone, no head lag when pulled to sit
4 m		
5 m	Kisses, eats solid food, fear vocalizations (van Lawick–Goodall), sits erect momentarily, creeps, stands with hand held, allogrooms	Top level reach, ticklish, rolls from supine to prone
6 m	Pivots sitting, fear of strangers (Hayes), smiles to chimpanzees (Lemmon)	Lifts head when supine, sits erect momentarily, lifts head when pulled to sit, fear of strangers when mother present
7 m	Sits steadily	Obtains Gesell ring by string, stands with hand held
8 m	2 ft from mother	Stands holding rail, fear of strangers, crawls on stomach
9 m		Waves bell, sits steadily, sit to prone, creeps
10 m	Spontaneously waves bell, puts cube in cup, releases cube in cup, tries tower of two blocks, threat display	Puts cube in cup

TABLE III—*continued*

Age	Chimpanzee	Human
11 m	Tower of two cubes, points to wants, eats with spoon	Pivots sitting
12 m	Spontaneous scribble, steady walking	Releases cube in cup, tries tower of two blocks
13 m		
14 m		
15 m	Looks at pictures	Tower of two cubes, points to wants
16 m		
17 m		
18 m		Threat display, spontaneous scribble, looks at pictures

mothers' stomach until about six months old. Motor control when in an erect position, sitting or standing, is not so advanced. In the chimpanzee there is again a suggestion that the onset of fine prehension and manipulation are slightly earlier than greeting, fear and threat gestures, compared to the human, while gross motor control is earlier still. Again, this must be treated with caution, because the social data come from van Lawick-Goodall's wild chimpanzees while the adaptive behaviour is from Gesell tests on home-reared animals.

Table IV is drawn from Knobloch and Pasamanick's (1959a, b) study of Colo, a gorilla born at the Colombus Zoo. This is reproduced as the only recent attempt to give a primate Gesell Tests by experimenters experienced with human infants. They remark on (1) the relative precocity of this gorilla, as compared to the chimpanzee, in both motor and adaptive behaviour in the first months, (2) the gorilla's remaining, in adaptive behaviour, at roughly the level of a 40–44 week human, while home-raised chimpanzees behave at least like human (averbal) two-year-olds, and (3) spurts in the gorilla's adaptive behaviour. These spurts I think might reflect underlying advances in more general capacities such as object conservation. Unfortunately, there is little social data, because gorillas earn epithets ranging from Yerkes' "introverted" to Knobloch and Pasamanick's "autistic".

It would be fascinating to compare the development of infant orangutans with the other two great apes. In zoos, orang-utans are the most manipulative of the apes (Benchley, 1942; Parker, 1969; Rensch and Duecker, 1966) surpassing in problem solving even the chimpanzee. However, they are solitary in the wild, unlike any other higher primate.

TABLE IV. *Comparison of rates of development between gorilla and human infants.
After Knobloch and Pasamanick (1959a, b). w, weeks; m, months*

Age	Gorilla	Human
0 w		
2 w	Visually tracks object to midline when supine	
4 w	Head bobs when sitting	Visually tracks object to midline when supine, diminishes activity to bell ring
6 w	Tracks object past midline when supine, sustains head in zone III when prone	
8 w	Retains rattle briefly	Retains rattle briefly, tracks object past midline when supine, head bobs when sitting
10 w	Two hand approach, diminishes activity to bell ring, tracks object 180° when supine, arms activate on sight, brings object to mouth, looks from hand to object, rolls from supine to prone, head set forward when sitting, lifts head when pulled to sit, crawls on stomach	Arms activate on sight
12 w	Regards rattle in hand, one hand approach and grasp, eats solid food	Tracks object 180° when supine
14 w	Stands with hand held, stands holding rail	
16 w	Holds two cubes	Looks from hand to object, brings object to mouth, head set forward when sitting, sustains head in zone III when prone, regards rattle in hand
4 m	Retains two cubes as a third is presented, grasps pellet and bottle simultaneously, manipulates string holding ring, sits erect steadily, goes from sitting to prone, creeps	
5 m	Transfers object from hand to hand, grasps third cube, pivots when sitting	Two hand approach, grasps object if near the hand, rolls from supine to prone

TABLE IV—*continued*

Age	Gorilla	Human
6 m	Index finger to pellet, steady walking	Lifts head when supine, lifts head when pulled to sit
7 m		One hand approach and grasp, transfers object from hand to hand, holds two cubes, stands with hands held, retains two cubes as a third is presented
8 m	Sequential play with cubes	Stands holding rail, crawls on stomach, grasps a third cube, manipulates string holding ring
9 m		Sits steady, sitting to prone, creeps, grasps pellet and bottle simultaneously, cube into cup
10 m		Pokes bell clapper, index finger to pellets, sequential play with cubes
11 m	Pokes bell clapper	Pivots sitting
12 m		Scribbling, tries cube tower
Not seen:	Cube into cup, looks at pictures, scribbling, eats with spoon, cube tower	
24 m	Waves bell	

When two orang-utans happen on to the same fruit tree they neither greet nor groom each other, but feed indifferently and proceed on their separate ways (McKennon, 1971; Rodman, 1973). At some point their relative frequency of social and manipulative responses must diverge from all other primates'—perhaps the rates at which they advance in different spheres are shifted as well.

CONCLUSIONS

One distinguishing feature of early human development is the long period of perceptual learning. Long before he acquires any degree of motor competence the infant already possesses a well developed perceptual apparatus (Schaffer, 1971). Human infants begin to *recognize* objects between 3–6 months, as shown by visual fixation, the habituation of fixation, and cardiac deceleration when presented with novel versus familiar stimuli. It is only at about 7–8 months that a child can selectively manipulate novel stimuli whilst inhibiting reaching for familiar stimuli. At the same time, the child may begin to show fear of strangers, to seek for hidden objects and to seek for his absent mother. All this Schaffer sees as the growth of *recall*, the facility of free access to a central representation. In precocial birds on the other hand, the ability to recognize the mother object is usually taken to be synonymous with the ability to respond selectively. In this case by running away from strange objects.

Schaffer's paper is a cross-sectional account of a whole adaptive complex which appears in the human at about eight months. It is the sort of complex which should be compared with the nonhuman primates. A rhesus monkey can run to or from strangers before the onset of fear calls, a chimpanzee cannot. It may or may not inhibit reaching, we do not know for certain, but the rhesus begins to eat solid food at a third of the age when it is reported to give social fear calls. In contrast a chimpanzee begins eating solid food at about the same time as it gives fear calls. Presumably to eat very much the selective manipulation of familiar objects is necessary, though the first foods may not be recalled, just recognized as what the mother ape is currently taking.

To return, then, to the conclusions stated at the beginning, nonhuman primates are enough like people for a detailed comparison of infant behaviour to be feasible. When such comparisons are made, they will be of significance for further theoretical advances. One of the advances seems likely to be in organizing experiments in primate cognitive psychology under a Piagetian or neo-Piagetian rubric, which may bring a welcome degree of order to the primate work. A second advance would come in deciphering the relative rates of social, manipulative, and motor development in man and primate, to illuminate the nature as well as the evolution of infant competence.

REFERENCES

AINSWORTH, M. D. S. 1967. *Infancy in Uganda*. Johns Hopkins Univ. Press, Baltimore.

BENCHLEY, B. 1942. *My friends the apes*. Little Brown, Boston.

BOOTH, A. M. 1957. Observations on the natural history of the olive colobus monkey, *Procolobus verus* (van Boneden). *Proc. Zool. Soc. Lond.*, **129**, 421–430.

BOWER, T. G. R. 1969. Perceptual functioning in early infancy. In R. J. Robinson (Ed.), *Brain and early behavior*. Academic Press, London.

BRAINE, M. D. S. 1959. The ontogeny of certain logical operations: Piaget's formulation tested by non-verbal methods. *Psychol. Monogr.* No. 475.

BROWN, A. L. and LLOYD, B. B. 1971. Criteria of success: a developmental study of oddity learning. *Brit. J. Psychol.*, **61**, 21–26.

BRUNER, J. S. 1968. *Processes of cognitive growth: infancy*. Clark Univ. Press, Williamstown.

CLUTTON BROCK, T. 1971. Ecology of the red colobus monkey (*Colobus badius*) in the Gombe Stream Reserve, Tanzania. Paper presented at the joint meeting of the Association for the Study of Animal Behaviour and the Primate Society of Great Britain, London, November 1971.

CONNOLLY, K. and ELLIOTT, J. 1972. The evolution and ontogeny of hand function. In N. Blurton Jones (Ed.), *Ethological studies of child behaviour*. Cambridge Univ. Press, Cambridge.

DAVIS, R. T., LEARY, R. W., CASEBEER SMITH, M. D. and THOMPSON, R. F. 1968. Learning and perception of oddity problems by *Lemur* and seven species of monkey. *Primates*, **8**, 311–323.

DÖHL, J. 1968. Uber die fähigkeit einer Schimpansen Umweg mit selbständigen Zwischenzielen zu ünerblicken. *Z. f. Tierpsychol.*, **25**, 89–103.

FANTZ, R. L. 1967. Visual perception and experience in early infancy: a look at the hidden side of behavioural development. In H. W. Stevenson, E. H. Hess and H. L. Rheingold (Eds.), *Early behavior*. Wiley, New York.

FANTZ, R. L. 1968. Visual discrimination in a neonate chimpanzee. *Percept. Mot. Skills*, **8**, 59–66.

FLETCHER, H. J. 1965. The delayed response problem. In A. M. Schrier, H. F. Harlow and F. Stollnitz (Eds.), *Behavior of nonhuman primates*, Vol. 1. Academic Press, New York.

FOSSEY, D. 1971. More years with mountain gorillas. *Natl. Geographic*, **140**, 574–586.

GARDNER, B. T. and GARDNER, R. A. 1971. Two-way communication with a chimpanzee. In A. M. Schrier and F. Stollnitz (Eds.), *Behavior of nonhuman primates*, Vol. 4. Academic Press, New York.

GLUCK, J. P. and HARLOW, H. F. 1971. The effects of deprived and enriched rearing conditions on later learning: a review. In L. E. Jarrard (Ed.), *Cognitive processes of nonhuman primates*. Academic Press, New York.

HARLOW, H. F. and HARLOW, M. K. 1965. The affectional systems. In A. M. Schrier, H. F. Harlow and F. Stollnitz (Eds.), *Behavior of nonhuman primates*, Vol. 2. Academic Press, New York.

HARLOW, H. F., HARLOW, M. K., SCHULTZ, K. A. and MOHR, D. J. 1971. The effect of early adverse and enriched environments on the learning ability of rhesus monkeys. In L. E. Jarrard (Ed.), *Cognitive processes of nonhuman primates*. Academic Press, New York.

HAYES, C. 1951. *The ape in our house*. Harper, New York.

HAYES, K. J. and NISSEN, C. H. 1971. Higher mental functions of a home-raised chimpanzee. In A. M. Schrier and F. Stollnitz (Eds.), *Behavior of nonhuman primates*, Vol. 4. Academic Press, New York.

HINDE, R. A. 1971a. Some problems in the study of the development of social behaviour. In E. Tobach, L. R. Aronson and E. Shaw (Eds.), *The biopsychology of development*. Academic Press, New York.

HINDE, R. A. 1971b. Development of social behavior. In A. M. Schrier and F. Stollnitz (Eds.), *Behavior of nonhuman primates*, Vol. 3. Academic Press, New York.

HINDE, R. A. and SPENCER-BOOTH, Y. 1971. Towards understanding individual differences in rhesus mother–infant interaction. *Anim. Behav.*, **19**, 165–173.

ITANI, J. 1963. The social construction of national troops of Japanese monkeys in Takasakiyama. *Primates*, **4**, 1–42.

JOLLY, A. 1964. Choice of cue in prosimian learning. *Anim. Behav.*, **12**, 571–577.

JOLLY, A. 1972. *The evolution of primate behavior*. Macmillan, New York.

KAGAN, J. 1959. Continuity in cognitive development during the first year. *Merrill-Palmer Quart.*, **15**, 101–120.

KAPUNE, T. 1966. Untersuchungen zur Bildung eines "Wertbegriffe" bei neideren Primaten. *Z. f. Tierpsychol.*, **23**, 324–363.

KAWAMURA, S. 1958. Matriarchal social ranks in the Minoo-B troop: a study of the rank system of Japanese monkeys. *Primates*, **1**, 148–156.

KELLOGG, W. N. and KELLOGG, L. A. 1933. *The ape and the child*. McGraw-Hill, New York.

KLOPFER, P. H. 1972. Patterns of maternal care in lemurs: II. Effects of group size and early separation. *Z. f. Tierpsychol.*, **30**, 277–296.

KLOPFER, P. H. and KLOPFER, M. S. 1970. Patterns of maternal care in lemurs. I. Normative description. *Z. f. Tierpsychol.*, **27**, 984–996.

KNOBLOCH, H. and PASAMANICK, B. 1959a. Gross motor behavior in an infant gorilla. *J. comp. physiol. Psychol.*, **52**, 559–563.

KNOBLOCH, H. and PASAMANICK, B. 1959b. The development of adaptive behavior in an infant gorilla. *J. comp. physiol. Psychol.*, **52**, 699–704.

KÖHLER, W. 1927. *The mentality of apes*, 2nd ed. Routledge & Kegan Paul, London.

KOHTS, N. 1923. *Untersuchungen über die erkenntnis Fähigkeiten des Schimpansen aus dem zoopsychologischen Laboratorium des Museum Darwinianum in Moskau.* Nanka, Moscow.

LAWICK-GOODALL, J. VAN. 1968. The behaviour of free-living chimpanzees in the Gombe Stream Reserve. *Anim. Behav. Monogr.*, **1**, 165–311.

LAWICK-GOODALL, J. VAN. 1971. *In the shadow of man*. Collins, London.

LEHR, E. 1967. Experimentelle Untersuchungen an Affen und Halbaffen über Generalisation von Insekten- und Blütenabbit dungen. *Z. f. Tierpsychol.*, **24**, 208–244.

LEMMON, W. B. 1971. Deprivation and enrichment in the development of primates. In H. Kummer (Ed.), *Proceedings of the third international congress of primatology*, *vol. 3, Behaviour*. Karger, Basel.

LIPSITT, L. 1967. Learning in the human infant. In H. W. Stephenson, E. H. Hess and H. L. Rheingold (Eds.), *Early behavior*. Wiley, New York.

MARLER, P. 1969. *Colobus guereza:* territoriality and group composition. *Science, N.Y.*, **163**, 93–95.

MARLER, P. 1970. Vocalizations of East African monkeys. I. Red Colobus. *Folia Primat.*, **13**, 81–91.

MASON, W. A., SUZANNE, D. and THOMSEN, C. E. 1971. Perceptual factors in the development of filial attachment. In H. Kummer (Ed.), *Proceedings of the third international congress of primatology, vol. 3, Behaviour*. Karger, Basel.

MCKENNON, J. 1971. Orang-utan behaviour and ecology. Seminar given at University College, London.

MENZEL, E. W. 1969. Responsiveness to food and signs of food in chimpanzee discrimination learning. *J. comp. physiol. Psychol.*, **56**, 78–85.

MEYER, D. R., TREICHLER, F. R. and MEYER, P. M. 1965. Discrete training techniques and stimulus variables. In A. M. Schrier, H. F. Harlow and F. Stollnitz (Eds.), *Behavior of nonhuman primates*, Vol. 1. Academic Press, New York.

MIYADI, D. 1967. Differences in social behaviour among Japanese macaque troops. In D. Starck, R. Schneider and H. J. Kuhn (Eds.), *Neue Ergebnisse der Primatologie*. Fischer, Stuttgart.

MOWBRAY, J. B. and CADELL, T. E. 1962. Early behavior patterns in rhesus monkeys. *J. comp. physiol. Psychol.*, **55**, 350–357.

PARKER, C. E. 1969. Responsiveness, manipulation and implementation behavior in chimpanzees, gorillas and orangutans. In C. R. Carpenter (Ed.), *Proceedings of the second international congress of primatology, vol. 1, Behaviour.* Karger, Basel.

PIAGET, J. 1954. *The construction of reality in the child.* Basic Book, New York.

PLOOG, D. 1969. Early communication processes in squirrel monkeys. In R. J. Robinson (Ed.), *Brain and early behaviour.* Academic Press, London.

PRECHTL, H. F. R. 1965. Problems of behavioral studies in the newborn infant. In D. S. Lehrman, R. A. Hinde and E. Shaw (Eds.), *Advances in the study of behavior,* Vol. 1. Academic Press, New York.

PREMACK, D. 1970. A functional analysis of language. *J. exp. anal. Behav.,* **14,** 107–125.

RENSCH, B. and DOHL, J. 1968. Wählen zwischen zwei uber schaubaren Labyrinth-wegen durch einen Schimpansen. *Z. f. Tierpsychol.,* **25,** 216–231.

RENSCH, B. and DUECKER, K. C. 1966. Manipulier fähigkeit eines jungen Orang-utans und eines jungen Gorillas: Mit anmerkungen uber das spielverhalten. *Z. f. Tierpsychol.,* **23,** 874–892.

RODMAN, P. S. 1973. Population composition and adaptive organisation among orang-utans of Kutai Reserve. In *Comparative ecology and behaviour of primates,* R. P. Michael and J. H. Crook (Eds.), Academic Press, London and New York.

ROSENBLUM, L. A. 1968. Mother–infant relations and early behavioral development in the squirrel monkey. In L. A. Rosenblum and R. W. Cooper (Eds.), *The squirrel monkey.* Academic Press, New York.

ROSENBLUM, L. A. 1971. Infant attachment in monkeys. In H. R. Schaffer (Ed.), *The origins of human social relations.* Academic Press, London.

ROWELL, T. G. 1963. The social development of some rhesus monkeys. In B. M. Foss (Ed.), *Determinants of infant behaviour, II.* Methuen, London.

SCHAFFER, H. R. 1971. Cognitive structure and early social behaviour. In H. R. Schaffer (Ed.), *The origins of human social relations.* Academic Press, London.

SCHAFFER, H. R. and EMERSON, P. E. 1964. The development of social attachment in infancy. *Monogr. Soc. Res. Child. Dev.,* **29,** serial no. 94.

SCHALLER, G. B. 1963. *The mountain gorilla.* Univ. Chicago Press, Chicago.

SCHILLER, P. H. 1957. Manipulative patterns in the chimpanzee. In C. H. Schiller (Ed.), *Instinctive behavior.* Internat. Univs. Press, New York.

SPENCER-BOOTH, Y. and HINDE, R. A. 1971a. Effects of 6 days separation from mother on 18 to 32 week old rhesus monkeys. *Anim. Behav.,* **19,** 174–191.

SPENCER-BOOTH, Y. and HINDE, R. A. 1971b. The effects of 13 days maternal separa-tion on infant rhesus monkeys compared with those of shorter and repeated separations. *Anim. Behav.,* **19,** 595–605.

SPITZ, R. A. and WOOLF, K. M. 1946. The smiling response: a contribution to the ontogeny of social relations. *Gen. Psychol. Monog.* No. 34.

STRUHSAKER, T. T. 1971. Social behaviour of mother and infant vervet monkeys *(Cercopithecus aethiops). Anim. Behav.,* **19,** 233–250.

STRUHSAKER, T. T. and HUNKELER, P. 1971. Evidence of tool-using by chimpanzees in the Ivory Coast. *Folia primat.,* **15,** 212–219.

SUBRAMONIAM, S. 1957. Some observations on the habits of the slender loris, *Loris tardigradus* (Linnaeus). *J. Bombay Nat. Hist. Soc.,* **54,** 387–398.

TAKESHITA, H. 1961–2. On the delivery behaviour of squirrel monkeys *(Saimiri sciureus)* and a mona monkey *(Cercopithecus mona). Primates,* **3,** 59–72.

TWITCHELL, T. E. 1970. Reflex mechanisms and the development of prehension. In K. Connolly (Ed.), *Mechanisms of motor skill development.* Academic Press, London.

WARREN, N. In press. African infant precocity. *Psychol. Bull.*

WEINSTEIN, B. 1945. The evolution of intelligent behavior in rhesus monkeys. *Genet. Psychol. Monog.*, **31**, 3–48.

WHITE, B. L. 1970. Experience and the development of motor mechanisms in infancy. In K. Connolly (Ed.), *Mechanisms of motor skill development*. Academic Press, London.

WOLFF, P. H. 1963. Observations on the early development of smiling. In B. M. Foss (Ed.), *Determinants of infant behaviour. II*. Methuen, London.

WOOLRIDGE, F. L. 1971. *Colobus guereza:* birth and infant development in captivity. *Anim. Behav.*, **19**, 481–485.

ZIMMERMANN, R. and TORREY, C. C. 1965. Ontogeny of learning. In A. M. Schrier, H. F. Harlow and F. Stollnitz (Eds.), *Behavior of nonhuman primates*, vol. 2. Academic Press, New York.

Sentence Structure in Chimpanzee Communication[1]

DAVID MCNEILL

University of Chicago

INTRODUCTION

THERE ARE NOW two experiments on teaching chimpanzees a human language that have been in some sense successful (Gardner and Gardner, 1971; Premack, 1971). It is an appropriate time to review these experiments in an attempt to determine what they have demonstrated.

What is the purpose of such experiments? The reasons given by the experimenters themselves are not the same, and my purpose, in this paper, is yet again different. It is a good idea, therefore, to describe these differences at the outset. Premack (1970, 1971, in press) states clearly that his purpose in attempting to teach a chimpanzee language is to validate what he calls a "functional analysis" of language. By this he means a transliteration of linguistic structures into a set of training procedures that one can follow to teach an animal (chimpanzee) these structures. Gardner and Gardner (1969, 1971) are less explicit as to their goals, but seem to be interested in demonstrating that behaviour that one would intuitively call "linguistic" can be invoked in some species other than *Homo sapiens*. These are different goals. The difference can be seen from the fact that, in principle, Premack's question could be answered within our own species. For example, except for moral and legal restrictions, Premack could raise a child without any human contact except in controlled experimental settings where the prescribed training procedures are used. Obviously, the Gardners' goal would not be met by such an experiment.

There is a third question that can be raised, which is the question that

[1] Preparation of this paper was supported by grant from the N.S.F. to David McNeill.

I will pursue in this paper. This concerns the possibility that language in our (or any other) species is to some degree a biological specialization. Typically, questions of biological specialization have depended on comparisons of species. However, species comparisons have not been possible with language. But now, for the first time, the question can actually be investigated with the Gardners' and Premack's experiments. The results, I believe, are more surprising and interesting than many would have anticipated.

Starting from the undeniable fact that only our species has the highly intricate structure we call language, one can ask whether any abilities can be isolated on which this unique biological distribution of language depends; or if it is a result of a general difference in cognitive ability between man and other species. This question is different from Premack's in that one aspect of any biological specialization for human language might well include a high degree of sensitivity to linguistic forms in the developing young. Clearly, it may be possible to find training procedures that instil certain linguistic structures in a chimpanzee even if it lacks such sensitivity. This has been done with many kinds of behaviour (Seligman, 1970). The question of biological specialization differs from the Gardners' question also because it is conceivable that the chimpanzee and man have abilities in common at some points, but at other points each has certain abilities not possessed by the other. In this case, some aspects of human language could be easily transmitted to a chimpanzee while others would be transmitted only with difficulty and, possibly, would be reconstituted in a form that is more natural for the animal.

In fact, Premack's and the Gardners' experiments taken together, suggest that the chimpanzee resembles man in a number of fundamental respects, but that each species has a distinct set of abilities, which are nevertheless linguistic in character. These differences, which may be the result of separate biological specializations, exist alongside a number of conceptual and other linguistic similarities between the chimpanzee and man.

Washoe

Washoe was estimated to be fourteen months of age at the beginning of the Gardners' experiment. She was kept at home, housed in a trailer, and was in the company of human adults during all waking hours. Apart from simulations of natural chimpanzee vocalizations, the only medium of communication was American Sign Language (A.S.L.), a system of manual gestures used by deaf people in North America (not to be confused with finger spelling). In A.S.L. typically one sign corresponds to one word, although occasionally signs correspond to groups of words or entire phrases. The Gardners' first report (1969) contains a list of the signs (words) that Washoe acquired in the order in which they appeared. The first twelve of these are as follows: *come-gimme* (one sign), *more, up, sweet, open, tickle, go, out, hurry, hear-listen* (one sign), *toothbrush, drink.* Only two signs denote physical objects (*drink, toothbrush*), the remaining ten referring to relations or actions. Object words were acquired later in Washoe's development. At first glance this appears to be different from the speech of children at a comparable stage, since with children the earliest words are almost exclusively object words. In an earlier publication (McNeill, 1970), I concluded that Washoe differed from children during the one word stage of development. However, it has recently been noted that the relatively numerous object words that children acquire are highly transitory, appearing for a few days and then often disappearing completely, to be replaced by other object words (Bloom, in press). Apparently, there is a constant circulation of object words during the single word stage. On the other hand, relational words (*more*, etc.) and action words, while much less numerous, are more stable. These new facts change the interpretation of Washoe's single word development. The Gardners adopted an extremely strict criterion for considering a sign to be part of Washoe's vocabulary. A sign had to be used at least once daily for fifteen successive days. If Washoe was like the subject described by Bloom, the Gardners' criterion would have had the effect of eliminating all object words in the early stages. If the same criterion were used with Bloom's data, the resulting vocabulary list would include, like Washoe's, no object-words and only relational and action words. Thus, while we still do not know whether Washoe had an early vocabulary of transitory object words, we do know that the stable part of children's early vocabulary is similar to the stable part of Washoe's vocabulary, both including only relational and action words. There is no evidence that the chimpanzee differs from children at this stage.

Washoe's combinations

Washoe spontaneously began to produce sequences of signs at an early point in training; 294 combinations had been recorded at the time of the Gardners' latest (1971) report. Interpretation of this remarkable phenomenon is unfortunately made difficult, but I think not impossible, by the Gardners' practice of disregarding the order in which Washoe made sequences of signs. Whenever the same signs were produced in succession, regardless of word order, the Gardners recorded it as the same combination. Apparently, changes in word order were frequent. This practice discards much of the information essential for determining whether the animal had developed syntactic patterns. The Gardners (1971) claim that Washoe committed no more order "errors" than children do (according to information collected by Brown, in press) but it is far from clear what this assertion means. The Gardners report no data for the comparison and we do not know what standard was used to determine an "error". In the case of child language, often what seems to be errors from the standpoint of adult grammar turn out to be completely systematic when one takes into account a child's own immature linguistic system (see examples in the various papers in Bellugi and Brown, 1964). It does not seem that the Gardners took this precaution into account in determining Washoe's "error" rate and comparing it to that of children.

Table I contains all examples of sign sequences by Washoe that the Gardners (1971) report. Assuming these ninety-one sequences are representative of Washoe's total output, there is sufficient information here to support certain conclusions about how Washoe put signs together.

TABLE I. *Sign sequences from Washoe* (*Gardner and Gardner, 1971*)

---

come-gimme (one sign) sweet
come-gimme (one sign) open
Greg tickle
Naomi hug
Naomi come
Naomi quiet
Naomi good
please out
hurry out
you me out
you Roger Washoe out
you me go out
you me go out hurry
Roger you tickle (= Roger, tickle Washoe)
you Greg peekaboo (= Greg, you play peekaboo)
catch me
tickle me
go in
go out
in down bed
drink red (= red cup)
my baby
listen food
listen drink (= supper bell)
dirty good (= potty)
key open food (= open the refrigerator)
open key clean (= open the soap cupboard)

TABLE I—*continued*

key open please blanket (= open the bedding cupboard)
please song
song dirty
please song good
come hug sorry sorry
sweet drink (= soda)

please sweet drink ⎫
gimme sweet drink ⎪
hurry sweet drink ⎬ a
please hurry sweet drink ⎪
please gimme sweet drink ⎭

up Susan ⎫
Susan up ⎪
mine please up ⎪
gimme baby ⎪
please shoe ⎪
more mine ⎪
up please ⎪
please up ⎬ b
more up ⎪
baby down ⎪
shoe up ⎪
baby up ⎪
please more up ⎪
you up ⎭

gimme key ⎫
more key ⎪
gimme key more ⎪
open key ⎪
key open ⎪
open more ⎪
more open ⎬ c
key in ⎪
open key please ⎪
open gimme key ⎪
it open help ⎪
help key in ⎪
open key help hurry ⎭
gimme food

a. The Gardners add that this request for soda was also made "by variations in the order of these signs". They do not say what the variations are, however. In particular, it would be of interest to know whether the recipient of the action (sweet drink) was always in final position, as in these examples.

b. Produced in a single situation, where an assistant, Susan, has placed her foot on one of Washoe's dolls.

c. Produced in a single situation where Washoe obtained a key from an assistant but was unable to open a door with it.

TABLE I—*continued*

---

gimme food gimme
more tickle
please tickle more
come Roger tickle
out open please hurry
you me in
you me out
you me Greg go
Roger Washoe out
you Naomi peekaboo
you tickle me Washoe
you me drink go
you me out look
hug me good (an apology)
Roger Washoe tickle
you peekaboo me
tickle me Washoe Roger
you me in
you me out
you me go
out you me Dennis (rare)
please me you go (rare)
you out me (late)

In evaluating this evidence, it is important to note that, while A.S.L. does not necessarily follow English syntax, Washoe's trainers tended to transliterate English order into sign, in particular, using the English order of subject-verb-object (Gardner and Gardner, 1971, p. 176). Hence, Washoe was presented with linguistic specimens that corresponded to the basic rules of English.

Washoe's meaning is generally clear in these examples. She conveys familiar concepts and seems to organize her perception of the world in ways that are immediately recognizable to adult humans. Specifically, she apparently perceives events in terms of agents and actions (*Greg tickle, Naomi quiet, Naomi hug*); actions and recipients of actions (*tickle me, catch me, gimme sweet drink*); locations (*in down bed, go in, key in*); ownership (*my baby, more mine*); instrumentality (*key open food, open key please*); and sequences of action (*you me drink go*).

Comparing Washoe to children, or even adults, in terms of the conceptual content of speech she shows a high degree of similarity. Each of the relations above can be found in the early speech of children. It must be concluded that there is no evidence here of any major species differences.

Washoe has an extensive and mostly appropriate use of several words that refer to conceptual relations. These are the signs that Washoe first acquired as single words; *more, up, out, in*, etc. In combinations, they permit her to encode various dynamic and relational interactions, such as leaving a room or locating an object in some particular way. Again, they are used in a way that resembles adult language.

In the context of these similarities between the linguistic processes of Washoe and human children, the differences that follow are particularly striking and significant.

Word order

Does Washoe follow any rules for arranging signs into sequences? In many respects, her sign sequences are clearly contrary to any use of word order to encode conceptual relationships. For example, each of the following can be found in Table I: a single conceptual relation represented by two different word orders (*up Susan, Susan up*); two conflicting conceptual relations with the same order in successive strings (*shoe up* where *shoe* probably is agent, *baby up* where *baby* probably is recipient); non-relational repetitions of referents in a single string (*You tickle me Washoe*); and chaos across several strings (*open gimme key, in open help, help key in, open key help hurry*). These examples suggest that the principles for arranging words to express conceptual relationships, if any, are sporadically applied. There is evidence, however, that other forms of regularity exist in Washoe's sign sequences.

The Gardners (1971) mention two arrangements they have observed in Washoe's signing. One of them is of little interest from a linguistic point of view, but the other is significant. The less interesting arrangement is a tendency for *you* to precede *me* in sequences such as *you me out*. The order of words in this case seems to have a purely mechanical explanation and does not reflect a rule of grammar in any sense. The sign for *you* is made by pointing away from the chest toward (and touching?) the addressee, whereas *me* is made by tapping one's own chest, and hence near the region of the chest where the sign for the action will be made next. Given that the sign for the agent precedes that for the action, the preference for the *you-me-action* order can be understood as the result of the greater mechanical ease of signing in this order than in the *me-you-action* order.

The second consistent order reported by the Gardners is the tendency, just noted, to place agents before action words, as in *Naomi hug*, and *you me out*. In contrast to the placing of *you* before *me*, this regularity appears to be genuine. The agent may be either the addressee (*you, Naomi*, etc.) or a non-addressee (always, *me*, i.e. Washoe herself). The non-addressee usage is secondary, in the sense that it occurs only in the context of the addressee usage and is limited to self reference (*me*), whereas the addressee usage also occurs alone and includes various referents. Beyond this pattern mentioned by the Gardners, a second apparently real pattern can be found in the examples listed in Table I. Washoe had a strong tendency, 80% in the examples, to place the recipient of an action after the action word, as in *gimme key* and *you tickle me Washoe*. In all cases the recipient is a non-addressee, who may be either animate (i.e. Washoe) or inanimate (some physical object).

Thus, there are two patterns in Washoe's sequences of signs, one with two versions (addressee and non-addressee), which may indicate some kind of linguistic structure. The following schemata represent all the discoverable information contained in these patterns (square brackets represent single signs, curly brackets indicate alternatives):

1. (Primary)   [Agent, Addressee, Animate] — [Action]
   (Secondary)   [Agent, Addressee, Animate] —
                 [Agent, Non-addressee, Animate] — [Action]
2. Action — $\left[\text{Recipient, Non-addressee, } \left\{\begin{array}{l}\text{Animate}\\\text{Inanimate}\end{array}\right\}\right]$

The primary version of schema (1) represents such strings as *Naomi hug* and the secondary version represents *you me out*. Schema (2) represents such strings as *gimme key* and *you tickle me*. Comparing only the *primary* version of schema (1) to schema (2), we can see that Agent and Recipient are redundant with respect to Addressee and Non-addressee. That is, Agents are always Addressees and Recipients are always Non-addressees. The converse redundancy also holds, Addressees always being Agents and Non-addressees being Recipients. Agents also are redundant with respect to Animateness and conversely, but Recipients are not thus redundant since there are both Animate and Inanimate Recipients.

Adding the secondary version of schema (1) simplifies matters considerably. In this version, Agent is no longer redundant with respect to Addressee, since there is also a Non-addressee Agent, the converse redundancy also has disappeared. The redundancy of Recipient with respect to Non-addressee and conversely, is similarly interrupted. Only the redundancy between Agent and Animateness remains. Since there can be animate Recipients in schema (2), this redundancy is asymmetrical and we can conclude that in schema (1), both versions combined, it is the Agent that is redundant with respect to Animateness and not conversely.

Because of the contradictory properties of the primary and secondary versions of schema (1), very little that is positive can be said about what Washoe might have been encoding in her sign sequences. But it is clear that she was not encoding the relation of Agent. As noted above, Agent is redundance with respect to Animateness in both versions of schema (1). There is, therefore, no evidence that Washoe arranged sign sequences so that agents came first. However, we are unable to say on what basis she did arrange sign sequences without further information.

The Gardners report that sequences such as *you me out* occurred early in Washoe's development, and were replaced later by somewhat more exotic sequences such as *you out me*. That is, the secondary version of schema (1) disappeared, and was replaced by schema (3):

3. [Agent, Addressee, Animate] — [Action] — [Agent, Non-addressee, Animate]

The component Agent, Non-addressee, Animate in schema (3) was always *me* or *Washoe*.

This schema coincides very neatly with schema (1) (primary version) and schema (2), and clarifies the significance of the order signs for Washoe. When schema (3) appeared in Washoe's signing, she consistently followed the pattern: Addressee—Action—Non-addressee. All other relations were either redundant (Recipient), occurred in all positions (Agent, Animate), or were not used distinctively in any position (Animate, Inanimate). The exotic string *you out me* has two agents, then, according to schema (3), but this fact did not determine its grammatical structure. Its structure was established by the addressee–non-addressee relationship. The only exception to this latter pattern is the string, *tickle me Roger Washoe*, listed among the Gardners' examples. However, it is not clear that the sign *Roger* was actually a name to Washoe, according to an unpublished summary of Washoe's diary that the Gardners have circulated, it originally meant "please".

The chimpanzee may therefore have imposed her own formula on the sentence structures she observed her handlers using. Washoe's formula does not capture what the handlers themselves encoded (agent, action, recipient), but instead emphasizes a novel relationship as far as grammatical form is concerned, that of an interpersonal or social interaction (addressee–non-addressee).

Negation and questions

Bronowski and Bellugi (1970) have pointed out that Washoe never incorporated questions or negatives into her combinations of signs. This omission is particularly striking because negatives and questions occurred as single word messages (showing that Washoe had the idea of negating and questioning) and Washoe's handlers used both negative and question forms in combinations, hence, providing Washoe with examples. Children, in contrast, incorporate questions and negatives into even the simplest word combinations, at a stage of development when the longest utterances are only two or three words. *No pocket* and *not truck* are typical negative examples, where *that pocket* and *that truck* are affirmative sentences at this stage. There are surely no reasons of length or complexity that prevent Washoe from producing equally simple negative sentences. The reason she did not must have something to do with the degree of internal organization they require. Early questions in child speech show a similar simplicity. They are formed either by uttering a sentence with a rising "question" intonation, resulting in a yes–no question (*see hole?*), or by combining a Wh-word with another word (*what doing?*). Again, there are no reasons of complexity or length to keep Washoe from producing such forms. This is particularly true of yes–no questions, which in American Sign Language (A.S.L.) are made merely by holding the hands for an extra moment at the completion of a sign gesture. Washoe was able to ask questions this way with single words. Doing the same with a sequence of words would not have been more difficult, if she had known how.

Encoding propositions about the physical world

The various characteristics of Washoe's signing discussed above can be unified in terms of a single observation: Washoe apparently does not use word combinations in a way that encodes conceptual relationships. The order of signs in strings, for example, was based on the social relations of addressee and non-addressee, rather than, as in the case of children, on the physicalistic notions of agent and recipient of an action. This is true despite evidence that the relations of agent, action, and recipient are intellectually within Washoe's grasp. A similar inability is shown in the absence of negatives from Washoe's strings. In particular, non-existence and denial, two semantic categories of negation that children use at an early age, presuppose some form of an underlying proposition in order to be meaningful. The absence of negative forms from Washoe's sign sequences implies that she was unable to encode such propositions. In the case of non-existence, there must be a proposition concerning existence, which is negated; *no pocket*, meaning that there is no pocket on an article of clothing, presupposes a proposition about the existence of a pocket. In the case of denial, there must be a proposition which makes a claim that is then said to be false; *not truck*, meaning that an object is not a truck, presupposes the claim that the object is a truck, which is then denied. Questions likewise depend on an ability to encode propositions by means of word patterns. Yes–no questions are requests for information about the truth or falsity of entire propositions, and Wh-questions are requests for information about parts of propositions. The absence of such questions from Washoe's sign sequences implies, again, that she did not encode propositions when she produced sequences of signs.

Thus, in general, whenever combinations of words serve in the language of adults or children to encode propositions or conceptual relations (components of propositions), it appears that Washoe has failed to use these syntactic patterns in her own linguistic performance. This is true despite the presence of examples of the missing linguistic patterns in the signing of her handlers. Properties of language that do not depend on this use of word combinations, on the other hand, were apparently acquired by Washoe without difficulty. This includes the acquisition of a vocabulary of relation words (*in*, *out*, etc.), and negation and questions using only one word. The Gardners (1971) repeatedly state that Washoe's signs are semantically associated in strings, but that there is no evidence that her signs are syntactically associated. The semantic association of signs implies a certain similarity of the conceptual processes of the chimpanzee and *Homo sapiens* and suggests that Washoe was able to bring these cognitive processes to bear on her sequences of signs. The lack of syntactic organization implies, however, that she could not use her conception of semantic relations to organize sign sequences. It is indeed the case that, as noted above, Washoe appears to convey information about agents, actions, and recipients. Thus, the grammatical differences between Washoe and human language users are presumably not due to some general cognitive difference between the chimpanzee and *Homo sapiens*. They arise from differences in the ability to use patterns of words to encode conceptual relations, which are themselves more or less shared between the species.

Sarah and the perceptability of linguistic structure

Premack's experiment with the chimpanzee he has called Sarah (Premack, 1970, 1971, in press) sheds light on the Washoe study by demonstrating a training method that can in some cases overcome the limitation on the chimpanzee's use of combinations, particularly the use of strict word order and negation. This method can be compared to the training "methods" parents successfully employ with children.

The most important result of Premack's experiment is that he was able to instruct Sarah on several of the syntactic forms that Washoe, acquiring linguistic information spontaneously, did not use. For example, Sarah was able to express the idea that two objects were not the same by spontaneously combining the sign for "not" and the sign for "same" (Premack, 1970). This implies some kind of propositional framework into which a negative operator was placed. Similar examples can be found for quantification (*some*, *all*) and for the conceptual relations of agent, recipient, and location, each of which is encoded by observing strict word order. As an illustration of what seems to be true grammatical knowledge, we can take the following example (Premack, in press). Sarah was first taught two alternative ways of encoding attributive statements: *red colour apple* and *apple is red*; these and all other utterances being "written" with bits of magnetized plastic placed vertically on a board, bits with distinct shapes and colours representing different words. These sentences were taught independently and at different times, and no attempt was made to link them until the following test was made. Drawing on previous training, in which Sarah had been taught to use chips meaning "same" and "different" in judging whether objects were the same, Premack now had Sarah judge whether *red colour apple* and *apple is red* are the same or different. She was able to do this immediately at her standard level of accuracy, about 80%. A judgement of "same" in this case could be made only on the basis that the two sentences have the same meaning for Sarah, i.e. on the basis of internal relationships that had been decoded from the structured arrays of words. Some sentences that she correctly called "different" are physically more alike than some sentences that she called "same".

These are impressive results. However, we must be cautious before we equate them with the process of acquisition shown by children. Premack has not attempted to simulate language acquisition. His interest has been in finding ways of instilling linguistic information in the chimpanzee, whether or not these are the ways such information is instilled in children. Premack's methods are based on the principle that, at any given time, exactly one element in the training situation should be unfamiliar to the learner, no more. By cascading a series of small steps in the correct order, complex structures can be built up. When learning the word *colour* (= "colour of"), at first Sarah had only the chip she was to learn to use before her, *colour*. She already knew that whenever the chip representing "?" occurred in a string, it was to be replaced by a word that would make the string into a correct statement. Hence, when she was shown *red ? apple*, and "?" could be replaced only with the word *colour*, her previous experience implied that *red colour apple* was true. It remained for Sarah to discover what it was, conceptually, about this statement that made it true. Such inferences evidently are possible for the chimpanzee. The second step of training presented alternative words, hence the need to respond selectively, and further steps required various kinds of generalization.

Adults talking to young children also adjust their speech to the presumed limitations of the child. Remarkably few studies have been made of this adjustment, however. In one of the few studies that exist, Snow (1972) observed considerable simplification of speech directed to two-year-olds, compared to speech to ten-year-olds. Sentences were more often simple declaratives, they were shorter, and they did not include as many pronouns. There was also a tendency to repeat sentences and sentence constituents in a way that set word groupings off. As an example of the latter, the following seems to be typical: "Put the red truck in the box now. The red truck. No, the red truck. In the box. The red truck in the box." Snow's procedure involved having adults instruct children on how to solve puzzles, the requirements of which would impose the kind of simplification and repetition she observed, so some of these effects may be artifacts of her method. But assuming that similar adjustments occur in normal adult speech to little children, we can see that there are certain similarities between the speech that adults direct to young children and the systematic training procedures used by Premack.

If one thinks of a scale of didactic speech, i.e. speech intended to instruct in language, Premack's "speech" to Sarah would be near (if not "at") one extreme and randomly chosen tape recordings of conversations on unrelated subjects would be near the other. On such a scale, the simplified speech of adults described by Snow would obviously be closer to Premack's end. However, the speech of adults to children does not follow the essential principle of Premack's method, that is that only one element should be unfamiliar at any given time. In the example of the repetitions mentioned above, the adult was simultaneously demonstrating declarative sentences, locative phrases, noun phrases, and noun phrases in relation to locative phrases. This discrepancy between Premack's method and the speech of adults to children would be largest at the earliest stages of development, when the child knows least about linguistic structure.

The position of a "training procedure" on the imaginary didactic scale above, influences the extent to which the procedure makes linguistic patterns explicit, and hence, inversely, the extent to which the learner must be able to perceive these patterns on his own. The conclusion to draw from Premack's experiment with Sarah therefore seems to be the following: at Premack's end of the scale, where there is only a single unknown, the word pattern being taught is made fully explicit. The chimpanzee must only be able to infer the significance (meaning) of the pattern. At the child's position on the scale, this inference is also required, but in addition, there must be an ability to perceive the syntactic patterns themselves when they are not made fully explicit. That is, the degree of simplification reported by Snow implies the presence of a perceptual sensitivity to syntactic forms on the part of young children which is not implied by the success of Premack's method. The patterns that children find on their own include precisely those that Washoe, receiving linguistic information from a point that appears to be close to the child's on the scale, is unable to acquire.

Thus, Premack's experiment complements the Gardners', by showing a difference between chimpanzee and children that is correlated with the ability to perceive and presumably use, syntactic patterns that encode conceptual relations. The conceptual relations themselves appear to be available to both species, a conclusion that Sarah's performance reinforces quite strongly.

A different grammatical system?

Attempts to teach chimpanzees English are based on the assumption that if the chimpanzee has any capacity for language-like communication it is for a language whose structure is basically similar to human language. The assumption implies that the chimpanzee is on the same evolutionary line as man, but has not progressed as far. However, such an anthropomorphic assumption is not necessarily correct. The chimpanzee may already have begun the evolution of a linguistic capacity but not along the line our own evolution has followed. If man's capacity for language itself is in part a biological adaptation to a certain range of life conditions, it is possible that another species has developed an adaptation to accomplish similar communicative effects under different life conditions. I will argue that chimpanzee is such a species. We obtain a glimpse in the Washoe experiment of what may be a fundamentally different linguistic framework, one that has a unique semantic basis and has rules that are unknown in any human language.

Human languages are extremely well adjusted to the problem of describing physical objects and relationships among physical objects. Every utterance, if it is a grammatical sentence, includes at a minimum, a phrase that refers to an object and another phrase that refers to a quality of the object or an action, with the sentence structure indicating the relationship between them. More elaborate sentences add further object phrases and additional relationships. All of this is highly familiar. The model of objects is of course extended beyond its natural base into realms where real objects and actions do not exist, e.g. to the domain of numerical relationships. Algebraic word problems, for example, are far more difficult to understand than ordinary sentences because in part they cannot be understood as being about objects, even though the sentence containing the problem is geared to describing objects and their relationships. Children, in their earliest speech, however, remain close to the basis of language and confine nearly all sentences to statements about objects and relationships among objects.

Because any human language is so well adapted to describing objects and their relationships, it is difficult for us to see that this facility is in a crucial degree the result of the structure of language, and not solely of the nature of the physical world. The great difficulties that have appeared with automatic pattern recognition by computers show how complex and latent the structure of objects actually is (cf. Neisser, 1967). It is not possible to explain the ease with which language describes objects and their relationships by falling back on another process, "the perception of objects", since this itself turns out to be hidden in obscurity and full of contradictions.

It is clear, however, that in speaking, one does not have to face the epistemological problems that are encountered in automatic pattern recognition. The most successful computer system to date for interpreting sentences from a natural language (Winograd, 1972) has built into it a correspondence between the physical world of objects and the grammatical world of noun phrases, predicates, etc. Pattern recognition is not an issue for this programme. It seems reasonable to speculate that the human capacity for language evolved under pressures to convey information about objects and their relationships in such a way that a similar correspondence exists in all members of the species, as part of their natural preparation for the use of language. Indeed, this correspondence is so close for human speakers, that it is difficult to notice when the correspondence does not hold, as in algebraic word problems, and it is especially difficult to imagine a linguistic system that is based on other principles, not on a model of the physical world. Yet the chimpanzee, apparently with very similar conceptual powers, seems to lack a parallel grammatical structure, and may have in its place a linguistic system based on social and personal interactions.

We have already seen one example of this system in the rule noted before, whereby Washoe put the word for her addressee first and the word for the non-addressee last, with an action word in between. This use of word order for addressee–non-addressee is no more arbitrary than the use of word order for action–recipient. The two ordering principles are, however, quite distinct. It is true, of course, that the agent–recipient sentences of English also often encode addressee–non-addressee. But the latter encoding is not the meaning of the grammatical structure. It is a concomitant meaning arising from the fact that addressees are often agents. For Washoe the situation seems to be reversed. Addressee–non-addressee is the meaning of the structure and agent–recipient is the concomitant meaning. This conclusion permits us to see a basis of organization within Washoe's utterances, which otherwise often appear chaotic.

Further examples from Washoe's signing suggest another principle that is grammatical in character but alien to the structural basis of human language. In their first report, the Gardners (1969) describe combinations in Washoe's signing which seemed to function as emphasizers. Words were added to strings not to convey new information but to make the basic message of the string more intense and emphatic. Examples are *please open hurry*, *gimme drink please*, *please hurry sweet drink*, and *open key help hurry*. Is there any grammatical principle involved in these strings? According to the unpublished summary of the diary the Gardners kept on Washoe's development, the longest sequences of signs she produced all included this kind of emphasis. Emphasizers were the main source of additional length in strings. We may speculate that she had a rule of the following kind,

$$S \rightarrow P^n$$

where S is a grammatical string, P is the basic meaning of the message and n is the number of occurrences of P and depends on Washoe's degree of urgency. An "organized" string according to this rule, consists of any number of signs in any order which convey a single meaning. This is not as vacuous as it first seems. A string may consist of repetitions (*more more more sweet drink*), different signs (*please out open hurry*) or both (*out out please out*). According to the rule above, all have the same grammatical (but not lexical) meaning: something is urgent to a degree that sets $n = 4$.

Beyond the addressee–non-addressee and emphasis rule, no other grammatical principle stands out. The order of words in Washoe's strings, apart from addressee and non-addressee, probably depends on the prominence of the things referred to. Since such prominence shifts with time and new situations, word order shifts also. This variability does not require any grammatical structure and does not appear to be part of Washoe's linguistic system. The addressee rule itself might be thought to be the result of a greater prominence of addressees compared to non-addressees for Washoe, except for the fact that, in a large number of cases, the most prominent part of Washoe's message, to judge from the part being emphasized, is the action, and yet still the addressee is mentioned first. The addressee rule as well as the emphasis rule, may have a different origin, a possibility we turn to next.

Aspects of chimpanzee life

Goodall (1965, van Lawick-Goodall, 1971) has written vivid descriptions of the life of free-ranging chimpanzees. From all this material, three observations stand out for our purposes. These have to do with the chimpanzees' lack of interest in physical objects, the importance of social interactions, and the effect of the dominance system.

Chimpanzees are intensely aware of one another. They seem to be in constant social contact through some means or other. This acute sensitivity to other chimpanzees contrasts with what seems to be a remarkable lack of interest in physical objects. Their attention often is not caught even by major new features of the physical environment. Goodall had the rather dangerous experience of chimpanzees almost colliding with her because the animals had not noticed her presence, in spite of her being in clear view. Other chimpanzees did not at first notice a newly arrived photographer, complete with equipment, whereas chimpanzees are ordinarily frightened of humans. Chimpanzee infants, whose play is remarkably like the rough and tumble play enjoyed by human infants, almost never play with physical objects the way human infants do so avidly, even from the earliest months of life.[2]

Chimpanzees are quite alert to selected aspects of the physical environment—the condition of feeding trees, for example, or the presence of the bits of grass they use for catching termites—and young chimpanzees show an interest in these too. What is lacking in the chimpanzee is the intense human curiosity about objects. There is no exploration of the physical environment unless there is a practical reason to carry it out.

The fact that Washoe did not absorb those linguistic structures that encode relationships among objects thus coincides with an indifference to the physical environment among wild chimpanzees. If the chimpanzee has indeed evolved a capacity for language-like communication, we should not expect it to resemble human language in structurally encoding physical relationships. In fact, it does not seem to do so. Conversely, we can see in the human's preoccupation with physical objects the basis for the evolution of a specialized communication system that encodes information about objects and their relationships.

The chimpanzees' social structure is complex and important to the animals. As Goodall points out, it is not less important to them than to us, and in some respects may be more important. Every chimpanzee is aware of the social hierarchy in which he finds himself and of his place

---

[2] Similar observations have been made of the mountain gorilla by Schaller (1963) and of the Hamadrayas baboon by Kummer (1968) and Omark (in preparation).

within it. This dominance hierarchy influences almost everything chimpanzees do—eating, relaxing, mating, even sleeping. If the chimpanzee has evolved a capacity for using grammatical structure based on social interactions, it is possible that the intense awareness of other chimpanzees can be encoded structurally. Corresponding to the human use of word order to encode agent–action, a relationship between object and an event, chimpanzees might use structural means to encode social relationships between individuals. Washoe's use of word order to encode addressee–non-addressee can be seen in this light. What for her was most salient in situations in which agents and recipients were being related to actions, may have been that there was an addressee and a non-addressee. It was this fact that she seized upon and made the basis of a grammatical rule.

The impact of the dominance hierarchy on the social interaction of chimpanzees is especially strong on appeasement and begging behaviour. A subordinate chimpanzee must perform an elaborate and finely graded ritual of appeasement if he wants to obtain a donation of, say, food from a more dominant chimpanzee. Even when not begging, a display of appeasement may be necessary from a subordinate animal to avoid giving offence and being attacked viciously. In chimpanzee interactions, it is essential for an individual to signal his intentions clearly to other animals, whether he intends to be subservient or aggressive or merely neutral, and to what degree.

Washoe's signing shows many examples of appeasement and begging. Among the latter, *please* combines with *come-gimme, out, drink, open, go*, and many other signs. *Come-gimme* (which is identical to the natural chimpanzee begging gesture) combines with *open, tickle, sweet, listen, more*, and many others. Appeasement was conveyed by *sorry, hug, please*, and *more* combining with lipsmacking. That is, Washoe used for begging and appeasement most of the signs that played a part in the rule, $S \rightarrow P^n$. This congruence suggests that the rule, with its flexible use of message length, is related to the need for chimpanzees to encode their intentions in social interactions precisely and clearly. Again, assuming that the chimpanzee has evolved a capacity to encode social relationships through structural means, Washoe may have been able to develop a rule for encoding the urgency of messages—begging and entreaties—by arranging signs into strings of definite length and indeterminate order.

Washoe and Sarah may be unique, Sarah because she has been taught, through rigorous means, to use word combinations for encoding propositional relationships; Washoe because she was exposed to A.S.L. However Washoe did not encode propositional relationships through word combinations in A.S.L., although she expressed these in other ways, and she reconstituted the linguistic information she was given along lines completely different from those her handlers presumably had in mind. It is conceivable that her ability to do this would not have been brought to the surface if she had not been given the stimulus of A.S.L., but it is also conceivable that free-ranging chimpanzees use a native linguistic system organized along the lines suggested by Washoe's reorganization of A.S.L. This question, obviously, can be answered only by those who can observe free-ranging chimpanzees leading their normal community life.[3]

REFERENCES

BELLUGI, U. and BROWN, R. (Eds.). 1964. The acquisition of language. *Monog. Soc. Res. Child. Dev.*, **29**, 5–191.

BLOOM, L. 1970. *Language development: Form and function in emerging grammars.* MIT Press, Cambridge, Mass.

BLOOM, L. *One word at a time: the use of single word utterances before syntax.* Mouton, The Hague. In press.

BRONOWSKI, J. and BELLUGI, U. 1970. Language, name and concept. *Science, N.Y.*, **168**, 669–673.

BROWN, R. *A first language.* Harvard Univ. Press, Cambridge, Mass. In press.

GARDNER, R. A. and GARDNER, B. T. 1969. Teaching sign language to a chimpanzee. *Science, N.Y.*, **165**, 664–672.

GARDNER, B. T. and GARDNER, R. A. 1971. Two-way communication with an infant chimpanzee. In A. M. Schrier and F. Stollnitz (Eds.), *Behavior of nonhuman primates*, Vol. 4. Academic Press, New York.

GOODALL, J. 1965. Chimpanzees of the Gombe Stream Reserve. In I. DeVore (Ed.), *Primate behavior. Field studies of monkeys and apes.* Holt, Rinehart and Winston, New York.

KUMMER, H. 1968. *Social organization of Hamadrayas baboons: a field study.* University of Chicago Press, Chicago.

V. LAWICK-GOODALL, J., 1971. *In the shadow of man.* Houghton Mifflin, Boston .

McNEILL, D. 1970. *The acquisition of language.* Harper, New York.

NEISSER, U. 1967. *Cognitive psychology.* Appleton-Century-Crofts, New York.

OMARK, D. Peer group formation in children. Dissertation in progress, Committee on Human Development, University of Chicago.

PREMACK, D. A. 1970. A functional analysis of language. *J. exp. Anal. Behav.*, **14**, 107–125.

[3] It will not be an easy matter to discover the properties of such a linguistic system, or even whether one exists. The medium may be gestural, but there seems to be no *a priori* basis for guessing what these gestures would look like. The structure of the language will presumably be built around various social interactions, not descriptions of the physical world, and the content of typical messages will probably consist of entreaties, demands, mollifications, and declarations of ownership and location. Linguistic regions may be quite small because of the small areas occupied by isolated reproducing communities. Goodall remarks that occasionally, the chimpanzees would abruptly change their activities and that she could not on these occasions discover what had triggered the change. Conceivably, a coded message had been exchanged, obvious to the chimpanzees but unnoticed by the human observer.

PREMACK, D. 1971. On the assessment of language competence in the chimpanzee. In A. M. Schrier and F. Stollnitz (Eds.), *Behavior of nonhuman primates*, Vol. 4. Academic Press, New York.

PREMACK, D. On animal intelligence. In H. Jerison (Ed.), *Perspectives on intelligence*. Appleton-Century-Crofts, New York. In press.

SCHALLER, G. B. 1963. *The mountain gorilla*. University of Chicago Press, Chicago.

SELIGMAN, M. E. P. 1970. On the generality of the laws of learning. *Psychol. Rev.*, **77**, 406–418.

SNOW, E. E. 1972. Mothers' speech to children learning language. *Child. Dev.*, **43**, 549–565.

WINOGRAD, T. 1972. Understanding natural language. *Cognit. Psychol.*, **3**, 1–191.

Mothers and Infants

Mother–Infant Interaction and the Development of Competence

MARY D. SALTER AINSWORTH and SILVIA M. BELL

The Johns Hopkins University

COMPETENCE IN INFANCY may be defined in three major ways, and in each case it is illuminating to consider the neonate as well as the older infant. First, competence may be defined in terms of cognitive abilities and motor skills. In these terms an infant, especially a neonate, must be assessed as incompetent and helpless, both absolutely and when compared with an older child or an adult. At the beginning, for example, he cannot reach out and grasp an object that interests him. He becomes more competent later when he can do so, and his competence in this regard can increase as his speed, precision, and control increases. This definition of competence is obviously useful when one is concerned with a child's development towards adult ability. On the other hand, it tends to minimize the effectiveness of an infant's behaviour and to neglect the extent to which it is preadapted to perform vital biological functions.

The second definition implies age- or stage-relevant assessment. An infant is competent to the extent that he functions well in the various situations that an infant normally encounters. As a neonate his competence rests on the adequacy of patterns of reflex activity (reflex schemata, or fixed action patterns), and hence upon the integrity of his neural, muscular, and sensory equipment. A competent neonate thus, for example, sucks well and cries lustily; a relatively incompetent one might suck or cry weakly. This view gives an infant his due as an infant, and also takes into account the fact that much of his competence rests, particularly at the beginning, upon the efficiency of his preadapted equipment. According to this view competence is most appropriately assessed relative to age peers. This is, of course, the core of the age-scale principle of assessing intelligence; it has been a useful principle. Its chief shortcoming, as applied to infancy, is that a baby's preadapted behaviours cannot be effective in performing the functions for which they were selected (in an evolutionary sense) should his environment depart unduly from the environment to which they were originally adapted. Thus it matters little how well a baby cries or roots or sucks if no one heeds the signal of his crying, and no one picks him up and makes a nutritive nipple available enough that he can find it and suck it.

A third view of competence views neonatal patterns as adapted to an environment that contains an accessible mother figure whose responsive reciprocal behaviour is to a substantial extent under the control of the infant's behaviour. This implies that at first an infant's competence rests, in most essential respects, upon the co-operation of his mother figure. This defines an infant's competence as his effectiveness. An infant is competent to the extent that he can, through his own activity, control the effect that his environment will have on him. This definition includes such matters as controlling when and how he is fed and control of his proximity to companions, as well as control of the continuation or recurrence of interesting sights and sounds or control of reaching out and grasping an interesting object.

This definition of competence implies a competent mother–infant pair—an infant who is competent in his pre-adapted function (as in our second definition) and a mother who is competent in the reciprocal role to which the infant's behaviour is pre-adapted. The infant in such a competent pair is effective in getting what he wants, at least in part, because he can influence the behaviour of a responsive mother. It is our hypothesis that this fosters the further growth of the competence of the infant both in absolute terms and in terms of increasing skill in enlisting the cooperation of others.

According to this view, an infant who is initially relatively incompetent in the sense of inefficient function may, when paired with a mother highly responsive to the signals implicit in his behaviour, gradually increase his effectiveness in dealing with his environment, both physical and social. On the other hand, an infant, competent enough in his pre-adapted behaviours, may be ineffective in getting what he wants, if paired with a mother unresponsive to his signals. As a pair, this couple is relatively incompetent. The infant himself, although competent in his initial functioning, is ineffective. Such initial ineffectiveness tends to hamper the further development of his sensorimotor and social skills, and hence adversely affects the development of competence relative to his more favoured age-peers. Finally, of course, an initially malfunctioning infant may be paired with an unresponsive mother; this is the condition with the poorest prognosis for the development of infant competence. In the ultimate biological terms of survival this third view of competence is the crucial one.

Furthermore, one facet of competence, important throughout the entire life span, is social competence—the ability of the person to elicit the cooperation of others. According to our third definition of competence, maternal responsiveness provides the conditions for a normally functioning infant to influence what happens to him by influencing the behaviour of his mother. This, we believe, fosters a general "sense of competence" (White, 1963), and a sense of competence—or confidence—influences the development of increased competence in other realms, whether viewed in age-relevant or in absolute terms.

CRYING, COMMUNICATION, MATERNAL RESPONSIVENESS AND SOCIAL COMPETENCE

Central to social competence is effective communication. So let us begin by considering communication in mother–infant interaction to which Richards (this volume) attributes primary significance. Perhaps the most important contributions an infant makes to mother–infant interaction are his signalling behaviours, especially crying, through which he can attract his mother from a distance into closer proximity. Although to a sensitive mother an infant's entire behavioural repertoire may have signalling value, it can scarcely perform this function if she is not close enough to perceive his other signals hence the special significance of crying as a signal.

These early signals at first imply no intent to communicate. It seems unlikely that communication can become fully intentional until Stage 4 of the sensorimotor period (Piaget, 1936) or until there is a shift from fixed-action patterns to goal-corrected behaviour (Bowlby, 1969)—that is, not until the last three or four months of the first year. Nevertheless, long before an infant can intentionally seek to influence the behaviour of his companions, he does in fact exert a measure of control through the expressive, signalling quality of his behaviour. Through interaction with them his signalling behaviour may become increasingly differentiated and effective in influencing their response to him.

Elsewhere (Bell and Ainsworth, in press) we have presented findings pertinent to the argument that the responsiveness of a mother figure to infant signals promotes the development of infant communication and hence the development of social competence. These findings emerged from a short-term longitudinal study of the development of infant–mother attachment in the first year of life. The subjects were 26 infant–mother pairs from white, middle-class, Baltimore families. They were observed in their own homes at intervals of three weeks, each visit lasting approximately four hours. The raw data are in the form of detailed narrative reports. A variety of coding, rating, and classificatory procedures have been used in the data analysis.

The signalling behaviour that concerned us in the above mentioned analysis was crying. Each instance of crying that occurred in the course of a home visit was coded. Among the particulars coded were: the duration of the cry, whether the mother responded to it or ignored it, and, if she responded to it, how long she delayed before responding. We were interested in ascertaining whether a mother's responsiveness was associated with a change in the incidence and duration of infant crying in the course of the first year. We were also interested in teasing out the direction of effects—a difficult matter in a naturalistic study which must use correlational procedures.

First, a word about our procedures. Our infant crying measures included fussing as well as crying, and very brief cries as well as full-blown, prolonged crying. There were two measures of infant crying: (a) the frequency of crying episodes per waking hour, and (b) the total duration of crying in minutes per waking hour. The two measures of maternal responsiveness that are relevant to this report are: (a) the number of crying episodes that a mother altogether ignored, and (b) the duration of maternal unresponsiveness—the length of time in minutes per waking hour that a baby cried without or before an intervention by the mother.

The first step in our analysis was to examine the stability of infant crying throughout the first year and to compare it with the stability of maternal responsiveness to crying over the same period. Do infants who cry relatively frequently at the beginning continue to cry relatively frequently throughout the first year? Are there constitutional differences in irritability that make some infants cry more than others both at first and throughout the first year? Our findings suggested that there is no stability in infant crying until the very end of the first year, and therefore no support for the view that babies who cry more than others at the end of the first year do so because they are constitutionally irritable.

Mothers were found to be substantially more stable in their responsiveness to infant crying than infants in their tendency to cry. Their responsiveness in each quarter-year was significantly related to their responsiveness in the previous quarter. This stability was particularly striking in regard to the duration measure, the length of time a baby cried without or before maternal intervention. The first and second quarters, as well as the third quarter, were significantly correlated with the fourth quarter.

The second step was to consider the intercorrelations between infant crying and maternal responsiveness. Table I shows the correlation

TABLE 1. *Episodes of crying ignored by the mother and frequency of crying. The figures in italics have been corrected to avoid confounding*

| Frequency of crying | Episodes ignored by the mother | | | |
	First quarter	Second quarter	Third quarter	Fourth quarter
First quarter	*−0·04*	0·34	0·48*	0·21
Second quarter	0·56*	*0·35*	0·32	0·29
Third quarter	0·21	0·39*	*0·42*	0·40*
Fourth quarter	0·20	0·36	0·52†	0·45*

* *p* 0·05.
† *p* 0·01.

between the number of crying episodes ignored by the mother and the frequency of infant crying episodes. There are three parts of the table upon which to focus. The first is the diagonal, which gives the correlation of maternal behaviour and infant behaviour in the same quarter. The second is the six-celled lower left portion of the matrix, which shows the correlation of maternal behaviour in each quarter with infant behaviour in subsequent quarters. The third part is the six-celled upper right portion of the matrix which gives the correlation of crying in each quarter with maternal ignoring in subsequent quarters.

Let us first consider the information on the diagonal. Here it was necessary to introduce a correction for the confounding of measures. The confounding consists in the fact that the number of crying episodes (within a quarter) includes those that the mother ignored as well as those to which she responded. The correction consisted of excluding from the infant measure those episodes that the mother ignored. After this correction is made it is evident that the extent to which a mother ignores crying and the frequency with which an infant cries are not significantly related either within the first or within the second quarter. Within each of the third and fourth quarters, however, babies who cry more frequently have mothers who more frequently ignore their crying.

The lower left portion of the matrix shows that from the beginning of the first year maternal ignoring in each quarter correlates significantly with infant crying in the subsequent quarter. (A correction was not necessary here, because the frequency with which a baby cries in one quarter is not confounded with the number of episodes which his mother ignores in another quarter.) Thus tiny babies do not respond immediately to maternal ignoring by crying more frequently, but from the end of the third month onward they tend to be more insistent in their crying as a result of the past history of mother's ignoring tactics. Finally, the upper right hand portion of the matrix suggests that there is no consistent tendency for an infant's crying in one quarter to be associated with maternal ignoring in the following quarter, until the fourth quarter.

These findings, together with the findings on stability, summarized earlier, suggest that maternal ignoring increases the likelihood that a baby will cry relatively more frequently from the second quarter onward, whereas the frequency of *his* crying has no consistent influence on the number of episodes his mother will be likely subsequently to ignore.

TABLE II. *Duration of mother's unresponsiveness to crying and duration of crying. The figures in italics have been corrected to avoid confounding*

| Duration of crying | Mother's unresponsiveness | | | |
	First quarter	Second quarter	Third quarter	Fourth quarter
First quarter	*0·19*	0·37	0·12	0·41*
Second quarter	0·45*	*0·67†*	0·51†	0·69†
Third quarter	0·40*	0·42*	*0·39*	0·52†
Fourth quarter	0·32	0·65†	0·51†	*0·61†*

* p 0·05.
† p 0·01.

Table II shows a comparable analysis of the relation between the duration of maternal unresponsiveness and the duration of infant crying. For intra-quarter comparisons, those shown on the diagonal, there was again a correction for confounding since the duration of an infant's crying includes both the time during which his mother was unresponsive and the time he continued to cry after she intervened. The corrected measure deals only with the time he cried after she intervened. When this measure is used, it may be seen that babies whose mothers are unresponsive in the first quarter do not cry more (after intervention) than those whose mothers are responsive. But within each of the second, third and fourth quarters, babies with unresponsive mothers do cry more.

For inter-quarter comparisons there is no confounding of measures and hence no correction. The lower left portion of the matrix shows that babies whose mothers were unresponsive in the first quarter tend to cry more in subsequent quarters, and that, generally, maternal unresponsiveness in one quarter is associated with longer duration of crying in subsequent quarters. The upper right-hand cells differ, however, from those of the previous table. It appears that by the second half of the first year infants who persistently cry for long periods tend to make mothers more than ever reluctant to respond. This suggests that a vicious spiral may have been established. Mothers who are unresponsive to the crying of their tiny infants have babies who cry more later on, which in turn further discourages the mother from responding promptly, and results in relatively increased infant crying.

These findings are of considerable interest in themselves, perhaps especially since they fail to confirm the common belief that to respond promptly to a baby's cry will strengthen his tendency to cry on subsequent occasions. But let us consider the findings within the context of the various concepts of competence. Even though crying may be age-appropriate at the beginning of the first year, substantially diminished crying is appropriate towards the end of the first year and later. It is evident that maternal unresponsiveness to crying does not diminish it. On the contrary, it tends to prolong this primitive form of signalling up to at least the end of the first year. If, however, an infant's competence is viewed as depending on his mother's cooperativeness, one might argue that a one-year-old (albeit to a lesser extent than a neonate) still must be able to signal effectively if he is to be deemed competent. What has happened to the signalling behaviour of infants whose mothers have been relatively responsive?

This question led us to assess infant communication in the fourth quarter of the first year. A seven-point rating scale was constructed, which took into consideration facial expression, gesture, and non-crying vocalizations. At the positive pole of the scale was a wide variety of

TABLE III. *Infant communication in the fourth quarter, crying and maternal responsiveness*

	Fourth quarter infant communication
Duration of crying	$-0\cdot71$†
Frequency of crying	$-0\cdot65$†
Mother's unresponsiveness	$-0\cdot63$†
Episodes ignored by mother	$-0\cdot54$†

† $P\ 0\cdot01$.

subtle yet clear modes of communication (as described by the observer in his narrative report, and without taking into account maternal response to the communication). At the negative pole was a limited variety in modes of signalling, and signals that were difficult to "read". (The seven-point scale was subsequently collapsed into a three-point scale, in the interests of obtaining good inter-rater agreement, but the poles retained this definition.) Table III shows the relationship between our ratings of communication and infant crying on the one hand and maternal responsiveness on the other. It may be seen that there are substantial negative correlations between infant communication and the frequency and duration of crying. Babies who cried little had a wider range of differentiated modes of communication than did babies who cried much. Furthermore, it is clear that those mothers who were responsive to infant crying, ignoring few episodes and responding with little delay, have infants who have more variety, subtlety and clarity of non-crying communication.

It is not suggested that this relationship is entirely attributable to maternal responsiveness to crying. There is good reason to believe that those mothers in our sample who are relatively responsive to crying are also responsive to a wide range of other infant signals. We assessed such responsiveness by a rating scale designed to measure a mother's sensitivity–insensitivity to infant signals. (The rating scale is reproduced in Ainsworth et al., in press.) Sensitivity–insensitivity ratings have significant negative correlations with maternal ignoring of crying episodes ($r = -0.41$; $p < 0.05$) and with duration of maternal unresponsiveness to crying ($r = -0.58$; $p < 0.01$). It therefore seems likely that it is a mother's responsiveness to non-crying signals as well as to the more obvious and urgent crying signals that facilitates the development of a differentiated repertoire of non-crying modes of communication. Thus maternal responsiveness to signals supports the development of social competence, in the sense that it promotes the development of a variety of communicative behaviours which are easy to read and hence are likely to influence the behaviour of others in a more differentiated way than an infant can through merely crying.

COMPETENCE IN DIRECT DEALING WITH THE PHYSICAL ENVIRONMENT

Important though social competence may be, one can further ask about the manner in which mother–infant interaction may influence those aspects of cognitive development that imply a direct interaction with the physical environment and the gaining of control over it—

rather than the indirect control gained through influencing the behaviour of others. There seem to be at least three important ways in which mother–infant interaction might influence the development of an infant's competence in direct interaction with his physical environment and the objects in it.

First, it seems reasonable to suppose that maternal behaviour might facilitate the development of abilities directly pertinent to an infant's dealings with his physical environment. Thus, for example, in the course of being held by his mother, his adjustment of posture to the shifts of position occasioned by her movements might well accelerate the acquisition of control over head and trunk musculature, which in turn would accelerate the development of locomotion, and consequent exploration and manipulation of his physical environment. Similarly, it has been suggested (Piaget, 1937, 1954) that the mother, in the course of interacting with him, is the one object who can serve as "aliment" simultaneously to many of the infant's schemata, and thus promotes their inter-coordination and his general development. It can be further argued (Bell, 1971) that the mother's initiative in introducing her child to stimulating conditions through play has an increasingly important role in the course of cognitive development from the end of the first year of life onwards.

Second, even when she is not in interaction with him, a mother may substantially influence the kind of experience an infant can have with his environment. For example, she may provide interesting objects for him to see when he is lying in his crib rather than a barren visual surround; she may tuck him up so his hands are not free, or leave him free to use his hands. When he has become mobile, she may give him freedom to explore interesting facets of his environment, or she may confine him in a playpen.

Third, a baby's experience with his mother may have an indirect effect on his dealings with the rest of his world through affecting his confidence. This confidence has at least two noteworthy aspects— confidence in her and confidence in himself. Trust in her may well be a necessary condition for him to venture forth to explore the world, this will be discussed later. Confidence in himself may also be affected by his experience with her, through fostering a "sense of competence". It seems reasonable to suppose that the more consistently an infant has experienced effective control of what happens to him as a consequence of his own activity, the more likely he is to approach a new object or new situation with the expectation that he can control its effect on him. Thus it seems likely that an infant whose mother's responsiveness has given him frequent experiences of affecting what happens to him (through affecting her behaviour) would have influenced his confidence in his own ability to act effectively on his environment.

When attempting to ascertain the effect of maternal behaviour on the development of an infant's competence it is very difficult to sort out those particular aspects of her behaviour that may have been responsible for any specific effect that might be attributed to her. Despite this difficulty, there are a few findings from our investigation of the development of infant–mother attachment and related studies which suggest generally that maternal behaviour can influence the development of infant competence.

Maternal behaviour and intelligence

The first of these findings relates to infant intelligence as measured by the Griffiths (1954) Scale. Whether or not such measures predict later I.Q. at least they may be accepted as valid assessments of developmental level in infancy, and as such may be considered overall measures of the level of competence achieved by an infant. In the course of our longitudinal study of the development of infant–mother attachment, the Griffiths test was administered at intervals of approximately nine weeks during the first year. The measure that concerns us here is the mean "General Quotient" for the tests undertaken in the fourth quarter-year.

The analysis of the relationship between maternal behaviour and infant intelligence is a reworking of the correlational matrix presented by Stayton et al. (1971), which was concerned with the relationship of infant obedience and infant I.Q. The correlation matrix is shown in Table IV. The first three variables were measured by nine-point rating scales. Maternal sensitivity–insensitivity to infant signals was mentioned earlier. This and the two other variables, acceptance–rejection and

TABLE IV. *Intercorrelations between maternal variables and infant I.Q.*

Variables	1	2	3	4	5	6
1. Sensitivity–insensitivity	...					
2. Acceptance–rejection	0·91†	...				
3. Cooperation–interference	0·87†	0·88†	...			
4. Frequency of verbal commands	−0·14	−0·05	−0·35	...		
5. Frequency of physical interventions	−0·44*	−0·38	−0·59†	0·62†	...	
6. Floor freedom	0·07	0·00	0·10	−0·03	0·07	...
7. Infant I.Q.	0·46*	0·45*	0·44*	0·06	0·06	0·46*

* p 0·05.
† p 0·01.

cooperation–interference, were described briefly by Stayton *et al*. The frequency of mother's verbal commands and the frequency of her physical interventions in lieu of, or to reinforce commands were derived from coding and refer to the mean number of such behaviours per visit. Floor freedom refers to the degree to which a baby was permitted to be free on the floor during his waking hours; two groups were distinguished, those given relatively much and those given relatively little floor freedom. It may be seen that four of the six maternal variables have a significant, moderate, positive relationship with infant I.Q.—floor freedom and the three rated variables.

TABLE V. *Stepwise multiple regression: infant I.Q. as criterion variable*

Step number	Variable entered	R with I.Q.
1	Sensitivity–insensitivity	0·46
2	Floor Freedom	0·63
3	Frequency of physical interventions	0·67
4	Cooperation–interference	0·70
5	Acceptance–rejection	0·70
6	Frequency of verbal commands	0·70

Table V shows the results of a stepwise regression using these six maternal variables, with infant I.Q. as the criterion variable. Although all three rated variables (sensitivity–insensitivity, acceptance–rejection, and cooperation–interference) were significantly related to infant I.Q. they were so highly correlated with each other that the addition of a second or third to the regression equation effected little or no increase in the multiple correlation coefficient. However, when floor freedom was added to the first of the rated variables, maternal sensitivity–insensitivity, the R was raised to 0·63. The addition of two other variables raised the multiple correlation coefficient to 0·70, and the addition of the last two variables effected no further increase.

The correlation matrix in Table IV was not originally assembled with the prediction of infant I.Q. in mind, and obviously omits a number of variables that ought to be included in such an analysis, for example, parents' education and occupation, stimulating nature of physical environment provided in the home, and parental encouragement of the acquisition of verbal and motor skills. Nevertheless the findings of the stepwise regression analysis are suggestive. Mothers who both are sensitive to infant signals *and* permit their babies freedom of movement to explore the world on their own account tend to have babies who are relatively accelerated in psychomotor development, whereas mothers who are insensitive to signals *and* who limit their infants' opportunity to interact with their physical environment tend to have babies who are relatively retarded in development.

The contribution of floor freedom to the development of competence seems obvious. The contributions of maternal sensitivity to signals is perhaps less immediately apparent. It suggests that the behaviour characteristic of the sensitive mother has, as Piaget proposed, a facilitating effect on the development of the infant's ability to deal with his physical environment. It also fits the hypothesis, advanced earlier, that a baby whose signals are responded to promptly and appropriately builds up a sense of competence—a confidence that he can through his own activity control what happens to him—and this confidence carries over into his transactions with his physical environment.

Substantial confirmation of these findings comes from two sources. First, Beckwith (1971) studied twenty-four adopted infants living in middle-class families, in order to control possible confoundings of

TABLE VI. *Correlation of I.Q. at two age levels with: stimulating potential of the environment, quality of the infant–mother attachment and several variables of maternal care*

	I.Q. eight months	I.Q. eleven months
Stimulating potential of environment: eight months		
Floor freedom	0·61†	0·34†
Toys	0·43†	0·13
Amount of play	0·14	0·04
Stimulating potential of environment: eleven months		
Floor freedom	0·56†	0·57†
Toys	0·45†	0·41†
Amount of play	0·21	0·34*
Quality of infant–mother attachment	0·55†	0·46†
Maternal variables		
Verbal stimulation	0·18	0·23
Frequency of punishment	−0·24	−0·34*
Education	0·16	0·08

* $P\ 0·05$.
† $P\ 0·01$.

genetic effects and maternal behaviour. She used two composite measures of maternal behaviour derived from time-sampled observations during home visits. One measure was "stimulation" which combined scores on verbal and physical contact; another was a measure of restrictiveness of exploration. A highly significant relationship was found between these measures and Cattell intelligence scores. Low maternal verbal and physical contact plus high maternal restrictiveness of exploration significantly lowered I.Q.

Second, one of us (S.M.B.), in the course of a longitudinal study of thirty-three black socio-economically underprivileged children, obtained findings of the relation between the quality of the infant–mother attachment, floor freedom and I.Q. which closely parallel those outlined above. The children in this study were tested repeatedly during the first two years of life on several measures of cognitive development, the Griffiths Scale and two tests of the object concept. In addition they were observed in free play and in interaction with their mothers for a two-hour period subsequent to each testing. An informal interview was also conducted with the mother in each session for the purpose of evaluating the stimulating potential of the home environment, parental education, and other pertinent factors. The findings relevant to the concern of this paper are presented in Table VI, and show the correlation between I.Q at two age levels, some of the variables assessed in interview, and a measure of the observed quality of the infant–mother attachment relationship.

At both eight and eleven months, floor freedom and a harmonious infant–mother attachment relationship were found to be highly correlated with I.Q. Availability of toys also showed a significant, but lower, correlation with I.Q. at both age levels. Amount of time that adults or other children spent in playing with the baby was positively correlated with I.Q. towards the end of the first year. Frequency of punishment was negatively and moderately correlated with development at eleven months. Parental education, in contrast, was not significantly correlated with infant I.Q. at either eight or eleven months.

This table presents only a part of the total matrix of variables reported by Bell (1971). The larger matrix was subjected to a factor analysis, with Varimax rotation. The first factor, which accounted for 52% of the variance, was defined primarily by high loadings on the cognitive tests, including I.Q., at the two age levels, the quality of the infant–mother attachment relationship, and floor freedom. Availability of toys at eleven months loaded primarily, but only moderately, on this factor. Since the quality of the infant–mother attachment relationship, observed in this study, is largely a function of the degree of maternal sensitivity characteristic of the transactions between mother and infant (Bell, 1970) the findings corroborate the conclusions of Ainsworth's and Beckwith's studies discussed above.

The use of the mother as a secure base from which to explore

We have often emphasized one significant outcome of infant–mother attachment, namely, that an infant can use his mother as a secure base from which to explore his world (Ainsworth, 1967; Ainsworth and Bell, 1970; Ainsworth *et al.*, 1971; Salter, 1940). The fact that a baby has become attached to his mother does not mean that he constantly seeks to be in contact, close proximity, or even in interaction with her. On the contrary, he may leave her often on his own initiative and may move about, interested in investigating his surroundings and the objects and other people in it. He keeps track of his mother's whereabouts, however, and tends to return to her briefly from time to time before moving off again. He may go out of sight in the course of his explorations, showing no sign of fear, presumably because he knows where his mother is and expects her to remain accessible to him. But should his mother get up to leave the room, he may well abandon his explorations and scuttle after her, or perhaps merely gravitate to where she now is. It is her presence that provides him with a secure base from which to explore.

The secure-base phenomenon may be viewed within the context of Bowlby's (1969) control-systems model of attachment behaviour. There are at least two systems of behaviour that are in dynamic balance with each other, attachment behaviour that promotes proximity to an attachment figure and exploratory behaviour (including locomotion, manipulation, visual investigation, and exploratory play) that promotes acquisition of knowledge of the environment and adaptation to environmental variations. The balance is tipped towards exploration by complex, novel, or changing features of the environment, provided that these are not so sudden, intense, or strange as to provoke alarm. The balance is tipped towards proximity seeking by a number of conditions, both intra-organismic and environmental. Important among the environmental conditions that heightens a child's attachment behaviour are alarm and threatened or actual separation from the attachment figure. Obviously, if attachment behaviour were constantly activated at a high level a child's development would be greatly hampered for he would not be attracted away from his attachment figure to explore his world. Perhaps not so obviously, if his exploratory behaviour constantly overrode his attachment behaviour then his survival would be threatened, unless his mother were constantly vigilant to retrieve him from danger.

An optimum balance between exploratory and attachment behaviour would seem to be a favourable condition for cognitive development and thus, for the development of competence. It is by no means easy to study the attachment–exploration balance, however. Our first attempt to do so prompted us to devise a strange-situation procedure (Ainsworth and Wittig, 1969). When observing a baby at home it was not clear whether it was his mother who was providing the secure base for his exploration of his whole familiar home environment. In an unfamiliar laboratory situation, however, it was intended to tip the balance towards exploration by providing an attractive display of toys at a distance from the mother. If a baby left his mother to explore the toys when she was present and ceased to explore when she was absent, it could be inferred that her presence provided security for his exploration. A majority of one-year-olds, both in our longitudinal sample and in Bell's (1970) project, did in fact behave as our hypothesis predicted they would (Ainsworth and Bell, 1970). There were striking individual differences, however, especially (a) in the extent to which attachment behaviour replaced exploratory behaviour during the brief separation episodes of the strange situation and in the reunion episodes that followed, and (b) in the intensity and quality of attachment behaviour in the reunion episodes.

Babies were classified into three groups chiefly in terms of their attachment behaviour in the reunion episodes (Ainsworth et al., 1971). Group A infants tended neither to maintain contact with the mother nor to seek proximity to her even in the reunion episodes following brief separation, but rather conspicuously avoided proximity to her and interaction with her. Group B infants' attachment behaviour was heightened by separation; in the reunion episodes they actively sought to be near the mother, to gain and to maintain contact with her, or, at least to establish interaction with her. The attachment behaviour of Group C infants was also heightened by separation but was of highly ambivalent quality.

In an attempt to throw light upon these individual differences, assessments were made of the behaviour of mother and infant at home. Maternal behaviour was rated on four nine-point rating scales; sensitivity–insensitivity to infant signals, acceptance–rejection, and cooperation–interference, which were mentioned earlier, and also accessibility–ignoring. Whereas all the mothers of Group B infants were above the median on each of four scales, the mothers of both Group A and Group C infants were below the median on all scales. Group A mothers were especially rejecting, whereas Group C mothers were not, although they were either strongly interfering or very inaccessible.

In regard to infant behaviour we tackled the difficult job of assessing attachment–exploration balance as it appeared in behaviour in the familiar home environment. In advance of this analysis symmetrical findings were expected, with a majority showing a smooth balance between attachment and exploratory behaviour but with some having the balance tipped towards exploratory behaviour with less than average attachment behaviour, and others having the balance tipped towards attachment behaviour with less than average exploratory behaviour. The findings (reported by Ainsworth et al., 1971) did not turn out precisely according to expectation. It seemed to be not so much the quantitative ratio of exploratory to attachment behaviour that was significant as the smoothness of the transition from one to the other, and the quality of the attachment behaviour when it was activated.

The strange-situation classification showed remarkable congruence with the classification of attachment–exploration balance at home. At home all but one of the thirteen Group B babies showed at least a fairly smooth kind of transition between exploratory and attachment behaviour. They were not especially clingy; they enjoyed physical contact with their mothers when it occurred, but they were content to be put down and to move off into independent activity. They tended to follow their mothers about in a casual way, but tended not to be distressed by minor everyday situations in the familiar home environment. Three infants (two A and one B) did seem to have the balance tipped towards exploratory behaviour with relatively infrequent attachment behaviour. But the remaining eight subjects (four A and four C) seemed not so much to show below average exploratory behaviour as disturbances in the infant–mother attachment relationship. Their attachment behaviour was ambivalent, and they were more insecure than the average, crying relatively frequently, and especially prone to separation anxiety.

One of us (S.M.B.) is currently studying the quality of investigative behaviour and exploratory play, and its relation to maternal behaviour and to the quality of the infant–mother attachment relationship. In the course of studying the cognitive development of black underprivileged children mentioned earlier (Bell, 1971), infants were observed with their mothers in a free-play situation for a two-hour period several times in the first three years of life. Each session was subsequently coded for infant exploration and for maternal behaviour. The coding of infant exploration consisted of: (a) noting all the behaviours shown by the child and all the toys explored in the course of the session, and (b) ascertaining the number of different schemata exhibited and the cognitive level of the play. The coding of maternal behaviour referred primarily to: (a) the qualitative and quantitative engagement of the mother with the toys and the child during his exploration, and (b) the quality and quantity of her transactions with him unrelated to his exploration. The analysis of these data is still underway but results obtained for the last quarter of the first year indicated that there is a substantial relationship between an infant's competence and his mother's behaviour. Infants who had frequent harmonious transactions with their mother in the course of the play session, and whose mothers were generally responsive to their initiations of interaction (whether directly related to exploration or not), tended to explore more toys and, more important, to display more behavioural schemata in the course of play. In addition, infants who experienced frequent prolonged periods of play with their mother, or main caretaker, outside the observed play session, explored more toys and displayed a greater number of schemata and a more advanced level of play in the play session itself, than did infants whose mother figures did not characteristically spend time playing with them. The findings of this study suggest that variety of exploration and level of behavioural repertoire are associated with the general quality of the infant–mother relationship and also with the amount of time that a child spends in play and in one-to-one interaction with a significant attachment figure.

Mother–infant interaction and the development of the concept of the object

One of us (Bell, 1970) compared the development of the concept of inanimate objects as permanent with the development of the concept of persons as permanent objects. A scale of object permanence was developed, based on Piaget's (1937) detailed observations, and a parallel scale of person permanence. The subjects were thirty-three infants of white, middle-class families who were tested on these two scales three times between the ages of $8\frac{1}{2}$ and eleven months. Attention was directed towards the horizontal decalage between the two measures of development of the object concept. The hypothesis was that infants who had enjoyed relatively harmonious interaction with their mothers in the course of the first year would be accelerated in person permanence in contrast with the concept of permanence of inanimate objects, while the reverse would hold for infants who had experienced relatively disharmonious interaction. The assessment of the degree of harmony of mother–infant interaction was indirect; the strange-situation technique was used to classify the infants, and as reported above, it is clear that Group B infants have more harmonious mother–infant interaction than do either Group A or Group C infants.

Twenty-four of the thirty-three infants in this sample could be classified in Group B in regard to strange-situation behaviour. Twenty-three of these had a positive decalage, being more advanced in the development of person permanence than in the development of the concept of the permanence of inanimate objects. One of them showed no decalage. None of the babies classified in either Group A or in Group C had a positive decalage. Four Group A babies showed a negative decalage, and one no decalage. Three Group C babies showed a negative decalage, and one no decalage. It was concluded that babies who have had a harmonious interaction with mothers sensitive to their signals, and who have developed an attachment relationship of normal quality, tend to develop person permanence in advance of inanimate-object permanence.

Once the relationship between the type of decalage and quality of attachment had been established, it was of interest to determine if those babies who had a positive decalage differed from the others in terms of the maximum level of the object concept they had achieved. For this analysis the negative and no decalage groups were combined. Fig. 1 shows the mean scores on person permanence and object permanence

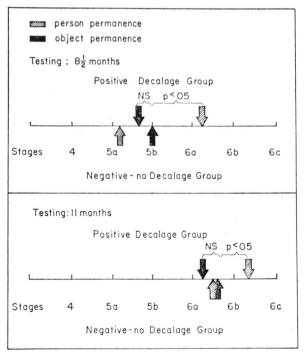

FIG. 1. Mean scores on object and person permanence for the positive and negative–no decalage groups at $8\frac{1}{2}$ and eleven months.

at $8\frac{1}{2}$ and eleven months. At both ages it may be seen that the person-permanence scores of the positive decalage group are significantly in advance of the object-permanence scores of the negative and no decalage group. At $8\frac{1}{2}$ months the positive decalage group was facile in coping with the visible displacements of persons, and thus had nearly reached stage 6 in person permanence, although they were just beginning stage 5 in object permanence. The negative and no decalage group was significantly better in object permanence, and had scarcely begun to search for hidden persons, and hence were at the beginning of stage 4 in person permanence. By eleven months the majority of babies in the sample had begun to cope with invisible displacements of inanimate objects and thus had entered stage 6. Babies in the positive decalage group had also completed the higher substages of stage 6 in regard to person permanence, and thus had acquired an ability to handle complex invisible displacements of one type of object. About half of the babies were retested at $13\frac{1}{2}$ months. Of these, a significantly higher number in the positive decalage group had completed the object-permanence scale than in the negative–no decalage group (Fisher, $p < 0.01$). In addition, the rate of development with respect to both object and person permanence was found to be significantly faster for the positive decalage group (Fisher, $p < 0.05$). This study indicated that the environmental circumstances that affect the quality of an infant's attachment to his mother — namely, maternal characteristics of perceptiveness, appropriateness and contingency of responding subsumed under the label "sensitivity" —affect also an important aspect of cognitive development in the first two years of life.

Continuing with her work in this area, Bell undertook a study to evaluate the importance of the mother–infant relationship in affecting cognitive development, relative to ethnic and socio-economic factors. One aspect of the project (Bell, 1971), which was outlined in an earlier section of this chapter, aimed to study black under-privileged infants using procedures similar to those utilized in the (1970) study of white, middle-class infants. The results of the second study directly parallel those obtained in the first. There was a perfect correspondence between type of decalage and quality of infant–mother attachment; only those infants who had a positive decalage had had a harmonious relationship with the mother. Those infants who had a positive decalage were significantly more advanced in the development of the object concept than were the negative–no decalage group.

In addition, a comparison of the middle-class and socio-economically deprived samples revealed no differences in the level of the object concept at eight months, but significant differences in the level of both object and person permanence at eleven months, differences which favoured the middle-class sample (t significant at 0·01 level for both tests). But when the decalage subgroups were compared across socio-economic level, there were no differences in the level of the object concept at either eight or eleven months for those infants who had a positive decalage and had experienced a harmonious relationship with the mother. On the other hand, those infants in the low socio-economic sample who had experienced a disharmonious relationship with the mother were significantly inferior to the middle-class infants who had experienced disharmony. These findings suggest that, whereas the environmental conditions associated with socio-economic deprivation have a detrimental effect on cognitive development, a harmonious infant–mother relationship can act as a buffer protecting a child from their detrimental effect, and, in fact, is the single most important factor alleviating socio-economic disadvantage.

SUMMARY

Several sets of evidence have been offered to support the hypothesis that cognitive and social development are intimately interrelated, and that mother–infant interaction influences both. A mother's prompt responsiveness to her baby's signals tends to foster the development of varied and clear modes of communication and thus the development of one facet of social competence. Sensitive maternal responsiveness to infant signals, especially when combined with giving a baby freedom to explore his physical environment, facilitates the overall development of competence as measured by a general intelligence quotient. The quality of mother–infant interaction affects both the quality of a baby's attachment relationship with his mother and at least one important specific aspect of cognitive development, the development of the concept of the object. The balance between exploratory and attachment behaviour has been considered, and it has been suggested that the significance of this is not so much quantitative as qualitative. That is, the significant individual differences lie not so much in the relative quantities of attachment and exploratory behaviour as in the quality of each and the smoothness of the transition from one to the other. Evidence has been presented that the quality of mother–infant interaction influences the quality of the infant's attachment relationship to his mother, and that it also influences the level and quality of exploratory behaviour and play. These findings from one set of related studies have accomplished little more than demonstrating a relationship between mother–infant interaction and the development of competence. Further research is presently under way to yield more detailed knowledge of which specific aspects of the mother–infant relationship interact with other variables, both environmental and organismic, to affect the development of specific aspects of competence.

Acknowledgements

This paper has been prepared while one author's (M.D.S.A.) research was supported by the Grant Foundation and the others' (S.M.B.) by the Office of Child Development (grant number OCD-CB-49) but acknowledgements are due also to the agencies which supported the earlier research upon which the paper is based, grant number 62-244 of the Foundations' Fund for Research in Psychiatry, USPHS grant number R01 01712, and grant number OEG-3-70-0036 of the Office of Education. We acknowledge with gratitude Donelda J. Stayton, our colleague in much of this research, whose study of infant obedience formed the basis for the analysis of the relationship of maternal variables to infant I.Q. in one of the samples, and Inge Bretherton who initiated and carried through that analysis. We also thank the many other research colleagues and student assistants who helped to collect and to analyse the data summarized in this paper, in particular Carolyn Bates whose enthusiasm and dedication were invaluable in enlisting and maintaining the cooperation of S.M.B.'s sample.

REFERENCES

AINSWORTH, M. D. S. 1967. *Infancy in Uganda: infant care and the growth of love.* Johns Hopkins University Press, Baltimore.

AINSWORTH, M. D. S. and BELL, S. M. 1970. Attachment, exploration, and separation: illustrated by the behavior of one-year-olds in a strange situation. *Child Dev.*, **41**, 49–67.

AINSWORTH, M. D. S., BELL, S. M. V. and STAYTON, D. J. 1971. Individual differences in strange-situation behaviour of one-year-olds. In H. R. Schaffer (Ed.) *The origins of human social relations.* Academic Press, London.

AINSWORTH, M. D. S., BELL, S. M. V. and STAYTON, D. J. Infant–mother attachment and social development: socialization as a product of reciprocal responsiveness to signals. In M. P. M. Richards (Ed.), *The integration of a child into a social world.* Cambridge University Press, Cambridge. In press.

AINSWORTH, M. D. S. and WITTIG, B. A. 1969. Attachment and exploratory behavior of one-year-olds in a strange situation. In B. M. Foss (Ed.) *Determinants of infant behaviour IV.* Methuen, London.

BECKWITH, L. 1971. Relationships between attributes of mothers and their infants' I.Q. scores. *Child Dev.*, **42**, 1083–1097.

BELL, S. M. 1970. The development of the concept of object as related to infant–mother attachment. *Child Dev.*, **41**, 291–311.

BELL, S. M. 1971. Early cognitive development and its relationship to infant–mother attachment: A study of disadvantaged Negro infants. Report prepared for the U.S. Office of Education, Project No. 00542.

BELL, S. M. and AINSWORTH, M. D. S. Infant crying and maternal responsiveness. *Child Devel.* In press.

BOWLBY, J. 1969. *Attachment and loss*, Vol. 1. *Attachment*. Hogarth Press, London; Basic Books, New York.

GRIFFITHS, R. 1954. *The abilities of babies*. University of London Press, London.

PIAGET, J. 1936. *The origins of intelligence in children*, 2nd ed. International Universities Press, New York, 1952.

PIAGET, J. 1937. *The construction of reality in the child*. Basic Books, New York, 1954.

PIAGET, J. 1954. *Les relations entre l'affectivite et l'intelligence dans le developpment mental de l'enfant*. Centre de Documentation Universitaire, Paris.

SALTER, M. D. 1940. *An evaluation of adjustment based upon the concept of security*. University of Toronto Studies, Child Development Series, No. 18. University of Toronto Press, Toronto.

STAYTON, D. J., HOGAN, R. and AINSWORTH, M. D. S. 1971. Infant obedience and maternal behavior: the origins of socialization reconsidered. *Child. Dev.*, **42**, 1057–1069.

WHITE, R. W. 1963. *Ego and reality in psychoanalytic theory*. International Universities Press, New York.

The Development of Psychological Communication in the First Year of Life[1]

M. P. M. RICHARDS

The University of Cambridge

INTRODUCTION

DURING THE PAST five years, Judy Bernal and I have been concerned with a longitudinal observational study of mother–infant relations in the first year of life. Details of the methods and assumptions employed in this work and some of the preliminary results have been described elsewhere (Bernal, 1972; Bernal and Richards, 1971; Richards and Bernal, 1972). The data collection for this study is now complete and we are involved in the analysis of results. This analysis not only requires a theory of a more formal kind than we used in data collection but it also provokes its elaboration—one enters a kind of accommodation–assimilation relationship with theory. In this paper I want to describe the current stage of this theoretical development and some of the observations that have led to it. I realize that this theorizing is not worked out and is oversimplified but I hope that, at least, it will provide others with an object for attack.

What we require is a descriptive and explanatory structure for the development of the social relations of infants and we are attempting to build this around a concept of psychological communication. We prefer communication to the concepts of attachment (Ainsworth, 1969; Bowlby, 1969) that have been used so widely in the discussions of early social relationships. The latter are unduly restrictive and cannot easily be used as a basis for the discussion of the range and subtlety of the infants' relationships which we have observed. Furthermore concepts of

[1] The mother–infant interaction project is carried out jointly with Judy Bernal and is supported by a grant from the Nuffield Foundation. Our thanks also go to the mothers and children for their patience and cooperation.

attachment seem to underemphasize the infant's active role in his socialization and his considerable communicative skills.

The development of these communicative skills takes the infant from a beginning where others pre-suppose some of his actions and regard the rest of his behaviour as random and purposeless, to the highly sophisticated skills of the egocentric one-year-old, well able to transmit complex intentions and wishes without more than a rudimentary use of speech. I will trace, at least in outline, the process by which these skills develop and the ways in which they closely parallel the infant's cognitive development. A development that moves from a stage where there is recognition of events with only the simplest of internal representation, to a point where the representations are highly differentiated, specific and permanent so that people are perceived individually, distinct from one another and from the self. This level of individual perception, coupled with an elaborated communicative competence and differentiation of affect, allows the infant to invest varying amounts of interest and emotion in his various specific relationships.

A THEORETICAL DESCRIPTION

The infant is an organism predisposed to become an adult and predisposed to be social (Berger and Luckman, 1967). He is not social at birth—but not an untamed savage—and he cannot develop social behaviour except in the context of a social world. To put it another way, there are features of the neonatal organism which, in combination with (and only in combination with) the social worlds which infants generally inhabit, make it highly probable that a social adult will emerge. I am not postulating any mysterious goal-directedness, indeed as biologists (e.g. Waddington, 1969) have made clear, programmes for means and not ends are specified epigenetically. I am merely pointing to the fact that there are features of the infant's behaviour and biological structure that will lead the child in a social world in a predictable fashion towards adult systems of functioning (Trevarthen, 1972). In this sense we must look both to infancy (and the embryo) and the child's social world for the origins of social behaviour. We must bear in mind that social relations for the child are drastically different from those of any adult.

At birth, the infant possesses cognitive mechanisms which lead to his being attracted by the perceived features of other persons. Similarly, adults and children probably have unconscious biological pre-adaptations of action and perception, as well as conscious intentions, that lead them to infants, towards whom they act in ways which are quite different from anything seen in encounters between peers. The first stage in social relations is therefore a mutual attraction and attentiveness of infants and others which brings about the first fleeting social interchanges. The attractiveness of adults for infants arises from the selective tuning and preadaptation of their perceptual systems to characteristics of adults. As Schaffer (1971, p. 37) has put it, we "conceive of sociability as being rooted in the infant's perceptual encounters with his environment". In the auditory sphere, artificial sounds which share features of adult speech seem particularly attractive to infants (Eimas et al., 1971; Eisenberg, 1969; Freidlander, 1970; Hutt et al., 1968; Trehub and Robinovitch, 1972). In the visual system, the perception of movement is both phylogenetically and ontogenetically primitive (Trevarthen, 1968) and ensures that attention will be paid to other humans. More specifically, three-dimensional moving percepts which share features of the human face hold great interest for the neonate. Elements with high contrast, moving relative to the whole stimulus object, command most fixation and scanning—properties exemplified by the eyes within the face. Several authors (Robson, 1967; Spitz, 1965) have emphasized the role of eye-to-eye contact in early social contacts and have described the way in which an infant's gaze is fixed on the mother's face during feeding[2]. Observations suggest that the later patterns of mutual visual regard develop from these early fixations.

Adults and children are assiduous in their attempts to gain a neonate's attention, sometimes making few concessions to the two-sidedness of their relationship with the infant. Prominent features of early interchange with the infant are attempts to gain face-to-face and eye-to-eye contact (this is part of the mother's rather stereotyped response to her infant at birth, see Klaus et al., 1970) and to elicit any behavioural response from the infant which can be interpreted as intentional responsiveness. People talk a lot to newborns and will try repeatedly using voice, rocking and stroking of the infant's face to elicit smiling. If smiling occurs "spontaneously", it is often dismissed as "wind" rather than being regarded as a social action. Here we see the beginning of what Shotter (1972) has called the "mutual power to complete one another's intentions".

---

[2] In our own observation, eye-to-face (or eye) contact is common during bottle feeding in the first ten days but is rarely seen in breast feeding as the mothers seem to hold infants with their heads too turned in to their bodies to make it possible. However, some casual observations and comments from mothers suggest that this position adopted while breast feeding may be an artifact of our observational methods. The infant may be held in the turned-in position in order to hide the breast from the observer. In any event, at the next follow-up observation, at eight weeks, eye-to-eye contact is a very striking feature of both breast and bottle feeding.

To the extent that a mother can appreciate the intentional structure in her
baby's rudimentary movements, she can complete their intention and in
some manner satisfy his needs for him. But the mother too, pursues intentions within the inter-active scheme; she wants her baby to suck, to stop
crying, to acknowledge her by looking into her eyes, to grasp her finger,
etc., and she discovers strategies and tactics via which she can "elicit"
these responses—she cannot, of course, elicit the whole pattern of responses
from the child as a pattern, he must already have the power to structure
his activity so, and she simply discovers a way of making him manifest
that power.

The fundamental needs of the infant for food, warmth, and sensory
stimulation through movement, all work together to foster contact
with adults which will entail social exchanges. From an early age different
kinds of crying are elicited under different conditions and these may
have different meanings for the caretaker (Bernal, 1972; Wasz-Hockert
et al., 1968; Wolff, 1969). A crying infant is more likely to be picked
up (Moss and Robson, 1968), and the infant's state at the moment of
encounter with the mother can be an important determinant of her
response in some situations (Levy, 1958). Beyond this, many mothers
feel that their babies should be held and perhaps rocked and talked
to even when they are not crying. Being held is especially important for
fostering interchange. Many observers have noted that the contact
provided by holding is particularly effective in producing visual alertness
in the infant (e.g. Korner and Grobstein, 1966; Korner and Thoman,
1971) and so leads to more visual exploration of their human companions. From birth, the infant will turn towards the source of a
human voice—another preadaptation that will lead to social contacts.

Not only do we have evidence that from a very early age the various
characteristics of persons are perceived by the infant as a gestalt whole
(e.g. Aronson and Rosenbloom, 1971) and that social actions such
as smiling (cf. Wolff, 1963) are elicited by the presence of an adult
rather than by some invariant stimulus feature of people, but also there
are rather different modes of behaviour when infants interact with
people rather than objects (Trevarthen and Richards, 1972). If we accept
the view that the power of completion of intentions has relevance in
development, it is important to demonstrate that the infant employs
different strategies of behaviour when dealing with objects, to those he
employs when dealing with people in early communicative interchanges.

Early social interchanges of mother and child involve precise temporal
organization at many levels. In the neonatal period when an infant's
attention is fleeting there are only brief periods when there is interest in
social contact. The mother comes to recognize these periods and concen-

trates her social attentions at these times. After a month or so many more differentiated forms of temporal organization become apparent involving precisely phased alternation and synchrony.

As argued elsewhere (Richards, 1971; Wolff, 1967), there is good evidence for the endogenous patterning of neonatal behaviour of the kind postulated by Lashley (1951) to account for the serial order properties of adult behaviour. The mother adapts to these rhythms of the infant and the infant to her rhythms. An example of the latter process is seen during feeding in the neonatal period. Infant sucking is organized in a series of sucks separated by a pause from another group of sucks (Kron *et al.*, 1968). Episodes containing many groups of sucks and pauses are terminated by much longer gaps in which the nipple may be expelled from the baby's mouth. This serial organization of sucking patterns the mother's behaviour so that her movements of the infant tend to fall in the intra-episode pauses (H. Kaye, personal communication) and talking and smiling to infants, at least during breast feeding, is generally confined to the inter-episode intervals.

More complex timing relationships soon develop, and may be seen for example, in the mutual smiling games played from about six weeks onwards (Richards, 1971). Often these games may last for many minutes but if the mother fails to respect the timing structure, the infant is quickly reduced to fussing and active avoidance of the mother's face and so terminates the game.

As the mutual phasing of the interaction becomes more complex, its description is technically more difficult and we know almost nothing of this aspect of behaviour in the latter half of the first year. All we can say is that it is an important aspect of communication between adult and infant, and that the evidence suggests that quite precise phasing of behaviour is one of the earliest of the infant's cognitive accomplishments. However, though temporal patterning exists at many levels in the organization of behaviour—from the distribution of feeds during the day and night to the moment to moment organization of sucking—we should not assume that all phasing depends on the same underlying mechanisms.

TOWARDS A THEORY

At this point, I want to consider the growth of communicative skills at a rather more theoretical level. It is probably clear from the language I have been using that I regard communication as something beyond interaction; it is not simply a two-sided modification of behaviour or responsiveness to signals, but involves notions of mutuality, reciprocity, and inter-subjectivity.

Here, at least in broad terms, I would support Piaget and Inhelder's (1968) view and argue that the development of communication, as an element of intelligence, "proceeds from action as a whole in that it transforms objects and reality, and that knowledge, whose formation can be traced in the child, is essentially an active and operatory assimilation". Piaget, in contradiction to many other theorists, does not see this development as stemming from a passive process of reception and conditioning.

The child's actions take place in a social world and I would agree with Piaget that the essential feature in social development is the child's relationships, not his attachment to his mother as is often stated. In other words, it is not so much the presence or absence of the mother that is important to the child but the opportunity to indulge in reciprocal social interchange with familiar and unfamiliar persons—the first is of course usually provided by the mother in the Western family setting.

There is a close correspondence between the development of social relations and the stages in the construction of the object (Bell, 1970; Gouin-Decarie, 1962; Schaffer, 1971; Wolff, 1960). The evidence seems to support Piaget's view that "affectivity" is not a cause or effect of cognitive development but both are aspects of a single system. Piaget also proposes that affect may be considered as the energizer of cognitive structures, "when behaviour is studied in its cognitive aspect, we are concerned with its structures, when behaviour is considered in its affective aspect, we are concerned with its energetics. While the two aspects cannot be reduced to a single aspect, they are nevertheless inseparable and complementary" (Piaget and Inhelder, 1968, p. 21). The notion expressed here seems very close to Freud's idea of libidinal energy with all its attendant difficulties. This raises a large and ramifying question which I will not deal with in detail. However, there seems no reason why the affective component of behaviour should be separated in any way from its cognitive structure and be considered as more than an element of the schemata of social exchange. The further assumption made by Piaget seems unwarranted by the evidence, at least in the early part of development after birth. My view is much closer to that of Vygotsky (1966) who argues that the "central fact of consciousness which is characteristic of early childhood (is the) union of affect and perception. At this age perception is generally not an independent feature but an initial feature of a motor-affective reaction; i.e. every perception is in this way a stimulus to activity" (p. 11). During the first year, as is widely agreed among analytic and cognitive theorists, the child proceeds from a stage where there is a lack of differentiation between the self and the physical and social environment, towards "the construction of a group of exchanges or emotional investments which attach the differentiated self to other persons and things" (Piaget and Inhelder, 1968, p. 21). At first there is no consciousness of self, no boundary between the world of experience and the world of external reality, but by the first birthday a clear boundary has been formed and the child behaves towards people in a highly specific and differentiated manner.

The newborn has but the simplest sensory-motor schemata which allow some temporal consistencies in behaviour. This we must assume from the evidence of habituation and conditioning in the neonate (Fitzgerald and Porges, 1971; Lipsitt, 1963; Sameroff, 1971). By three months these schemata have become sufficiently elaborated to provide recognition through the action of effective patterns. Many observations have provided evidence of the recognition of adults and the differentiation of familiar and unfamiliar patterns of caretaking by this age (Schaffer, 1971; Wolff, 1963; Yarrow, 1967). This elaboration proceeds to a stage about three months later when object permanence and stranger anxiety appear. Now recognition and recall appear and so make possible a vast elaboration of relations involving complex emotional differentiation within relationships with specific people. There is a rapid growth of the rules and modes of communication and increasing subtlety in what is communicated. The individual variation in the patterns of behaviour manifest in social situations increases but all share the common features of complex communication with specific partners. In descriptive terms, our knowledge of this period is extremely sparse, much more so than in the earlier period, but the broad features seem clear. Now the infant may play a much more positive role in his relationships and can exercise choice in the times and situations in which social exchanges occur. He may move over long distances to gain physical proximity to adults, or to avoid them, and so initiate and regulate social contacts. He has some newly developed action patterns which seem particularly effective, for example, the raising of the arms and clinging to the adult's clothes which often leads to him being picked up. Also his primitive vocalizations. But, in spite of this increase in the infant's social power, we should note that his world is still bounded by his family or significant others who act as the interpreters and mediators of the wider social world.

Imitation, both by adults of the child and by the child of adults, becomes a very striking feature of social exchanges during the latter part of the first year. This may be very important in the development of specific relationships with adults because imitation provides very precise correspondences between the actions of the two partners, and so, in

Piagetian terms, provides a direct relationship between the schemata of the child's own action and those of his adult partners. In these imitative exchanges the self is modified to meet external reality, so that the child's self is modified to that of the mother and the mother's self is modified to meet the social reality of the child. Other important features of behaviour at this stage may be interpreted in the same manner. Children often point to objects, sometimes with an accompanying vocalization. This frequently leads the mother to point to the same object and name it. Other sequences may be initiated by the mother pointing and naming things, often, for example, using pictures in a book as well as actual objects. Another common game is the exchange of goods. The child offers an object to the mother. She takes it and then returns it to the child, frequently acknowledging the gift with an expression of gratitude and naming the object. It seems likely that further observation will reveal many other sequences of this kind which involve close correspondence and alternations of child and adult actions, or interchange with peers.

In this very brief and somewhat inadequate account of the growth of social relationships in the first year I have discussed development at a species level on the basis of observations made in Europe and the United States. I have not considered individual differences. The explanation of individual variation may involve quite other factors than those required in an account at the species level though most behaviourist psychology fails to make this distinction and only concerns itself with statistical differences in behaviour between groups. I believe that much greater knowledge is required of the generalities of early human social relations before we can begin to investigate the origins and consequences of differences at all effectively. The outline of development I have sketched is intended to apply to all children except those suffering from gross biological abnormalities. I would argue that some degree of communication between child and adults will always be found except where there is either something about the child that prevents development—for example, congenital blindness, or something about the social context which rules out contacts with others. I would regard all major disruptions of the developmental process, those described in some autistic children for instance, as traceable to one or both of these processes.

AN ILLUSTRATIVE EXAMPLE

Against this background, I want to discuss a specific interaction situation in order to amplify some of the points made earlier and to illustrate some of the problems that are encountered by a communication perspective. My example, at first sight, seems to be the simplest inter-action of mother and infant in the neonatal period. The baby cries, the mothers goes to him, picks him up and feeds him. The baby stops crying. This we can illustrate in diagrammatic form (Fig. 1). However, as it stands this diagram is too simple because it takes too much for granted and hides many of the things that need to be explained. First of all, it leaves out the observer, an important person who is involved in the sequence. Just as the mother has to interpret the baby's behaviour so does the observer. He also has to decide that the baby is crying and crying in a way that demands attention. If such a judgment is not made independently of what the mother does, description can only be made via the mother and so, from the baby's point of view all objectivity is lost. Crying for food becomes only that crying which results in feeding.

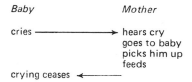

FIG. 1. An example of mother–infant interaction in the neonatal period.

But how does the observer (or mother) decide what the baby wants? A psychological training does not give immediate access to knowledge of the physiological or social needs of infants, however this ignorance does not preclude the recording of the baby's behaviour independently from the mother's responses.

Clearly the mother has to presume the baby's needs from his behaviour. She has to decide that crying is related to hunger and this is largely a matter of cultural knowledge (which is usually shared by the observer). Certainly there are biological constraints here too; no one supposes that smiling indicates hunger in infants but there is no automatic link between the baby's cries, his need for food and the mother's response. These links begin with some structures but their specification during the infant's development depend on the ways in which the mother and other caretakers respond (or do not respond) in interaction sequences. The cultural nature of our assumptions about crying babies is demonstrated by observations of mothers in other parts of the world where babies are carried for most of the day on the mother's body (Blurton Jones, 1972). For example, among the Zhun/twasi bushmen (Konner, 1972) crying does not seem to be an important signal for feeding. Instead mothers seem very conscious of the movements of the baby, who is in direct contact with her skin, and use these as an indication of the need for food.

When a baby becomes restless he is slid round the body so he can reach a nipple.

The importance of the social definition by adults of infants' signals is further illustrated by our observations in Cambridge. Some mothers believe that babies turn "blue" around the mouth when they have wind. If this signal is perceived by the mother a prolonged period of rocking, patting and carrying may postpone the time when the infant is replaced in his cot. However, I have never been able to see this blueness and the evidence linking "wind" to any physiological need state is doubtful at best.

The analysis of our observations (Bernal, 1972) has shown that mothers do not operate on any simple cry equals hunger principle. Time since last feed is an important determinant of a mother's response to a crying baby. Mothers vary in the exact way in which the interval since the last feed influences their response and in how consistent they are from day to day. This is partly a function of their social situation, previous experience of caretaking this and other infants and their own childhood experiences. Some follow the generally given advice of four-hourly feeds very closely while others modify this pattern in accordance with what is happening in the home. Yet others make no attempt to fit a four-hourly pattern and feed more frequently, though very few approach a true demand routine and feed at every cry. In view of these considerations the diagram can be redrawn (Fig. 2).

After the first few weeks another factor enters the picture as the mother begins to acknowledge the baby as a person and she begins to assume that there is a more complex relationship between crying and internal need states. This is illustrated by the situation where the mother does not pick up her crying baby and comments that he is not crying because he is really hungry but because he wants to be fed or simply wants attention. The implication of the mother's action is that only "genuine" physiological needs should be satisfied. The mother is not merely acknowledging the emergence of autonomy in her baby but also behaving as if, at least, some manifestations of his independence must be denied and brought under social control. Here the mother does not seem to be cooperating in the way described by Shotter (1972) in completing her baby's intentions. However, I do not think the idea of completion of intention should be taken too simply. In this situation the infant is still able to learn a good deal about himself and the actions and intentions of others and most importantly, the way his desires must reflect social sanctions. The latter effect is not, of course, confined to cases where the mother seems consciously to acknowledge his wishes and then deny them but is potentially present, for example, every time

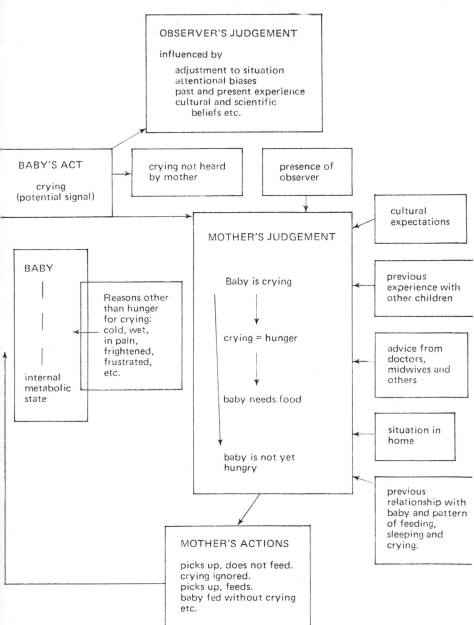

FIG. 2. This diagram is highly simplified and is only intended to indicate the sorts of conceptual categories that can be employed in the analysis of the communication system. Many loops are omitted and arrows should inter-connect almost all the boxes. It is left to the reader to complete the diagram, if he so wishes.

he cries and is not heard or when the mother delays picking up her baby because she is in the middle of washing up.

CONCLUSIONS

In this paper I have tried to explore some of the ways in which the growth of social relations in infancy is illuminated by an approach based on a notion of the development of communication. One clear advantage of such a viewpoint is that it demonstrates that many things that have been often considered simple are more complex and problematic and it does not allow the covering up of problems by a recourse to assenting the presence of biologically based signalling systems. In order to understand development we must understand the intra-penetration of the social and the biological. I believe that this approach can be taken much further but in order to do this we not only need more elaborate theory but much more observation. The details of mother–infant interaction and communication have seldom been recorded and without this knowledge I believe that further understanding will be limited.

REFERENCES

AINSWORTH, M. D. S. 1969. Object relations, dependency and attachment: a theoretical review of the mother–infant relationship. *Child Dev.*, **40**, 969–1025.

ARONSON, E. and ROSENBLOOM, S. 1971. Space perception in early infancy: perception within a common auditory–visual space. *Science, N.Y.*, **172**, 1161–1163.

BELL, S. M. 1970. The development of the concept of object as related to infant–mother attachment. *Child Dev.*, **41**, 291–311.

BERGER, P. L. and LUCKMAN, T. 1967. *The social construction of reality.* Allen Lane, London.

BERNAL, J. F. 1972. Crying during the first 10 days of life, and maternal responses. *Develop. Med. Child Neurol.*, **14**, 362–372.

BERNAL, J. F. and RICHARDS, M. P. M. 1971. The effects of bottle and breast feeding on infant development. *J. Psychosom. Res.*, **14**, 247–252.

BLURTON JONES, N. 1972. Comparative aspects of mother–child contact. In N. Blurton Jones (Ed.), *Ethological studies of child behaviour.* Cambridge Univ. Press, Cambridge.

BOWLBY, J. 1969. *Attachment and loss*, Vol. 1. Hogarth Press, London.

EIMAS, P. D., SIQUELAND, E. R., JUSCZYK, P. and VIGORITO, J. 1971. Speech perception in infants. *Science, N.Y.*, **171**, 303–306.

EINSENBERG, R. B. 1969. Auditory behavior in the human neonate. *Internat. Audiol.*, **8**, 34–45.

FITZGERALD, H. E. and PORGES, S. W. 1971. A decade of infant conditioning and learning research. *Merrill-Palmer Quart.*, **17**, 79–117.

FOSS, B. M. (Ed.). 1969. *Determinants of infant behaviour*, Vol. 4. Methuen, London.

FREIDLANDER, B. Z. 1970. Receptive language development in infancy: issues and problems. *Merrill-Palmer Quart.*, **16**, 7–51.

Gouin-Decarie, T. 1962. *Intelligence et affectivité chez le enfant*. Delachaux et Niestlé, Neuchatel.

Hutt, S. J., Hutt, C., Lenard, H. G., Bernuth, H. V. and Muntjewcuff, W. J. 1968. Auditory responsivity in the human neonate. *Nature, (Lond.)*, **218**, 888–890.

Klaus, M. H., Kennell, J. II., Plumb, N. and Zuehilke, S. 1970. Human maternal behavior at the first contact with her young. *Pediat.*, **46**, 187–192.

Konner, M. J. 1972. Aspects of the developmental ethology of a foraging people. In N. Blurton Jones (Ed.), *Ethological studies of child behaviour*. Cambridge Univ. Press, Cambridge.

Korner, A. F. and Grobstein, R. 1966. Visual alertness in neonates: implications for maternal stimulation and early deprivation. *Child Dev.*, **37**, 867–876.

Korner, A. F. and Thoman, E. B. 1972. Visual alertness in neonates as evoked by maternal care. *J. exp. Child Psychol.*, **10**, 67–78.

Kron, R. E., Ipsen, J. and Goddard, K. E. 1968. Consistent individual differences in the nutritive sucking behavior of the human newborn. *Psychosom. Med.*, **30**, 151–161.

Lashley, K. S. 1951. The problem of serial order in behavior. In L. A. Jeffress (Ed.), *Cerebral mechanisms in behavior*. Wiley, New York.

Levy, D. M. 1958. *Behavioral analysis*. C. C. Thomas, Springfield.

Lipsitt, L. P. 1963. Learning in the first year of life. In L. P. Lipsitt and C. C. Spiker (Eds.), *Advances in child development and behavior*, Vol. 1. Academic Press, New York.

Moss, M. A. and Robson, G. S. 1968. The role of protest behavior in the development of mother–infant attachment. American Psychological Association Meeting, San Francisco.

Piaget, J. and Inhelder, B. 1968. *The psychology of the child*. Routledge and Kegan Paul, London.

Richards, M. P. M. 1971. Social interaction in the first weeks of human life. *Psychiat. Neurol. Neurochir.*, **74**, 35–42.

Richards, M. P. M. and Bernal, J. F. 1972. An observational study of mother–infant interaction. In N. Blurton Jones (Ed.), *Ethological studies of child behaviour*. Cambridge Univ. Press, Cambridge.

Robson, K. 1967. The role of eye-to-eye contact in maternal–infant attachment. *J. Child Psychol. Psychiat.*, **8**, 13–25.

Sameroff, A. J. 1971. Can conditioned responses be established in the newborn infant. *Develop. Psychol.*, **5**, 1–12.

Schaffer, H. R. 1971. *The growth of sociability*. Penguin, Harmondsworth.

Shotter, J. 1972. Prolegomena to an understanding of play. *J. Theor. Soc. Behav.* In press.

Spitz, R. A. 1965. *The first year of life*. Internat. Univ. Press, New York.

Trehub, S. E. and Robinovitch, M. S. 1972. Auditory–linguistic sensitivity in early infancy. *Develop. Psychol.*, **6**, 74–77.

Trevarthen, C. B. 1968. Two mechanisms of vision in primates. *Psycholog. Forschung*, **31**, 299–337.

Trevarthen, C. B. 1973. Behavioral embryology. In E. C. Cartnette and M. P. Friedman (Eds.), *The handbook of perception*. Academic Press, New York.

Trevarthen, C. B. and Richards, M. P. M. 1972. Two modes of visual response in infants. In preparation.

VYGOTSKI, L. S. 1966. Play and its role in the mental development of the child. *Soviet Psychol.*, **5**, 6–18.

WADDINGTON, C. H. 1969. The theory of evolution today. In A. Koestler and J. R. Smythies (Eds.), *Beyond reductionism*. Hutchinson, London.

WASZ-HOCKERT, O., LIND, J., VUORENKOSKI, J., PARTANEN, T. and VALANNE, E. 1968. *The infant cry: a spectrographic and auditory analysis*. Clinics in Developmental Medicine, No. 29. S.I.M.P./Heinemann, London.

WOLFF, P. H. 1960. The developmental psychologies of Jean Piaget and psychoanalysis. *Psychol. Issues*, **2**, monog. 5.

WOLFF, P. H. 1963. Observations on the early development of smiling. In B. M. Foss (Ed.), *Determinants of infant behaviour*, Vol. 2. Methuen, London.

WOLFF, P. H. 1967. The role of biological rhythms in early psychological development. *Bull. Menninger Clin.*, **31**, 197–218.

WOLFF, P. H. 1969. The natural history of crying and other vocalisations in early infancy. In B. M. Foss (Ed.), *Determinants of infant behaviour*, Vol. 4. Methuen, London.

YARROW, L. J. 1967. The development of focused relationships during infancy. In J. Hellmuth (Ed.), *Exceptional infant*, Vol. 1. Special Child Publications.

The Growth of Skills

Hierarchical Structure in Skill Development

JOHN ELLIOTT and KEVIN CONNOLLY

University of Sheffield

COMPETENCE IS TAKEN to relate to the organization underlying the child's behavioural adjustment to his environment. The origins of such competence lie in human evolution, and the manner in which it affects successful adjustment to the demands of the environment is implied in the study of intelligence. The organization of behaviour and its adaptive significance to the organism is of central concern in evolutionary biology, in psychology and in education.

The human newborn requires a number of functioning behaviour patterns for its initial adaptation to extra-uterine life; for example, it must suck in order to ingest food. Certain components of the infant's behaviour are preadapted in the genome. The centrally coordinated complex of movements which make up swallowing provide an example (Doty and Bosema, 1956). For the most part the patterns of behaviour exhibited by the child cannot be correctly described as preadapted in the genome with anything like the specificity seen in the case of swallowing.

THE NOTION OF SKILL

To an extent skill is synonymous with efficiency. It refers to the organization of actions into a purposeful plan which is executed with economy. Even in the case of such relatively imprecise concepts as "social skills", the essence of the skill lies in the ability to achieve a goal. Unlike efficiency, however, skill carries connotations of task difficulty. A broad description of skill therefore is "an ability to achieve defined goals with an efficiency beyond that of the inexperienced person". This description supposes that skill entails an ability—a competence—which underlies assessed performance on specific tasks. The nature of this underlying competence is the concern of this paper.

As Bruner (1970) has argued, the development of skill entails the solution of problems, and in thinking of skill acquisition and problem solving separately we may be using a distinction that has little justification from the perspective of the child. The nature of the difference becomes clearer, however, if the implications of the description of skill given above are pursued. If skill is thought of as entailing a programme of events directed at a goal, we may conceive of the basic unit of skilled performance as the sub-routine (Bruner, 1970; Connolly, 1970, 1973; Fitts and Posner, 1967). A sub-routine is an act, the performance of which is a necessary but not sufficient condition for the execution of some more complex, hierarchically organized sequence of sub-routines of which it is a member. A correctly organized sequence of actions constitutes what is generally considered as a skill, such as walking, tool-using, or singing. The sub-routine thus gains its significance as an act from the context in which it occurs. Thus if skill is modular, the distinction between problem-solving and skilled performance might be the distinction between the organization and the execution of sub-routines. Solving a problem may entail the question of the most suitable, or perhaps the only suitable, sequence of actions out of the many available to the person. This is not the same question as how efficiently the chosen sequence is performed, in terms of smoothness, speed and accuracy. The two questions relate to separate aspects of skill and performance not unlike that employed by psycholinguists.

THE ANALYSIS OF SKILL

Lashley (1951) drew attention to the importance of considering the organization, or syntax, of sequentially occurring acts. The idea of a syntax of behaviour under various names (grammar, plan, programme) has become influential, following the use of cybernetic ideas in psychology. The concept of control has been particularly useful, since it relates to the problem of determining a sequence of operations which are not intrinsically determinate. If an operation is not determined by the one before it, in what Miller et al. (1960) would call a chain, then it is a problem to decide how it is determined. The concept of feedback control is useful here, because it allows us to suppose that what determines a sequence might be whether or not successive operations reduce the discrepancy between the state of affairs external to the operator, and some model or envisioned representation of what that state of affairs ought to be. Miller et al., in offering the TOTE (Test Operate Text Exit) unit to describe this process, supply a logically respectable structure for the description of goal directed, intentional behaviour. Once the idea of a model "in the head" is accepted, against which successive acts can be evaluated, it is no longer necessary to think that for the goal to control and determine behaviour entails a ridiculous reversal of cause and effect in time (Hull, 1943).

Computer programmes may or may not have the flexibility implied in an ability to approximate to a goal state: they need not be chains in which each operation determines the next. It is an interesting question to ask to what extent our own behaviour shows a degree of chaining. Miller *et al.* (1960) draw a parallel between instinctive acts in animals and overlearned motor sequences in man. One of the characteristics of instinctive behaviour in animals is the stereotyped nature of the sequence of acts involved. The chain of actions is not re-ordered, rather it is released. The parallel with neonatal swallowing actions already mentioned is obvious but Miller *et al.* maintain that practised adult skills may also show considerable similarity. These have in effect come to entail chains of responses which have become controlled by specific releasers. Such overlearned chaining of acts allows the chain to be available for use by the subject without engaging his continuous attention. Consequently we may think of skilled operators as using plans which entail the use of several such overlearned chains, and which themselves take up the operator's information processing capacity. Such sub-routines may thus be thought of as hierarchically organized in the pursuit of activities that are voluntary with respect to their guiding plan. Practised sequences of acts would be definable as subroutines, comprised in turn of lower order behavioural elements available to more than one higher order sequence. Even common and seemingly trivial everyday tasks such as using a spoon might thus reflect an underlying organization involving substitution and the sequencing of acts at several levels. Such tasks would then reflect a structure of skill transcending the demands of the specific task or tasks on which the constituent acts had been practised.

Tinbergen's (1951) ideas concerning the organization of instinct also entail a hierarchical structure. He suggests hierarchical levels of instinct, within each of which more specific alternative behaviours, contigent upon the state of the animal and on external releasers, are nested, down to the level of motor units.

The concept of a hierarchically organized repertoire of practised movements available for the pursuit of goals raises the central question of the feedback control mechanisms responsible. The value of the concept of feedback is that it is applicable to any system, living or not, where the system output is used to vary the input. When considering skilled performance, therefore, it is necessary to bear in mind that a number of feedback loops may be entailed at quite different levels, and embodied in quite different systems (Fitts, 1962). A number of models have appeared in the literature (Bernstein, 1967; Hein and Held, 1962; von Holst, 1954; McKay, 1962). They offer an interesting insight into the structure of biological control systems, but it is likely that any overall model of skill performance will need to call on several such models to cope with the different kinds of feedback involved. The term feedback does not relate to any particular model, and other labels will have to be used to refine the concept for use in particular contexts. Some such refinement has already been made. Annett and Kay (1957) have suggested the terms intrinsic and extrinsic knowledge of results to distinguish between knowledge of performance inevitably available to the subject as a result of his movements, and terminal knowledge of results giving information about the consequences of action. Similarly, Miller (1953) has distinguished between action feedback, where information on performance is available to the subject and may modify his action as it proceeds, and learning feedback, the more conventional knowledge of results, where the results of an action are only available after its completion and can thus only affect future actions. This distinction parallels that between feedback and feedforward[1], and a similar distinction has been made by Mittelstadt (1964) in discussing orientational control systems in animals and man. It might also be profitable to refer to feedback concepts in the context of control systems, for instance, relating to:

   (i) Attention.
   (ii) Neuromuscular control.
   (iii) Perceptual processes.
   (iv) Task related results in progress.
   (v) Task related results on completion.

Items (i) to (iii) relate to the apparatus of neuromuscular control entailed in all motor skill. Items (iv) and (v) relate to feedback in the context of a particular task. Any impairment in the development of abilities on the first three items may be a limiting factor on the level of achievement in the last two. A detailed examination of particular skills should reveal the control system appropriate, to describe shortcomings in performance. The ability to anticipate, for example, is essential to the smooth sequencing of acts. It is apparent that we do not have to monitor

---

[1] Feedforward: "A method of control in which disturbances affecting the output variables are anticipated and compensating fluctuations of the input variables are generated. A knowledge of the *dynamics of the process* is necessary to achieve the correct compensation" (Metham, 1969).

the individual components of a practised sequence (that is attend to them) except under abnormal circumstances or when unusual contingencies arise. The emergence of smooth sequencing thus implies a transfer of attention from the control of individual acts to the control of the sequence. We may therefore speculate that when the control of an act no longer requires an attentional feedback loop, but becomes a feedforward mechanism, the act is available for sequencing purposes. In so far as sequencing abilities seem less easy with the younger children, reported below, we might legitimately speculate that this is due to an overloading of attentional mechanisms in younger subjects. Thus we arrive at Bernstein's (1967) interesting suggestion that achievement of control entails a reduction in the "degrees of freedom" in the action system being controlled.

To recapitulate briefly, a central problem for the study of behaviour concerns its organization. Practised patterns of behaviour become themselves constituents for new patterns directed at new objectives. The ability to grasp an object, for instance, once established, is incorporated into a sequence of acts which may involve the object in being transported between locations, or used as a tool. The concept of a sub-routine, which we may think of as the quantum of skilled performance, leads to the view expressed by Bruner (1970) that skill is modular in organization. Once mastered, sub-routines are inserted into new plans of action. The precision grip, once matured, is employed in using a range of tools, a pencil, a brush, a needle, and so on. This modularization of behaviour frees the organism's available central processing capacity for use in the smooth execution and control at a higher level of progressively more complex tasks.

An interesting example is provided by the boiled egg problem. Consider a young child given the task of eating a boiled egg with a spoon; we shall assume that he knows something of the properties and uses of a spoon. He must first grasp the spoon appropriately and then carry it to the egg. Once in the correct location, where the limits of tolerance are quite fine, he must adjust the orientation of the spoon by intrinsic movements of the hand and then exert carefully controlled force through it to the egg. Having loaded the spoon he must transport the egg back to another target, his mouth. Transporting objects to his mouth is something the infant is well practised at, and the existence of this sub-routine enables him to attack the problem of maintaining the orientation of the spoon. Nevertheless, the overall demands which this task imposes on the child are substantial as is evident from the distribution of egg on and around his person. The ultimate smooth performance of such a task is contingent upon the acquisition of sub-routines and their efficient combination. An appropriate grasp on the spoon is necessary for balancing it, and to enable the child to make the necessary intrinsic finger movements to adjust the orientation of the spoon and dig it into the egg. These hand skills are fundamental to all actions involving manipulative activity and it is to the relationship between the anatomy of the hand and manual skill that we now turn.

THE ANATOMICAL BASIS OF SKILL

The anatomy of our bodies imposes limitations and confers potential on our capacity for movement. Anatomical mechanisms must be understood when the cause of specific skill disability is being investigated, also they are seen as determining in part the degrees of freedom potentially entailed in a task. As long as we have an option of performing the simplest task by various combinations of movements, a knowledge of what combinations are in fact available is essential to the study of the structure and development of sub-routines.

These remarks may be illustrated by observations drawn from our own work on normal and pathological hand function in children (Connolly and Elliott, 1972, and unpublished material). We have been concerned with the development of hand function as expressed in the grasps used by young children. Emergence of the ability to make effective use of the prehensile potential of the hand might be taken to reflect the development of a general manual skill underlying various manipulative tasks. A general facility of this kind would comprise a range of grasping patterns and movements along with a set of rules for applying them to objects and situations. The four-year-old child shows a repertoire of about eight grasps on various tasks (Connolly and Elliott, 1972; Connolly, 1973). Different grasps having different implications for the movements of the grasped object that are then possible.

It has become customary to make a distinction between power and precision grips in referring to the grip configuration of the human hand (Napier, 1956). These grips are distinguished with respect to the degree and nature of opposition of the thumb, and the extent of rotation and adduction of the fingers (Fig. 1). Napier argued that the type of grip employed is determined by the amount of force required to accomplish a given task. However, Landsmeer (1962) has pointed out that the precision grip is not really a grip, in the sense that the object so held it not locked or restricted by contact with the palm, but held more distally in the digits, thus allowing them to manipulate or move the object. We have found the term *intrinsic* movement of the hand useful for referring to a movement of this sort, one that is made by the digits to control an object held in the same hand. It is clear that a power grip greatly limits the range of movements which can be made with an object, since intrinsic movements are much reduced if not impossible. It is not surprising, therefore, that in a sample of forty-nine nursery-school children (aged between two years ten months and four years ten months) we discovered that the incidence of grips which allowed intrinsic movements showed a

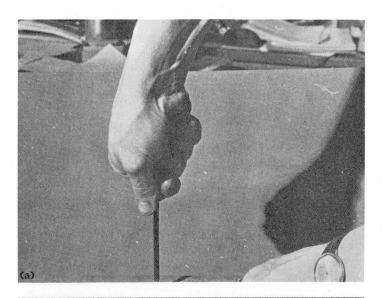

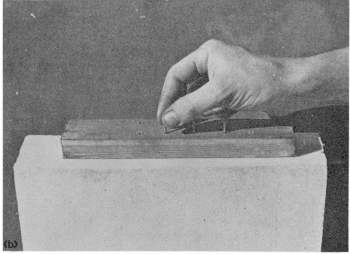

FIG. 1. Power (upper) and precision (lower) grips made by an adult.

significant age-related increase (Connolly and Elliott, 1972). This finding was based on observations of children using a paintbrush and was not related to the incidence of particular lines in the painting. We concluded that even at around four years, the child is still developing the use of his hands in ways that are likely to have great benefits for his ability to use tools, and that this is revealed by an examination of the scope and limitations of the various grips he has available at that age.

The posture adopted by the hand in any grip, and the movements which it makes, are definable anatomically. Supination of the hand, extension of the index finger and true opposition of the thumb are examples of anatomically specified events. Mastery of manual function implies a mastery over these components and their organization. An infant's early endeavours to use its hands may be seen as an attempt to acquire mastery of the possibilities permitted by his developing neuro-muscular system. The fact that acts of this sort may be defined in terms of structure and movement, or position, does not affect or specify the functions of these abilities once mastered. Because a grip may be defined independently of the uses to which it may be put, it is tempting to avoid describing it in terms of the theory of skill developed in the previous section. However, the importance of the study of hand function remains despite the availability of anatomically exact descriptions, since the persistent question in the analysis of skill in this context as elsewhere is the way in which available actions, albeit constrained by the structural considerations of anatomy, are perfected and put to use in various

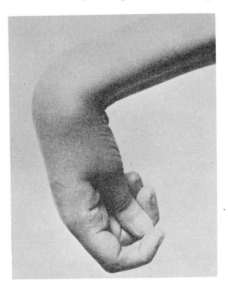

Fig. 2. An example of the thumb-in-palm syndrome from a child with cerebral palsy. The thumb cannot be abducted, and is only capable of slight extension. The limitations this imposes on the use of the radial hand may be exacerbated by poor ability to rotate or extend the wrist.

contexts. The more complex the skill (the greater the complexity and variety of the acts entailed) the more remote the sequence is from the constraints of anatomy in so far as the alternative possibilities are more numerous. The principle is not different, however, and may profitably be extended to the level of grip analysis in an attempt to understand basic features of motor skill in general. The truth of this proposition emerges when attention is directed at cases where manual skills have developed abnormally.

Cerebral palsied children frequently exhibit varying degrees of impairment in the control of the upper limbs. Involvement of the hand may take the form of excessive flexion of the wrist, accompanied by a flexion of the thumb across the palm, the "thumb in palm" deformity (Fig. 2) (Keats, 1965). A movement to close the hand may take the form of an undifferentiated synergic flexion of all digits. This makes the picking-up of objects extremely difficult, even assuming that the child is able to extend sufficiently and separate the digits initially. Some of our subjects have shown an ability to develop what we would describe as sub-routines to cope with their disability as best they can. For instance, one boy in an attempt to overcome an inability to voluntarily extend his digits developed the habit of "wiping" them back with his other hand and so forcing an extension which was then used in picking up an object. He also amazed us by the variety of grips that appeared in the course of a simple manipulative task. These apparently had been developed as a set of general purpose grips for use in a variety of tasks and were quite different from those of normal subjects. Other subjects had also developed particular grips which they regularly used in certain kinds of tasks. The abnormalities of these grips were generally traceable to abnormal or missing components as compared with the normal repertoire of manual movements. In all cases, the manual peculiarities of these handicapped children were related to the underlying neuromuscular deficit. But the resulting constraints had been overcome in a way characteristic for a particular child and describable in terms of constructed sub-routines. Objectively, the children's manual performance was often very poor, but given the limitations of their hands their behaviour showed the characteristics of skill.

An approach which attempts to analyse manual skills into their constituent sub-routines would be of value in the evaluation and treatment of handicap. So far little has been done to provide any detailed analysis of the handicapped child's manual function (but see Holt, 1965). The approach usually employed in assessing the hand function of cerebral palsied children consists in an examination of their ability to perform a range of common tasks; can the child fasten shoes, use a knife and fork, handle coins, etc. Such assessment procedures are valuable as a practical guide to the limits of the child's independence but evaluation on a pass/fail basis gives little insight into the nature of the difficulty or the reasons for any failure. A more detailed analysis designed to examine those basic functions which are constituents of everyday tasks would provide a much better basis for any extrapolation to other activities, it would also provide valuable information for diagnosis and for the evaluation of therapeutic procedures including surgery.

THE DEVELOPMENT OF BIMANUAL COORDINATION

The hand is the most prominent instrument of skill possessed by man and the variety and complexity of tasks which can be carried out using two hands is enormous. The study of how skilled activity is acquired must take into account the serial structure of acts and the growth of bimanual activities provides a useful approach to understanding the general development and organization of skilled behaviour.

An examination of day-to-day tasks reveals limitations on the ways in which the two hands can be used in combination by adults. A movement of one hand may only be simultaneously and purposefully combined with a movement of the other when the two components are sufficiently well practised and do not require continuous monitoring. The movements are lawfully related within the demands of a task, which is in itself within the attentional capacity of the operator. That is to say the movements made by the two hands must comprise part of some overall task the attainment of which is monitored. These points may be illustrated by reference to commonplace examples.

Sequenced Movements

Some keyboard skills such as typing require that any particular movement be made with one hand only (at a given time) although varying sequences of letters necessitate a varying distribution of movements between digits and between hands. In typing the novice monitors individual movements but as skill is acquired he attends to longer and longer sequences of letters which can be run off thus reducing the need for continuously monitoring the individual movements making up the sequence. Initially the unit is the letter, then the word and finally with the skilled typist the unit becomes a phrase, as shown by Bryan and Harter (1899) in their studies on telegraphy. Thus movements of the two hands become combined into a smooth sequence.

Piano players have the option of using the hands simultaneously as well as successively. However, there always remains a rhythmic relationship determining the timing of sequential or simultaneous movements, and this is one of the most essential features of the task. It is notoriously difficult to play at different rates with the two hands when the ratio of the rates is not a whole number.

Simultaneous Movements

There are several types of combination found where both hands are in use simultaneously.

(a) We may find one hand performing a controlled movement while the other performs a holding function, exerting pressure but not movement. There is then a division of labour across the hands as between manipulation and support (Bruner, 1970). The use of a knife and fork exemplifies this case. Connolly (1973) has also presented observations showing a marked division of labour of this kind in four-year-old children screwing together a large nut and bolt. The division of labour reflected in the different grips used for manipulation and support is shown in Fig. 3.

(b) One hand performs the manipulatory function and the other performs a rhythmic or cyclical movement in which little or no monitoring is needed. The use of an old-fashioned manually operated mangle is an interesting example. The winding of the mangle entails little monitoring, since, in Bernstein's (1967) phrase, the "degrees of freedom" of the

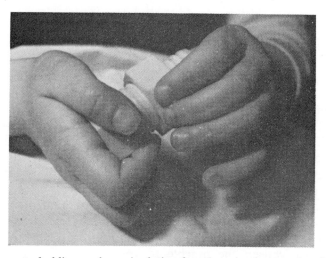

FIG. 3. Separate holding and manipulative functions in the two hands (child of 3 years). The left hand rotates the nut with movements of the opposed thumb and fingers. The right hand holds the bolt rigid in a palmar grip with pseudo-opposed thumb. Compare with Fig. 4.

movement needed are greatly reduced by the mechanical structure of the apparatus. The path of the handle as it revolves is determined, and all that is needed is an application of force roughly in the direction of revolution.

(c) Both hands make the same movement, or symmetrical movements. Anatomically speaking, symmetrical movements of the two hands are identical and it is easier, when learning to play the piano, to learn diverging scales with both hands, than parallel scales.

These limitations do not fix an absolute range of possible combinations of movements. The possibilities are affected by training. A skilled motor mechanic may be tightening up a wheel nut with one hand while reaching for and fitting a further nut with the other hand. The acquisition of such a skill is very probably due to the abolition of the need to continuously attend to the turning of the first nut, as a result of prolonged experience. The act of screwing up a wheel nut finger tight thus becomes a sub-routine and in accordance with the first of our limitations stated above it may be simultaneously and purposefully combined with a movement of the other hand.

The goal of the investigations reported below was to observe the natural development of bimanual coordination, with an apparatus that allowed the investigator to arrange the task requirements such that various difficult combinations or sequences of movement were needed for success.

Apparatus

The apparatus is shown in Fig. 4. It consisted of a tray 8 in. square mounted on a box within pivoted frames and converted from a commercially produced toy, the Labarynth Game, manufactured in Sweden by Brio. The tray could be tilted by turning two knobs set in adjacent sides of the box. The direction of tilt of the tray was a direct function of the direction of twist of the knob. Thus a marble placed on the surface of the tray could be made to roll in directions parallel to the sides of the tray by moving one knob at a time. In order to make the marble traverse a diagonal, it was necessary to employ both knobs simultaneously. With the subject positioned at one corner of the box so that he controlled a knob with each hand, turning each knob in an opposite rotation caused the marble to traverse the saggital diagonal— to travel towards or away from the child. Turning both knobs in the same direction caused the marble to traverse the frontal diagonal, travelling in frcnt of the subject from side to side.

Given this basic apparatus it was possible, by using replaceable trays, to present to the subject a variety of tasks. Basically these took

Fig. 4. The apparatus in use on task 6. Upper, child aged 3½ years, holding the knob in a power grip with palmar contact. Movement of the knob depends on movements at wrist and shoulder.

Lower, child aged 7 years. The digital grip allows knob adjustment to involve thumb and finger movements.

These age related differences are characteristic.

the form of mazes through which a marble had to be guided. The six different tasks used were designed so as to make different requirements on the subjects. They are described below, and illustrated diagrammatically in Fig. 5.

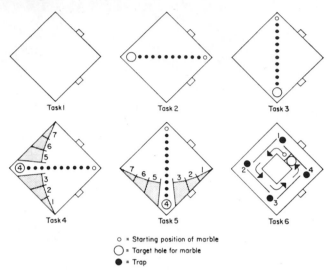

FIG. 5. Plan view of the trays used in each task. Dotted lines indicate the most direct path to the target. Arrows indicate the required path in task 6. The subject was positioned to the right of a tray, at the corner between the two knobs.

The Tasks

Task 1, free play. A blank tray was put on the box and the child invited to explore for himself the possibilities of the apparatus. The range of movements and the way they were used was noted.

Tasks 2 and 3, unrestricted diagonals. A tray with a hole at one corner was used, with a marble placed at the diagonally opposite corner. The subject's task was to get the marble into the hole. A diagonal line was painted on the tray to provide a perceptual link between starting point and goal, but the subject was not explicitly asked to make the ball travel along it. Tasks 2 and 3 differed in the orientation of the diagonal. In task 2 the saggital diagonal was used, and in task 3 the frontal diagonal. The experimenter recorded the course of the marble and the movements used for six trials.

Tasks 4 and 5, restricted diagonals. Tasks 2 and 3 were called unrestricted diagonal tasks because the subject was not obliged to use the diagonal to achieve the goal. In tasks 4 and 5, however, though the same diagonal paths were used as in tasks 2 and 3 respectively, there were added a number of traps which prevented subjects from getting the marble from start to goal by using one hand at a time. The marble had to be got away from the edges of the tray in order to reach the target. As may be seen from Fig. 5, the sides of the tray proximal to the target hole were partitioned into a total of seven compartments, the central one of which contained the target hole. Each partition subtended an equal depth: this was done in order to avoid making some of the partitions, or traps, harder to extricate a marble from than others.

There are three kinds of movements which can bring success to this task.

The experimenter noted the successive positions of the marble over four trials. A trial terminated when the marble was holed, but many subjects did not achieve even one success on this task.

Task 6, sequential operations. Task 6 was designed to require subjects to make sequential movements across hands in order to achieve success. The marble had to change direction four times, and this necessitated a left–right–left–right sequence of hand turning, with the second movement of a hand being the reverse of its first. Accurate anticipation was essential in this task. The marble ran into a trap if the correct movement in the sequence was not timed to anticipate the point at which the marble had to turn a corner. It was not enough to observe the consequence of one movement before initiating the next—it was essential that a prediction be made whilst the marble was *in transit* and a new movement initiated to coincide with the end of the effect of the previous movement.

The experimenter recorded errors and the nature of the movements used over four trials. As with tasks 4 and 5 the difficulty of the task frequently meant that no successes were scored.

Although some of these six tasks proved difficult, subjects, especially older children, were remarkably persistent.

TABLE I. *Age of children in the three groups making up the study. All the subjects in group C were from one school. Subjects in groups A and B were drawn in roughly equal numbers from a nursery school and a playgroup*

Group	Median age	Age range
A	3.28	2.50–3.51
B	4.30	4.02–4.45
C	6.05	5.27–6.14

Subjects

Three groups of sixteen subjects, eight boys and eight girls in each group, were drawn from three Sheffield schools, two Nursery Schools and one First School. Ages of groups in years and weeks are given in Table I.

Subjects in Groups A and B were drawn roughly equally from a nursery school and a playgroup.

All subjects in Group C were from one school.

Design

Each subject performed on all six tasks, in one of two possible orders:

1   2   3   4   5   6

or

1   3   2   5   4   6

Task 1 lasted until the subject seemed to have exhausted his inventiveness. Tasks 2 and 3 contained 6 trials each. Tasks 4, 5 and 6 each continued until subjects showed signs of boredom or until four "goals" had been achieved.

Procedure

The children were collected from classroom and playground and brought into a familiar room. After a few children had done the task, word got around, and there was little reluctance on the part of children invited to participate. The child was seated at a low table before the apparatus, and the experimenter demonstrated the movements of the marble on the blank tray (task 1). The child was invited to play with it himself, and from then on the experimenter simply substituted tasks as appropriate, telling the child to get the marble into the hole, and demonstrating this in task 6 and other tasks if the child had difficulty.

Results

For any task, the marble is wholly controlled by rotation of the knobs. There are four responses available; pronation or supination of right or left hand, corresponding to the four possible ways of turning the two knobs. Turning the knobs could be achieved by other means such as wrist flexion. This was virtually never seen, but it should be noted that it is the turning of the knob in a particular direction that defines the function of an act. It turned out to be the case that the anatomy of the movement involved showed little variety outside the four responses.

The child hence has two discrete movements or sub-routines for each hand, and two kinds of combination available. When both knobs are turned in the same direction, a pronation and a supination are involved, and we will describe such a case as an asymmetrical movement of the two hands (AS). If, however, the two knobs are turned in opposite directions, the two hands are either both pronated or both supinated, depending upon the directions of turning. This movement will be referred to as a symmetrical movement of the two hands (S). These two-handed movements could in turn be regarded, if practised, as sub-routines which could themselves be inserted into further sequences of movement. Some of the tasks made demands upon the child's ability to combine movements in this way; others examined his ability to use movements sequentially.

Task 1, Free Play

In this task the aim was to ascertain the movements spontaneously employed free from the constraints of the specific tasks. In first showing the children the apparatus in use, the experimenter always used all combinations of single and combined hand movements, without drawing attention to any particular one.

TABLE II. *Task 1, subjects' spontaneous preference for hand use*

Group	(n)	One hand	Two hands (S)	Two hands (AS)
A	(16)	15	11	1
B	(16)	11	12	5
C	(16)	13	11	6

Table II shows the results in terms of whether a child exhibited any of the following; a use of one hand at a time; a use of both hands in a symmetrical movement; a use of both hands in an asymmetrical movement.

Most children of all ages were seen to use one hand and two hands symmetrically. Few children used asymmetrical movements. Every subject, except one in group A, could use both hands simultaneously on request, and in every case the resulting movement was symmetrical. A number of interesting qualitative observations were made.

(i) It was almost always the case that the marble travelled in a straight line. This indicates that even when both hands were used at once, their relative rate of change of movement did not vary greatly.

(ii) Movements tended to be abrupt and discrete. On the whole movements were not made until the outcome of the previous movement had been observed and the marble come to rest.

(iii) Young children tended to perseverate in turning the knob or knobs in one direction after this had ceased to have any effect on the marble (because it had come to rest), or in turning the knob or knobs back and forth, moving the marble to and fro on an unvarying path.

(iv) Older children gave the impression of systematically trying out the possible routes the marble might take, and how their movements controlled it. Younger children gave an impression of a somewhat more random approach to the properties of the apparatus.

Tasks 2 and 3, Unrestricted Diagonals

In these tasks, the subject is asked to move the marble from one corner of a blank tray to a target hole in the diagonally opposite corner. In task 2 the relevant diagonal is saggital along the subject's line of sight, in task 3 it is frontal—across his line of sight.

The most efficient method of accomplishing the task is by a movement with both hands simultaneously, symmetrically in the case of task 2 and asymmetrically in the case of task 3. The most efficient method is taken to be that which moves the marble directly to its target hole along the appropriate diagonal. However, the target may also be reached by causing the marble to move along two adjacent sides with appropriate successive movements of the hands. The actual movements of the hands are the same for simultaneous or successive combinations of the hands. The interest of the results of this task lies in whether such movements are in fact employed simultaneously or successively, and whether or not the alignment of the diagonal, and hence the necessary combinations, affects this.

The alignment of the diagonal joining the start and target points on the tray affects the movements required for success in the following way. Irrespective of whether the movements of the hands are simultaneous or successive, when the marble is to be moved to a target on a saggital diagonal (task 2) the two hands must make the same movements—pronations or supinations depending upon the direction of movement. In task 3, when the marble has to be moved frontally across. the line of vision, the hands must make different movements—a pronation followed by a supination or vice versa, depending upon the direction of movement required.

On each trial, the following measures were taken.

(i) Whether the subject used both hands in succession or simultaneously, for the three movements ending in success.

(ii) Whether, for simultaneous movements, they were symmetrical or asymmetrical.

(iii) The number of discrete marble movements, whether of one or both hands, needed for success. Movements of the two hands together scored as one movement for this measure. Many subjects made inefficient movements, taking the marble in inappropriate directions, so that the movement score is a likely indicator of task difficulty.

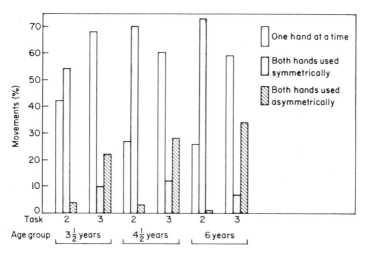

FIG. 6. Tasks 2 and 3. For each age group, the histograms show the frequency of occurrence of the different movement combinations as a percentage.

Figure 6 shows the percentage of the three different types of movement occurring in each task at each age level. The six trials are summed for each subject. From the figure it is clear that for all groups the pattern of movements differs sharply between the two tasks. In neither task are the distributions random. All six histograms in the figure reveal significance within group differences in the frequency of occurrence of types of movement ($p < 0.01$ or 0.001), Friedman analyses of variance for ranks (Siegel, 1956). It is noticeable that while on task 2 the symmetrical movement with both hands is preferred by every group, on task 3 the use of two hands is successive not simultaneous. Further, the asymmetrical movement, which would be the most efficient simultaneous movement, is not the most preferred as the symmetrical movement is in task 2.

There is an increasing use of two hands simultaneously among older children in task 2. Though not significant this trend is more marked than in task 3, and appears to reflect an increasing preference with age for symmetrical movement of both hands.

There was no evidence that appreciable learning occurred during the six trials, such that the frequency of utilization of the various movements was changing as the child continued with a task.

Turning to the mean movements required to hole the marble six times, these scores can be used as a measure of the relative difficulty of the tasks. A three-way analysis of variance (factors; task, age and sex) revealed that; subjects used more movements on task 3 than on task 2 ($p < 0.01$), in either task, older children used fewer movements than younger ($p < 0.05$), and there were no differences attributable to the sex of the subject, and no significant interactions.

It appears clear, therefore, that task 2 is the easier and that task 3 is the harder, for all groups, with the older children consistently doing better. It seems probable that this result is attributable at least in part to the greater incidence of the symmetrical two-handed movement in task 2, since this is a successful movement and will cut down the total movement score. There remains to consider the question of whether the greater difficulty in task 3 is due to the difficulty of combining supination and pronation in a single movement, or to the difficulty of using pronation and supination in different hands whether in combination or sequentially.

Figure 7 shows mean trials for each group in which the type of movement was one hand singly, both hands together, or mixed sequences.

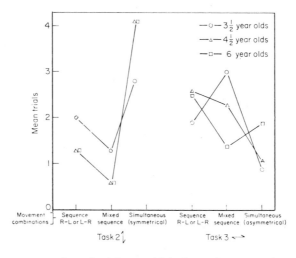

FIG. 7. Gives mean number of trials on which the various movement sequences or combinations were employed by the three groups of children. Tasks 2 and 3.

Mixed sequences are those in which the subject used neither a simple right–left sequence of two movements (H, one hand at a time) nor a successful combined movement (S or AS as appropriate to the task), but used an inefficient assortment of more than two movements.

The younger subjects exhibited relatively few successful asymmetrical movements and relatively more mixed sequences. The younger children also showed the smallest number of two movement sequences (pronation–supination or vice versa). The older subjects showed more asymmetrical (AS) movements and more discrete sequences of two movements (H), and far fewer mixed sequences. It appears, therefore, that the youngest group of subjects compared with the oldest have difficulty with either using asymmetrical movements successfully, or with generating satisfactory two movement sequences. This leads us to the view that the greater difficulty of task 3, as measured by total movements of all kinds, is due at least in part to the difficulty of using pronation and supination with different hands, whether simultaneously or successively.

This analysis of the data reflects more accurately the subjects' use of efficient strategies. The use of two hands in two successive movements or in a single bimanual response of the appropriate type (S or AS) both constitute efficient performance in contrast to the use of any other movement combination. It can be seen from Fig. 7 that on task 2 the older two groups of subjects use more symmetrical movements and fewer single two movement sequences than do the youngest group. The increase in symmetrical movements with age is significant ($p < 0.05$), though the decrease in two movement sequences is not (Kruskal–Wallace analysis of variance by ranks). Also significant is the less frequent use of inefficient multiple movement sequences in older subjects. The pattern is different in task 3. None of the changes with age are significant, but not only do the youngest subjects again use more multiple movement sequences, they use fewer asymmetric sequences and fewer simple two-movement sequences. Indeed by contrast with table 3 the mixed sequence is the commonest type of movement for this group.

It seems clear that when efficient movement combinations are involved the incidence of both simultaneous and successive asymmetrical combinations are less in the younger subjects with a correspondingly increased frequency of inefficient mixed sequences. (The within group variance for the $3\frac{1}{2}$ year old group along is significant on task 3, $p < 0.01$, Friedman's analysis of variance by ranks.) Consequently though younger children do show an appreciable frequency of asymmetric combinations (Fig. 6) on task 3 and do not differ from the older in this respect, the pattern of efficient responses shown in Fig. 7 suggests that the difficulty of task 3 (as measured by mean movements of all kinds) is at least partly due to the difficulty of any usage of pronation and supination with different hands whether combinatorial or sequential.

Tasks 4 and 5, Restricted Diagonals

Tasks 4 and 5 were identical to tasks 2 and 3 respectively, for each subject, except that the presence of partitions (traps) adjacent to the target prevented the use of the simple two-movement sequence that could easily be used in tasks 2 and 3 (see Fig. 5).

In tasks 4 and 5, the movements that the subject made were not directly recorded. The experimenter instead noted the successive points on the tray visited by the marble. The start point was labelled S, the target hole diagonally opposite it, 4. Numbers 1 to 3 and 5 to 7 designated the partitions of the tray other than the target partition, 4. Points S, 1 and 7 thus represent the three corners of the tray other than that containing the target hole.

Table III shows for each age group the mean number of times that the marble visited each of the labelled points. Since subjects were able to

TABLE III. *Mean scores for each group for each point on the tray in tasks 4 and 5*

	Group	S	1	2	3	4*	5	6	7	Total excluding 4
Task 4	A	29·0	18·9	3·1	2·3	2·6	2·9	1·8	11·7	69·7
	B	17·4	8·9	2·0	2·3	3·8	2·4	1·8	12·6	47·3
	C	12·3	4·8	1·9	2·1	3·8	1·8	1·1	5·7	29·6
Task 5	A	23·4	22·8	1·4	1·3	1·9	2·1	2·8	23·8	77·6
	B	25·4	24·4	3·1	3·1	3·5	3·2	3·5	23·4	86·1
	C	23·7	20·4	2·8	2·6	3·5	2·8	3·6	20·5	76·6

* Maximum score = 4.

TABLE IV. *Mean scores per cent for each group for each point on the tray in tasks 4 and 5*

	Group	S	1	2	3	5	6	7
Task 4	A	41·6	27·2	4·5	3·2	4·2	2·5	16·8
	B	36·7	18·8	4·2	4·9	5·0	3·8	26·6
	C	41·6	16·0	6·5	7·0	5·9	3·8	19·2
Task 5	A	30·2	29·3	1·9	1·6	2·7	3·6	30·7
	B	28·4	28·4	3·6	3·5	3·7	4·1	27·2
	C	26·7	26·7	3·6	3·4	3·7	4·7	26·9

continue at the tasks until they had succeeded in holing the marble four times, but since not all persisted in this, there is considerable variation in individual subjects' scores. Table IV therefore shows the data of Table III converted to mean score per cent, thus indicating better the relative frequency of the scores for each point.

It is clear that the main difference between these tasks lies in the frequency of the scores S, 1 and 7 and in the total number of movements made. The relation between S, 1 and 7 scores is a measure of the extent to which the marble is being kept to the edges of the tray, for the more it does so, the more it will tend to visit point S as often as it visits either point 1 or point 7. Hence if we calculate the value of scores $(1+7)-S$, and call this value d, then the more the marble is kept to the edges of the tray, the more d will tend to zero. Table V gives the value of d for the three groups on each task.

Inspection of Table IV reveals that in task 4 the marble was being kept to the edges very much more than in task 5. This difference is probably attributable to the occurrence of symmetrical movements of both hands in task 5. Initially the subjects tended to use one hand at a time in attempting these tasks, and this naturally caused the marble to travel from S to 1 or 7 and back. However, in task 4 a symmetrical movement of both hands tended to lead to the same result. Having tilted the tray considerably in attempting to use one hand, the use of both was not adequate to compensate for the resulting bias, and the marble tended to continue along the edges of the tray as a result. In the case of task 5, however, a symmetrical movement tended to take the marble from 1 to 7 direct, for in this task these points were in the line of sight. This would account for the markedly higher proportion of scores for these points in this task, and hence the higher d scores shown in Table V.

TABLE V. *Values of* d *for the three age groups on tasks 4 and 5.* d = *mean scores per cent* $(1+7)-S$

	Group	d
Task 4	A	$+2\cdot4$
	B	$+8\cdot7$
	C	$-6\cdot4$
Task 5	A	$+28\cdot8$
	B	$+27\cdot2$
	C	$+26\cdot9$

The children were not very successful at these tasks, though they were persistent. Among strategies resorted to were perseveration in turning knobs after the marble had come to rest in a trap, rapidly reversing or changing the movements, or making vigorous and excessive movements. Many children obtained apparently accidental successes in this way. However, if overall the total number of movements made in pursuit of the tasks is examined (Table III) it can be seen that fewer were needed for success in task 4 than in task 5. Taking total movements per subject, for each task as a measure of their relative difficulty, a three-way analysis of variance (factors; task, age and sex) revealed that (i) subjects used more movement on task 5 than on task 4 ($p < 0.01$), (ii) age effects were confined to the age × task interaction ($p < 0.05$). This is interpreted to indicate that on task 4 but not task 5, older subjects used fewer movements. (iii) No other effects or interactions were significant.

The finding that more movements overall are used in task 5 is comparable with the similar finding for task 3, and is interpreted as indicating that subjects found this task more difficult.

These tasks were not wholly satisfactory in that the use of one hand led to a bias in tray tilt which was not rectified by the subsequent use of both hands. Hence subjects found that neither kind of movement was reliable in achieving the goal, and experienced excessive difficulty with the task. Competent performance necessitates an ability to compensate for unequal prior movements of separate hands.

Task 6, Sequential Operations

Task 6, unlike the preceding ones, imposed upon the subjects strict temporal limits on the sequencing of movements. Successfully manipulating the marble around the maze and into the goal required not only a sequence of operations, but anticipation of the time at which the next movement was due. The construction of the apparatus was such that the subjects were not able to pause and plan the next move while the marble was at rest. Although the entire sequence did not have to be preprogrammed, it was necessary for the subject to make a movement at exactly the correct time in the overall sequence.

This task proved exceedingly difficult for the youngest group of subjects. Table VI shows the number of subjects succeeding in each group. This number increases significantly with age ($\chi^2 = 7.1$, $p < 0.05$).

Four error positions could be distinguished, 1 being the trap position nearest to the starting point, and 4 the farthest from it (Fig. 5). Table VII shows the mean errors at each point for each group and Table VIII

TABLE VI. *Subjects succeeding in task 6. Successful subjects are those completing at least one successful sequence out of a possible 4*

Group	n	Subjects succeeding	Mean success per child (max. 4)
A	16	3	0·6
B	16	12	2·9
C	16	14	3·5

TABLE VII. *Mean errors at each error position for each group*

Group	Error position number 1	2	3	4	Total
A	12·0	17·7	3·9	0·3	33·9
B	7·3	13·9	6·8	4·4	32·4
C	4·5	10·3	7·9	3·6	26·3

TABLE VIII. *Mean errors per cent at each error position for each group*

Group	Error position number 1	2	3	4
A	35·4	52·2	11·5	0·9
B	22·5	42·9	21·0	13·6
C	17·1	39·2	30·0	13·7

gives the mean errors per cent. The data in Table VIII are represented graphically in Fig. 8.

The distribution of errors is not random. Friedman's analysis of variance by ranks within each group is significant for each group (groups A, B, $p < 0.001$; group C, $p < 0.05$). The differences between groups on each error were also tested by the Friedman analysis. Differences with age on errors are not significant, except in the case of error position 4 ($p < 0.01$, Median test). It is clear that older children are better at the task than the younger, in that they tend to score more late errors, that is, they proceed on average further round the tray before failing.

Errors at later positions in the sequence necessarily involved successes at earlier positions, an error at position 3 necessarily entailed success at positions 1 and 2. A corrected error score was therefore calculated on the proportion of errors to successes at each error position. These

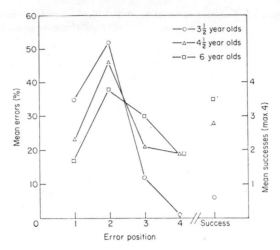

FIG. 8. Mean errors % at each of the four error positions on task 6. Error positions are illustrated in Fig. 5.

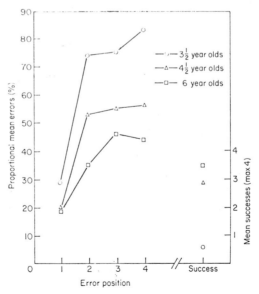

FIG. 9. Proportional mean errors (%) at the four error positions. Details in text.

proportional error scores are shown in Fig. 9, expressed as a percentage value for each group at each error position. The distribution of errors thus calculated is significantly different both within and between groups for every error position.

The sequence of movements entailed in task 6 involved the alternate use of the hands, while requiring *double alternation* of supination and pronation. A sequence always required a left-hand movement to start the marble. Four possible sequences were used (Table IX), counter-balanced among subjects within each group as shown below. The

TABLE IX. *Sequences of pronation and supination used in task 6. P = Pronation, S = Supination, L = Left, R = Right*

| Hand | Sequence | | | |
	1	2	3	4
L	P	S	S	P
R	S	S	P	P
L	S	P	P	S
R	P	P	S	S
L	P	S	S	P

sequence was determined by the location of the start point on the direction of travel of the marble. An error occurred whenever a given movement was not followed by the movement appropriate for that sequence. Thus in sequence 1, errors in position 1 occurred when an initial left-hand pronation was not followed by a right-hand supination: with sequence 4, on the other hand, two successive pronations are necessary to avoid error 1. An analysis was conducted to ascertain if the probability of errors at particular points was affected by the sequence of movements required of the subject.

Subjects' error scores at each position were dichotomized according to the sequence of movements needed at that particular position. Thus for error position 1, subjects in sequences 1 and 3 (Table IX) had to make a pronation followed by a supination, or vice versa, to avoid the trap. Error scores for such subjects represented failure to produce an asymmetric (AS) sequence of movements. Similarly, subjects in sequences 2 and 3 made errors if they failed to produce a succession of two pronations or supinations, a symmetrical (S) sequence. Table X gives the mean error scores for subjects of all ages combined. It can be seen that the need for an asymmetrical sequence led to a higher error rate at every position, significantly so in the case of positions 1 and 2.

TABLE X. *Mean error scores for subjects at each error position, dichotomized by type of sequence required. Significances were calculated by Mann–Whitney U test, data from all age groups being combined*

| Error position | Mean errors | | P |
	Asymmetrical	Symmetrical	
1	11·3	4·6	$<0·001$
2	17·5	10·5	$<0·05$
3	6·6	5·6	NS
4	3·6	2·0	NS

The results indicate that the greater difficulty of asymmetrical combinations found in the preceding tasks also had an effect over and above the difficulties of temporal sequencing in the present task.

The overall distribution of scores shown in Table VIII still requires explanation, particularly the tendency for error position 2 to attract most errors. The most likely explanation of this aspect of the distribution is that children learned that a single movement of the left hand would simply start the marble, and that what it did at the first turn depended on a right hand movement. This movement could precede the arrival of the marble at the corner. Thus it was a relatively simple matter to learn to avoid the first error, with the proviso that if supination and pronation was entailed it was harder. However, to avoid error 2 the child had to learn to reverse the movement of the left hand that had been needed to start the marble. This seemed a difficult thing to do. The children tended either to move the left hand further in the wrong direction, or to reverse the right hand movement. It thus seemed that the difficulty at error position 3 was that in order to avoid it the child had to revert to the hand first used, whilst using a different movement, and this was responsible for the majority of the difficulties, independently of whether or not a supination–pronation was involved (i.e. regardless of the sequence of movements appropriate) (Table X).

With error position 4, it is likely that the overall low score for errors reflects partly on the fact that children who could master error 3 were probably becoming quite proficient at the task, and partly on the fact that by the time any such mastery was manifest the child was likely to be rather satiated with the task, particularly as it was the last in order of the six. However, it should also be noted that if a child biased the tray with a right-hand movement before commencing to roll the marble with the left hand, it could obtain error 3 by simply reversing the left-hand movement as soon as the marble turned the first corner. This would obviate the apparently difficult problem of making a reversed movement of the left hand after an interpolated movement of the right. It is impossible to say how often this occurred, but the fact that it occurred at least sometimes indicates that the only certain measure of ability to sequence movements of alternate hands is to be found in the scores of error position 4. The numbers of subjects who succeeded in achieving this at all are given in Table XI, and it can be seen that the numbers increase with increasing age though the effect is not significant ($\chi^2 = 4.2$, $p < 0.1$).

TABLE XI. *Number of subjects in each group succeeding in achieving error position 4*

Group	n	Subjects reaching error position 4
A	16	5
B	16	10
C	16	14

TABLE XII. *Per cent mean responses of each type of movement for each group (task 6): incomplete data*

Group	n	Left hand only	Asymmetrical movement	Symmetrical movement	L–R sequence	Other (mixed)
A	14	11·0	3·0	47·5	37·0	1·5
B	10	29·4	0·7	15·4	53·8	0·7
C	12	8·2	2·8	13·1	37·9	18·0

The greater facility of the older groups at this task was achieved by their greater use of discrete movements of the appropriate hands. The youngest group showed a considerable tendency to attempt the task with the use of symmetrical movements of both hands, with added emphasis on alternate hands as needed. Success was in fact possible by this method. Some data were collected on the movements used by individual subjects, which are presented in Table XII. This table shows the greater use of sequential movements by older subjects. Sequential constraints still operate with younger subjects in respect of the timing of movements, but there are no difficulties of the sort found in a succession of discrete one handed movements as discussed above.

Table XIII shows the same data for subjects achieving the target only, and it will be noticed that the two successful subjects in group A both

TABLE XIII. *Per cent mean scores of various types of movement response, derived from successful subjects only where data available*

Group	n	Successful subjects	Left hand only	Asymmetrical movements	Symmetrical movements	Sequenced movements	Other (mixed)
A	—	2	—	—	100	—	—
B	—	6	—	—	4·2	91·6	4·2
C	—	11	—	—	10·0	62·5	27·5

used symmetrical movements, whereas these were rare amongst the older subjects.

In summary, it is clear that the movements needed on task 6 were not different from those required of the children in other tasks and which they were motorically competent to make. However, the youngest children found the task an exceedingly difficult one. They were less able than the older children to sequence movements which entailed a successive use of different hands. And for all the children it was generally the case that if a sequence of movements required the child to change both the hand and the direction of turn (anatomically defined), then that sequence proved more difficult. It seems that the difficulty in sequencing movements is at least partly a function of the compatibility of the movements to be sequenced.

DISCUSSION AND CONCLUSIONS

The experimental data presented in this paper suggest that with advancing age the development of a competence in skill is manifested in the kinds of ways in which simple movements can be combined and used. It seems clear that considerations of compatibility make certain combinations of movement, whether in sequence or simultaneously, harder for younger than for older children. At $4\frac{1}{2}$ years, moreover, the child has a better ability to turn together with the correct timing movements which the $3\frac{1}{2}$ year old executes only as individual components. Indeed, on task 6 it was clear that some enterprising members of the youngest group of subjects were able to achieve success with a strategy that did not exceed their competence in this respect, but which was superseded by more successful methods in older subjects.

The fact that asymmetrical movement combinations were harder for younger children argues against the view that differential difficulty of combinations is solely a matter of experience—that subjects become more practised at the types of movement which entail symmetrical bimanual movement through the demands of environmental manipulanda. For if true, this view would imply that the younger child, with his lesser experience of purposeful manipulation, should manifest a lesser differential difficulty as between symmetrical and asymmetrical combinations. Such is not the case. Some combinations, it would seem, are from an early age more equal than others. In this respect there is a parallel between the emergence of pronation/supination combinations as usable sub-routines and the emergence of precision grips of the sort detailed by Connolly and Elliott (1972). Indeed, it remains a matter for investigation whether there is any connection between the form of grip used on the apparatus and the difficulty of the task as measured by error rates or movement combinations attempted. One could predict that a regression would occur, from precise to less controlled grips, as the child's information-processing capacity becomes more burdened with difficult task demands.

A further matter for future investigation is the relation between the direction of tilt of a tray and the direction of turn of a knob. In the present experiment the direction of tilt always corresponded to the direction of turn of the knob. The two could therefore be described as showing a compatible relationship. Introduction of the reverse (incompatible) relationship might be expected to produce an effect if the compatible arrangement reflected a lawfulness in object relations already familiar to the child. Work currently in progress with adults suggests that incompatible relationships produce an adult performance not dissimilar to that of children with compatible relationships. This suggests that adults have certain expectancies about such relationships, which when disconfirmed, require attention to be switched to mastering the new relationship at the expense of the combination of movements in pursuit of the task goal.

More fundamentally, the prospect of varying the effects which a given movement, anatomically defined, has on the environment allows a distinction between anatomical and operational sub-routines to be made and examined. An anatomical sub-routine is a unit of behaviour definable in anatomical terms such as pronation of the hand. However, behaviour is more often defined in relation to its goal, for example, turning a knob, in any instance of which a variety of goal directed anatomical movements might be involved. Such units, which would in themselves comprise one or more anatomical sub-routines, we shall call operational sub-routines. An operational sub-routine, being defined by its effect on the environment, will have a different effect in different circumstances. The prospect of varied compatibility is to vary the effect of a given anatomical sub-routine, thus in effect defining a new operational sub-routine. Consequently it seems likely that the known effects of incompatibility in stimulus-response relationships (Fitts and Deininger, 1954; Fitts and Seeger, 1953) may be describable within the framework of skill we have proposed. The distinction between acts defined anatomically and those defined by their consequences reflects a distinction between the analysis of movement capabilities and that of function (see Connolly and Elliott, 1972, for a discussion of this point with respect to grasping). Any further analysis of skill in terms of its components is likely to have to acknowledge this distinction.

The work which we have reported was aimed at discovering something of the organization of anatomical sub-routines in the pursuit of operational sub-routines for a given task. Future studies will be necessary to ascertain if the organization of operational sub-routines reflects a comparable structure. Further experiments must also be made in order to ascertain the extent to which these levels of ability are characteristic of other skilled tasks, and the extent to which features of skill competence are to be found in other areas of ability. Wood *et al.* (in press) have reported an investigation into the combinatorial abilities of young children on a task entailing the construction of a toy by the intellectual application of a sequencing rule. They found a similar progression to that which we have described in the ability to combine learned acts or truth statements relating to the toy's structure. Along with our findings these encourage us in the belief that the analysis of various human abilities will profit from the application of the form of descriptive analysis described.

This paper has dealt with the natural history of skill, and the descriptions appropriate to it, as well as the details of a particular instance. The work reported is appropriately described within the framework of a modular theory of skill, but we believe further that the value of such a theory is that it enables performance to be described in terms of the relations between acts as well as in terms of the acts themselves. In an understandable emphasis on the attempt to describe behaviour in terms of stimulus and response, the psychologist may have improperly avoided a necessary analysis of the relations between responses. It is notoriously difficult to define a response—a signature written with the toes is still a signature—without resorting to the language of purpose. Clearly, theories which seek to show how the concept of purpose can be reconciled with a knowledge of a defined and finite set of molecular acts are likely to provide a more promising foundation to studies of more complex human behaviour. Indeed, though it is commonly claimed that psychology is the study of behaviour, we feel a more appropriate definition might be the study of the organization and function of behaviour, lest we be led back anew to an emphasis on observable responses at the expense of an understanding of the relations between them and their significance to the organism.

REFERENCES

ANNETT, J. and KAY, H. 1957. Knowledge of results and "skilled performance". *Occupat. Psychol.*, **31**, 69–79.

BERNSTEIN, N. A. 1967. *The coordination and regulation of movement.* Pergamon Press, London.

BRUNER, J. 1970. The growth and structure of skill. In K. Connolly (Ed.), *Mechanisms of motor skill development.* Academic Press, London.

BRYAN, W. L. and HARTER, N. 1899. Studies on the telegraphic language. The acquisition of a hierarchy of habits. *Psychol. Rev.*, **6**, 345–375.

CONNOLLY, K. 1970. Skill development: problems and plans. In K. Connolly (Ed.), *Mechanisms of motor skill development.* Academic Press, London.

CONNOLLY, K. 1973. Factors influencing the learning of manual skills by young children. In R. A. Hinde and J. S. Hinde (Eds.), *Constraints on learning.* Academic Press, London.

CONNOLLY, K. and ELLIOTT, J. 1972. The evolution and ontogeny of hand function. In N. Blurton Jones (Ed.), *Ethological studies of child behaviour.* Cambridge University Press, Cambridge.

DOTY, R. W. and BOSEMA, J. F. 1956. An electromyographic analysis of reflex deglutition. *J. Neurophysiol.*, **19**, 44–60.

FITTS, P. M. 1962. Factors in complex skill training. In R. Glaser (Ed.), *Training research and education.* University of Pittsburg Press, Pittsburg.

FITTS, P. M. and SEEGER, C. M. 1953. S–R compatibility: spatial characteristics of stimulus and response codes. *J. exp. Psychol.*, **46**, 199–210.

FITTS, P. M. and DEININGER, R. L. 1954. S–R compatibility: correspondence among paired elements within stimulus and response codes. *J. exp. Psychol.*, **48**, 483–492.

FITTS, P. M. and POSNER, M. I. 1967. *Human performance.* Brooks/Cole, Belmont, California.

HEIN, A. and HELD, R. 1962. A neural model for labile sensory-motor coordinations. In E. E. Bernard and M. R. Kare (Eds.), *Biological prototypes and synthetic systems.* Plenum Press, New York.

VON HOLST, E. 1954. Relations between the central nervous system and the peripheral organs. *Brit. J. Anim. Behav.*, **2**, 89–94.

HOLT, K. S. 1965. *Assessment of cerebral palsy*, Vol. I. Lloyd-Luke, London.

HULL, C. L. 1943. *Principles of behavior: an introduction to behavior theory.* Appleton Century-Crofts, New York.

KEATS, S. 1965. *Cerebral palsy.* Thomas, Springfield, Illinois.

LANDSMEER, J. M. F. 1962. Power grip and precision handling. *Ann. Rheum. Dis.*, **21**, 164–170.

LASHLEY, K. S. 1951. The problem of serial order in behavior. In L. A. Jeffress (Ed.), *Cerebral mechanisms in behavior: the Hixon symposium.* Wiley, New York.

MCKAY, D. M. 1962. Theoretical models of space perception. In C. A. Muses (Ed.), *Aspects of the theory of artificial intelligence.* Plenum Press, New York.

MEETHAM, A. R. 1969. *Encyclopaedia of linguistics, information and control.* Pergamon Press, London.

MILLER, G. A. 1953. What is information measurement? *Amer. Psychol.,* **8**, 3–11.

MILLER, G. A., GALANTER, E. and PRIBRAM, K. 1960. *Plans and the structure of behavior.* Holt, Rinehart and Winston, London.

MITTELSTAEDT, H. 1964. Basic control patterns of orientational homeostasis. *Symp. Soc. Exp. Biol.,* **18**, 365–386.

NAPIER, J. R. 1956. The prehensile movements of the human hand. *J. Bone Jt Surg.,* **38B**, 902–913.

SIEGEL, S. 1956. *Nonparametric statistics for the behavioral sciences.* McGraw-Hill, London.

TINBERGEN, N. 1951. *The study of instinct.* Oxford University Press, Oxford.

WOOD, D., BRUNER, J. S. and ROSS, G. A study of the tutorial process. In W. J. Mehler (Ed.), *Handbook of cognitive development.* In press.

Cognitive Competence

SUSAN CAREY

Massachusetts Institute of Technology

MY PURPOSE IN this paper is to discuss the consequences of early competence in problem solving for the later cognitive and social achievements of a child. A distinction must be made between *overall* cognitive competence and *particular* cognitive achievements. The aim stated above implies that there *is* such a thing as the former—that general cognitive competence exists. I know much more about the latter, about how a child comes to master particular problems. I will therefore begin by outlining a theory of this process (A Model of Problem Solving in Early Childhood). This will provide a basis for discussing general competence in problem solving from the point of view of a child's early experience (General Competence and Early Experience).

A MODEL OF PROBLEM SOLVING IN EARLY CHILDHOOD

I believe that a theory of the acquisition of motor skills provides the basic outlines of a theory of the acquisition of particular cognitive achievements. Such a theory of skill acquisition has been sketched by a number of authors (Bernstein, 1967; Connolly, 1973; Elliott and Connolly, this volume; Welford, 1968). The particular formulation that has influenced me most is Jerome Bruner's (Bruner, 1969), but all these theories have many common features. They all agree that skills are goal-directed and therefore any model must include means/end analyses. Skills are analysable into constituents and one of the problems in the performance of a skill is the combination of its constituents. The learning of new skills involves learning new constituents, perfecting them through practice (Bruner's "modularization"), and the learning of new combinations. An essential component of Bruner's description of skill is that the modularization of components is a prerequisite for their combination in sequences of skilled activity. This implies that sometimes we should find *preadaptive* constituents; that is, elements of skills which have *not yet* been incorporated into successful sequentially organized acts. This is indeed the case (Bruner and Koslowski, 1972).

In order to show how such a theory of skill applies to cognitive competence, I will use the example of Piaget's conservation of quantity. Nobody can deny that conservation is a cognitive achievement; furthermore, it has the dubious advantage of extreme complexity, thereby providing a framework from which to emphasize different aspects.

The basic phenomenon is this: equal quantities of water are poured into two identical beakers and one is then poured into a different shaped beaker

The child is then asked "Do A and C have the same amount to drink in them, or does A have more or does C have more?" A young child, a non-conserver, maintains that C has less to drink than A. The same child, when older, judges that the two quantities are equal. It is this cognitive achievement that I want to relate to the achievement of motor skills. In order to do so, I must describe the task as the child sees it and identify its possible constituents. There are several ways in which this could be done, several levels of task description. Here, let us assume that the child's problem is answering the questions the experimenter asks. The units of analysis are each of the child's answers, each justification, he gives, each prediction he makes. The constituents of these tasks are those aspects of the situation which the child takes as relevant in generating his answer[1]. What *is* relevant to any particular judgement? The correct task analysis yields at least two constituents, whether the quantities were equal or not to start with and whether any liquid had been added or subtracted during the pouring. The child, of course, may be basing his judgements on a different analysis of the task; he may think that other information is relevant, for example, relative water levels. Evidence for what he thinks is relevant can be found in the pattern of his judgements in many variations of the task and also in the justification he gives for his judgements. Development consists of changing the task analysis, including more constituents and more interrelationships between them. Granting all this, there are several possible ways in which new constituents could be added. One is that new constituents are added piecemeal, one at a time, in successive complications of the system.

---

[1] Since the act is generating a judgment, strictly speaking, the constituents—the child's *noticing* that water levels are different or *relating* width to height—are the actual components of that act. But it is simpler to talk as if the constituents are part of the situation.

Several years ago Jonckheere, Cromer and I made an observational study. We were interested in whether judgements would be easier if the quantities were, in fact, unequal than if they were equal. Therefore, we included two conditions where water was added or subtracted after the pouring was completed

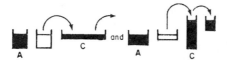

The finding that puzzled me was that several children maintained that A and C still had the same amount to drink. Notice that this finding calls into question these children's *correct* judgements on regular conservation tasks. Perhaps they had only one of the constituents of the correct answer; they knew that the original equality of the liquids was relevant but did not know that the addition or subtraction during pouring was relevant. This suggests that the development from non-conservation to conservation may be as follows:

1. Height alone is taken as relevant for amount judgements.
2. The original equality or inequality is taken as relevant.
3. The transformation (addition, subtraction or neither) is taken as relevant.

Once the child adds constituent 2 to his task analysis, he should no longer rely on constituent 1. Constituents 3 and 2 are not in that same relationship to each other; some children might pick up 2 before 3 and some others 3 before 2[2]. In the pretest of the studies summarized here, I included all cases necessary to demonstrate the piecemeal addition of the relevant constituents. Figure 1 shows the hypothetical patterns of judgements consistent with this view of development. The key groups are the intermediates, and the key responses are the false "same to drink" judgements.

The pretests revealed that there were pure non-conservers and pure conservers. Also, there were intermediates, 15% of whose judgements on tasks II (a and b) and III (a and b) were that A and C had the "same

[2] Evidence for the child's having constituent 3 but not 2 would be false "same to drink" judgements in the following situation: the two quantities start out *unequal* but none is added or subtracted

If the child says A = C in amount, he must lack constituent 2.

Type of task			Non-conservers, height the constituent	Intermedi-ates, one[1] relevant constituent	Intermedi-ates, one[2] relevant constituent	Full conservers, both relevant constituents
Regular conservation	Ia		C has more	A=C	A=C	A=C
	Ib		A has more	A=C	A=C	A=C
Some added or subtracted	IIa		A has more	A=C	C has more	C has more
	IIb	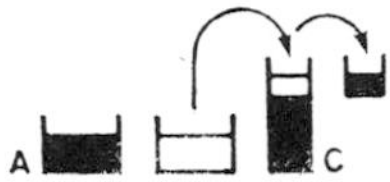	C has more	A=C	A has more	A has more
Not the same to start with	IIIa	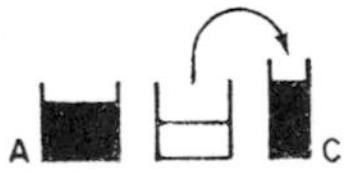	C has more	A has more	A=C	A has more
	IIIb	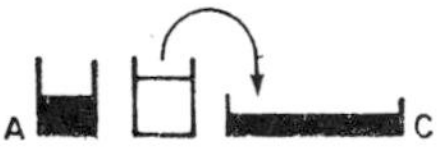	A has more	C has more	A=C	C has more

[1] These intermediates are basing their judgements on the original equality of the water *only*. Thus, they are correct on Tasks I and III, but not on II, when the transformation disturbs the original equality or inequality.

[2] These intermediates are basing their judgements on the nature of the transformation *only*. Thus, they are correct on Tasks I and II, but not on III. Mistakes on III are due to the fact that none was added or subtracted does not correctly imply that A and C are equal because A and B were not equal.

FIG. 1. Hypothetical patterns of judgements.

amount" to drink in them. Thus, these intermediates gave false "same to drink" judgements and might therefore have had only one of the relevant task analysis constituents.

The patterns made by the intermediates who were tested bear no resemblance to those shown in Fig. 1. Not one of the twenty who were tested made correct "same to drink" judgements systematically. There was no evidence for a piecemeal addition of the relevant constituents. Rather, the intermediate children had the same constituents as the conservers; they simply were not able to combine them into correct judgements and arguments. The chaotic patterns of judgements shown by all intermediates (correct judgements, judgements based on height, false "same to drink" judgements consistent with constituent 2 and also false "same amount to drink" judgements consistent with constituent 3 were all made by each intermediate child) is only a small part of the evidence for this claim.

The child's tasks include justifying his decisions. If the intermediate child differs from the non-conserver in having more constituents in his task analysis and from the conserver in having less, then his justifications should contain more arguments than non-conservers and fewer than conservers. To look at this, we must backtrack and briefly characterize the justifications given by the two extreme groups when they are asked "How do you know?" after a judgement. If they can think of anything at all to say, non-conservers characteristically mention only one argument—"because it's higher", "because it's more" (a reassertion of the judgement) being by far the most common response. In contrast, conservers' justifications are of several types, over half of which contain multiple arguments, as in "because that one had more to start with and you only poured it. It only looks less because it's in a wider glass". Among their justifications could be found statements of the two constituents in generating correct judgements, plus appeals to the appearance/reality distinction, suggestions of verification procedures, and explanations for changes in height in terms of width. What of the intermediate children? Their justifications were indistinguishable from the conservers—they showed all types and also gave multiple arguments on over half of their answers. But there was one important difference. In

Example 1: Judgement. "C has more to drink."
"How do you know?"
"Because B had more to start with."
(false)

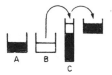

Example 2: Judgement. "C has more to drink."
"How do you know?"
"Because you took some out of there."
(inconsistent with judgement)

nineteen cases (contributed by thirteen children) the justifications were totally inappropriate. They were either false as in example 1 or inconsistent as in example 2.

No conserver ever made such bad arguments. Eighty per cent of these false and inconsistent arguments made by intermediates included at least one of the two constituents of the adult task analysis (inappropriately applied, of course). Thus, these children's justifications, as well as their chaotic patterns of judgements, support the view that they know what is relevant to the judgements, but simply are not skilled in putting it together correctly all the time. They do not systematically add constituents to their task analysis in a piecemeal way.

This leads to very inconsistent behaviour. Intermediates were significantly more likely to change their judgements than either of the other two groups, both spontaneously, and when given counter-suggestions[3]. Consider the following protocol on the "check test": Task—pour equal amounts in

Child 31. Poured the juice in the thinner glass a little higher (unintentionally). Said would choose the wider glass if thirsty because it had more in it. To equalize, took away some liquid from the thinner glass so they would be exactly same level. Then said would drink the liquid in the wider glass if thirsty, because it had more. Knew that the water from the wider glass would come higher when both were poured into the identical beakers. Maintained that really the two quantities were the same and one only appeared to be more when both were in the identical glasses.

Such inconsistency is common, but the point I would like to make now is that inconsistency is not a general property of the thinking of a child at a certain age or stage of development. It is task specific. Any child (or adult) would be inconsistent on *some* task which could be devised for him. Such inconsistency is found precisely in those cases where the child or adult knows several things which are relevant to some problem but cannot keep them all straight, or does not know all the relationships between them. For example, the check test is slightly harder than the conservation tasks. A child who passes all the conservation tasks, who is a consistent conserver, may well fail the check test, contradicting himself wildly.

[3] The standard Piagetian testing procedure includes a counter-suggestion to both correct and incorrect judgements. "Another little boy told me that they are really the same because they were the same in there and we only poured it. Was he right?" . . . "How could you convince him?"

It is important to remember that each intermediate made some correct judgements and some incorrect judgements; gave some valid justifications and some invalid ones. The descriptions I have given of intermediates, in terms of their not being able to combine skilfully the same battery of constituent information that the conservers infer their answers from, is open to two further interpretations. Perhaps the inter-mediates' right answers are not different from their wrong ones—random combinations of the same basic elements. That is, they know what information is relevant but cannot distinguish the valid inferences in this information from invalid ones. This view emphasizes the dif-ferences between intermediates and conservers; the conservers have structured the relevant information differently from the intermediates. This is the Piagetian view; that conservers think that conservation is necessary while intermediates do not (cf. Smedslund, 1961). The alter-native view, for which I will present evidence, states that there is no such structural watershed. First of all, the intermediates' reactions to counter-suggestions indicate that although they cannot consistently put the constituents together correctly, they recognize when they have done so. Their wavering at a counter-suggestion occurred only when their responses were incorrect and the counter-suggestions supplied correct judgements and justifications. Like conservers, intermediates never changed a judgement from right to wrong as the result of a counter-suggestion. As a second source of evidence, I would like to describe briefly an experiment which will further elucidate the skill model of cognitive competence.

The question asked in these experiments was what the reactions of children at different conservation levels would be if the water really changed in amount upon being poured into a new glass. What if a thimblefull became a bucketfull, or vice versa? I was interested in the answer to this question for two reasons. First, it provided a non-verbal way of probing for conservation. Perhaps even non-conservers would show surprise at such a violation of conservation. Secondly, it provided a direct test of whether conservers think conservation is necessary in a way that intermediates do not. Evidence for such a difference would be found if intermediates and non-conservers were not surprised when quantities changed, while conservers would indicate that they realize a trick had been played on them. Figure 2 shows the three tricks that were performed.

Reactions to the tricks were categorized into three categories—no reaction (level 0), a simple noting that the water level did not come to where it might have been expected (level 1), noting the discrepancy in an excited way, "That high!", "What happened?" (level 2). Only the level 2

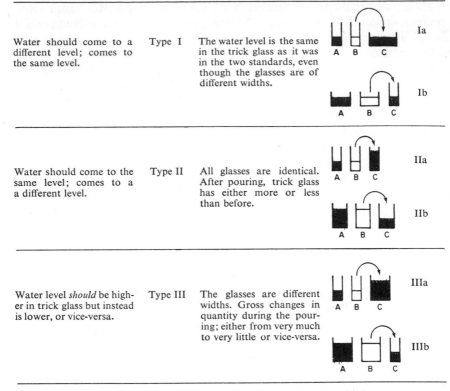

Water should come to a different level; comes to the same level.	Type I	The water level is the same in the trick glass as it was in the two standards, even though the glasses are of different widths.	Ia
			Ib
Water should come to the same level; comes to a a different level.	Type II	All glasses are identical. After pouring, trick glass has either more or less than before.	IIa
			IIb
Water level *should* be higher in trick glass but instead is lower, or vice-versa.	Type III	The glasses are different widths. Gross changes in quantity during the pouring; either from very much to very little or vice-versa.	IIIa
			IIIb

FIG. 2. The three trick problems presented to the children.

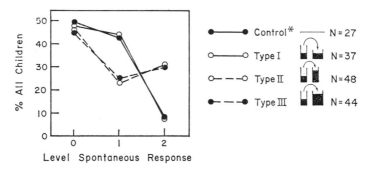

*Control pourings when FP was not exactly correct

FIG. 3. Per cent children showing each degree of surprise to the four pourings (control and three tricks).

reactions could be counted as "surprise". Figure 3 shows that there was very little surprise. The children's reactions to the trick where the water came to the same level in a wider or thinner glass as it had been in the standard (Type I trick) were indistinguishable from their reactions to a control pouring (no tricks) where the water level happened not to have been correctly predicted. There was slightly more surprise to the Type II and Type III tricks but even in these cases, 70% of the children's reactions were indistinguishable from their reactions to the control pouring. More important, conservers did not show significantly more surprise than the intermediates. Sixty per cent of the conservers had at least one level 2 reaction; 44% of the intermediates had at least one level 2 reaction.

Why did the conservers, who had correctly judged all six of the tasks on the pretest, accept without reaction the tricks in Fig. 2? To understand this, it is necessary to look at what the conservers did when presented with these tricks. When asked if there was still the same amount to drink, they said yes there was. Asked to justify their statement, they produced as fine a collection of false and inconsistent justifications as ever produced by the intermediates on the pretest. For instance, several children, upon seeing

said, "it came higher because it's so much thinner". Others claimed they saw me add some. Some children denied that the water level was higher; others said the two quantities were still the same because the water level was higher; yet others appealed to the blueness of the water, or the lips on the glasses. This might appear to prove that conservers think conservation is necessary even though they did not show more surprise than the intermediates. But the intermediates also maintained (falsely) that the quantities were still the same (see Fig. 4)[4] and produced a string of false and inconsistent justifications for their judgements.

These tricks present the children with a conflict between different constituents of the task analysis. First, the quantities were the same to start with and none was added or subtracted (as far as the child could see), and second, appearances dictated unambiguously that the quantities were now different. If any intermediate or conserver were shown the

[4] For the purposes of Fig. 4, the intermediates were broken up into three sub-divisions according to how many of the questions on the pretest they got right. LINTs (low intermediates) got only one or two judgements of the six pretest tasks right. Even they think conservation is as "necessary" as do conservers.

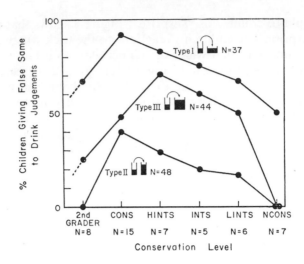

Summary:
   78% of all subjects say A and C have the same amount to drink on Type I tricks

   43% of all subjects say A and C have the same amount to drink on Type III tricks

   21% of all subjects say A and C have the same amount to drink on Type II tricks

* Differences between 2nd graders and conservers sig. at 0·05 level (Fisher exact test) on Type II tricks only.
   Differences between CONS, HINT, INT, LINT/ and NCONS sig. at 0·01 level (Fisher exact test) on Type III trick.
   Differences between CONS, HINT, INT, LINT/ and NCONS on Type II trick not significant ($p = 0·11$ Fisher exact).

FIG. 4. Percentage of subjects who said the two still had the same amount to drink on the three change tricks.

resultant quantities without the history, he would correctly judge the amounts unequal. Figure 4 shows that this conflict was not resolved in the same way on all three types of tricks. Type I tricks

yielded "same amount to drink" judgements 78% of the time; Type III tricks

in 43% of all judgements and Type II tricks

on only 21% of all judgements. This provides us with a puzzle. The actual quantity change and the appearance of inequality was the strongest in Type III tricks—the dimensions of one quantity were greater in both width and height. Why, then, were children more likely to judge the quantities equal in this case than they were when the dimensions of the two quantities differed only in one dimension (Type II tricks). A clue comes from the justifications they gave. Take

as an example. Many children, having judged the quantities equal, bolstered their answer with the argument that C was wider than A and that's why the water came higher! Their reasoning apparently was as follows—C looks more than A, something must account for this difference in appearance. Glass C is different from glass A, it is wider so this difference must account for the difference in appearance of the two quantities. In Type II tricks the two glasses were identical, so this form of reasoning was not available to them. There is nothing which can explain away the apparent change in amount, so in this case the children were less likely to deny that the amounts had changed. A similar argument accounts for the preponderance of "same to drink" judgements on Type I tricks, e.g.

The intermediates and conservers appealed to the equality of heights in bolstering their judgements that the amounts were equal.

The children were seeking local consistency. They did not immediately see that there had been a trick, so they hung on to anything which would allow them to dismiss the problem, even when they had demonstrated amply in other situations that they knew that water comes lower in wider glasses and that equal heights are not sufficient grounds for a judgement of equal amounts.

There was a difference between conservers and intermediates, an important one. After the child had made a judgement and offered a justification, I continued questioning, pointing out the inconsistencies. For example, on

one child said that the two quantities were the same because they were the same to start with and the quantity in C only looked more. Asked why it looked more, he said it was because the glass was wider. At that point, I asked whether water usually comes higher in a wider glass. He said, "Yes, . . . no, I don't think so—Hey, what happened?" This child was a conserver. Conservers were significantly more likely than intermediates to realize that there was something wrong, that there had been a trick, after such a line of questioning. The intermediates saw the contradictions; they often said "I don't know" when pressed in the above manner, but they were not sure enough of their expectancies to figure out that something impossible had happened[5].

It is clear that even "conservers" were "intermediates" when compared to adults on these problems. Adults immediately see the amounts as having changed in an impossible way. I looked at some second grade[6] "conservers" who were indistinguishable from my 5–7-year-old "conservers" on the pretests; their data is also plotted on Figs 3 and 4. Although they are more like adults than the younger children, even they do not always realize that the amounts have changed and that there has been a trick. Seeing that there was a trick was a slow process. The child had to notice that something was wrong, try to explain it away, fail, and draw the conclusion that it was not his fault that he could not explain it away. Only on the last point did the "conservers" and "intermediates" differ. The "intermediates" judgements and their initial attempts at understanding what was happening depended upon the

[5] My criterion for "surprise" was not too stringent. All children in this sample, including non-conservers, realized that there was a trick at some point in the procedure. If they had not seen it by the end of the three tricks described above, they were shown a whole pitcher being poured into a glass whose level did not change, and then water going up and down by itself.

[6] Second grade is between ages 7–8 years.

same task analysis that the "conservers" made. They simply were not as sure of each of the components; their expectanies were not as firm, and therefore, they were not able to draw the same conclusions.

Let me return to the skill analogy. I am claiming that making conservation judgements and justifications is a skill, the possible constituents of which are the separable sources of relevant information in the task analysis—original equality or inequality, the nature of the transformation, relative heights and widths of the liquid, etc. The intermediates had the same constituents as the conservers, they knew what was relevant and what inferences to draw from the relevance; they simply were less skilled in manipulating and integrating these constituents.

It is my contention that many, if not all, cognitive achievements are similar to those described above. One might ask how such intellectual skills differ from motor skills. First of all, the constituents of a motor skill are usually thought of as motoric acts (cf. Bruner's descriptions of the development of reaching). But even clear examples of motor skills require an analysis of the task, independent of the movements the person makes. Consider the game Elliott and Connolly describe in this volume. Part of the problem for the child is to figure out the two degrees of freedom of the apparatus and to learn to manipulate them simultaneously. Secondly, a more obvious difference between intellectual skills and motor skills is that in most motor skills there is a direct test of inappropriate task analysis or execution of the integrated act—the goal is either realized or it is not; in Elliott and Connolly's case, the ball either goes into the hole or it does not. In the conservation case, how is the child to know whether his analysis of relevant features and the inferences he draws from them is correct or not? Even on this point, there is no complete dichotomy between motor problems and intellectual problems. Most motor skills involve a constant, monitoring, feedback, but intellectual solutions must also ultimately be tested against reality. The constituents of task analysis must ultimately derive from the child's pursuits, his practical problems. Conversely, not all development of motor skills depends upon direct feedback from the environment. Consider a complex motor skill like skiing. Long after a learner is able to make it down a hill without falling, he is distinguishing good Stem Christies from bad ones—the good ones feel right, everything fits. In an intellectual task, such as making conservation judgements, the child's criterion for a good answer is his ability to make everything he thinks relevant consistent with that answer. This criterion, like that of "feeling right", does not depend upon a constant monitoring feedback.

In the above section, I have described the development of a particular cognitive skill and discussed its relationship to the development of motor skills. How, within this framework, are we to conceive of overall cognitive development? How do we conceive of the cognitive differences between three-year-olds and seven-year-olds? My answer is that age related cognitive differences are separable into two parts, in principle distinguishable from each other. First, there is a maturational component. One can conceive of this component as absolute information processing capacity: a younger child has a shorter memory, can handle fewer constituents at once, etc. The development of this processing space follows from the maturation of the nervous system. The second component is simply a battery of individual skills, bits and pieces of acquired knowledge, that the child has mastered in the way described above. The principles of acquiring these skills are the same no matter how old the person is; my first graders wrestling with the surprise tricks were not so different from a scientist whose head is swimming in confusing data (see Hanson, 1965). This process includes learning new constituents, their modularization, and their concomitant incorporation into larger structured wholes.

There is no doubt that seven-year-olds can solve cognitive problems that three-year-olds cannot solve. Two sources are suggested for the three-year-olds' relatively immature behaviour—first, a relatively limited processing machinery, and second, relatively limited knowledge from which to extract the variables to fit into that machinery. There two sources of immaturity are independent of each other; a child will get better just by getting older, even if he is not given practice which increases or reinforces his knowledge. Within the limits of his processing machinery, he can also be helped by being given practice in the constituent skills[7]. There are several situations where a child performs worse than might be expected which also can be interpreted in terms of an interaction between processing space and knowledge. Elliott and Connolly (this volume) described a case of a child's grip on a paintbrush showing a lag of over two years when compared with his grip on sticks he uses for some other purpose. Apparently, the requirement of painting with a brush reduces the degrees of freedom he can cope with in this grip (Connolly and Elliott, 1972). Anxiety also seems to reduce available processing space. This is the reason for the practice of familiarizing a child with the tester and the situation before an intelligence test.

The chacterization proposed here posits no qualitative cognitive differences between children at different ages. That is, the differences between three-year-olds and seven-year-olds cannot be expressed in

---

[7] All the experiments which succeed in teaching four-year-olds to solve Piagetian concrete operational problems (e.g. Bryant and Trabasso, 1971) can be seen as examples of the latter type of improvement.

terms of the former being pre-operational while the latter are operational, the former being iconic while the latter are symbolic, the former being tolerant of contradictions while the latter are not. Each of these broad distinctions (and many more as well) may well apply to the stages a child goes through in solving a particular problem, but this will be true of all ages. I cannot present here my full arguments for this position; rather let us consider the implications of this view for the question posed in this volume—what effects do early problem solving experiences have on later cognitive functioning?

GENERAL COMPETENCE AND EARLY EXPERIENCE

The first question to be considered is whether there is a general problem solving cognitive skill (or set of skills) of which individuals have a differing command. If so, what is the nature of this battery of skills, and does early experience help or hinder its development? Is such experience provided differentially by different social classes? I would argue against there being any such general, overall, cognitive competence correlated with social class. The argument will proceed first by considering and rejecting candidates for such basic skills and then by giving principal reasons to doubt their existence. Finally, the consequences of early competence, or lack of competence, in problem solving will be considered.

What are candidates for the general cognitive skills we seek? I will discuss three suggestions that have been made:

1. Basic linguistic capacities which underly all cognitive functioning.
2. General ability in acquiring new skills (according to the theory outlined in the first section). That is, general skill in considering alternatives, structuring a task, integrating multiple constituents, etc.
3. Personality factors with cognitive implications—sense of efficacy, goal setting and seeking, ability to delay gratification, etc.

The above are not sharply distinguishable from each other. Numbers 2 and 3 are very closely related, as goal seeking behaviour lies at the core of the theory of skill. They differ in that in the case of number 3, social and personality factors are assumed to interfere with cognitive functioning while in the case of number 2, the cognitive skills themselves are seen to be less developed.

Intelligence cannot be considered as a basic problem-solving skill. It is the wrong kind of construct, developed as an atheoretical predictive tool, it cannot be analysed into specific, named skills which in turn could be analysed into their constituent skills[8]. Intelligence is not a specific achievement like conservation, English syntax, arithmetic, or walking. I am not denying that there are social class differences in intelligence, nor that these may be important. Rather that the question being asked in this volume is whether there are specific basic cognitive achievements which are learned differentially by different people. If there are, one explanation for that difference might be intelligence differences. But, given the proper analysis of these basic skills into their constituents, the theory of skill acquisition outlined in the first section predicts that relative deficiencies in capacity, like processing space, can be compensated for by extra time and practice in the modularization of the constituent skills.

Let us begin with the first candidate—that there are basic differences in the linguistic capacities of different segments of the population. We must distinguish between true linguistic differences in language, in phonetics, syntax or semantics, and other cognitive differences which happen to be reflected in language. Linguistic differences between social classes which are supposed to have far-reaching cognitive implications are usually the latter. Most reduce to the second set of possibilities, type 2.

For example, consider the well-documented difference in the language used by mothers of different social classes in teaching their children (Bee *et al.*, 1969; Hess and Shipman, 1965). The language of the middle class mothers is characterized as more abstract, more structured and structuring than the language of lower class mothers. The former group uses language to dissect the task, to break it up into manageable subproblems; the latter uses language to plead, to complain, to order. Differences in the use of language are extremely important, but do not constitute evidence for a difference in *language* between the two groups of mothers. The theory of skill development outlined in the first section has implications for teaching—break the skill into its constituent parts so the child can modularize them; reduce the degrees of freedom while he learns to combine these constituents into higher order sequences. Such structuring is the goal of any modelling or teaching, whether mediated by language or not[9]. I believe that the same differences would be found between the above groups of mothers even if they had been

[8] There are many theories of the structure of intelligence in terms of hierarchy of capacities. But a capacity is different from a skill; a skill is content full, not content free. One can have an arithmetical capacity without knowing arithmetic; one cannot have skill in arithmetic without having practised and learned (as in the first section) multiple constituent arithmetical skills.

[9] Bruner discusses (in this volume) Susan Reit's training of young apes, necessarily nonlinguistic training, in just these terms.

told to help their children on the same tasks *without speaking to them at all*. What is being shown here, apparently, is a type 2 candidate for the difference between mothers from different social classes.

In the study of linguistic differences between children the work of Turner and Pickvance (1970) is important and revealing. They found that, given problems to solve (asked questions) children from higher socio-economic backgrounds express more uncertainty (say they don't know) more often than do those from lower socio-economic backgrounds. The former show that they are aware of more alternatives, can better formulate a problem, and are more likely to ask adults for help. Turner and Pickvance themselves point out that these differences obtain even when "verbal ability is controlled for". Thus, they do not think these differences in language reflect true linguistic differences. Indeed, these differences are paradigm examples of the type 2 hypothesis. I believe that Bernstein's distinction between restricted and elaborated codes is yet another example of this sort (Bernstein, 1961).

Working with much younger children, Tough (1970) found that three-year-olds from higher socio-economic backgrounds singled out more qualitatively different aspects of their environment, talked more about cause and effect, than did lower socio-economic three-year-olds matched in I.Q. and roughly for linguistic output. It is in this area that cognitive and linguistic differences overlap. What a child chooses to talk about reflects his immediate concerns and the degree to which he has structured his world. Vocabulary differentiation similarly reflects his understanding of his world—the modularization of his knowledge. Thus, these results are not simple linguistic differences. I do not want to appear to deny there are social class differences in truly linguistic development, certainly there are (Williams, 1970). Joan Tough has some good examples. For instance, the lower socio-economic class children in her sample were most likely to use pronouns like "he" or "it" to refer to objects and people in the field while higher socio-economic class children also used these pronouns to refer to things in the previous linguistic context. This is a syntactic advance. Indeed, we should not be surprised at evidence that children learn the rules of their language at differential rates, for language learning is an achievement which can be looked at in exactly the same terms as the achievement of other skills (see under A Model of Problem Solving in Early Childhood).

However, I see no way that such truly linguistic differences between individuals could form the basis of important differences in cognitive functioning. Rather, there are major reasons to doubt that they could have such a role. First of all, there have now been several studies of the relationship between cognitive development and linguistic development

(Carey, 1971; Cromer, 1968; Sinclair-de-Zwart, 1967) which have concluded that conceptual immaturity hampers linguistic development, rather than vice versa. Secondly, most of the phonetic, syntactic and semantic rules of language are mastered by the time a child is six years old; conceptual development never ends. Cazden and McNeill, in their contribution to this volume, discuss the "transparency" of language to the developing child. The child learning language appears to be learning about the world and picking up his language almost as a by-product. His parents' corrections of his speech are most often corrections of the content of his statements, of their truth or appropriateness, rather than their linguistic form. Complex as the task of formalizing the rules of a natural language is, none the less, the child easily masters it and the small differences in the rate at which individual children do so cannot be the basis of overall cognitive difference among people.

Although I reject truly linguistic differences as a viable possibility for differences in basic cognitive skills, these differences may well be very important to the learning of particular skills. Take learning to read, for example. As in the learning of any skill, learning to read places demands upon available processing space[10]. If a child's linguistic skills are relatively little modularized, then the language which is being read will occupy relatively more of his processing space, thus detracting from the development of reading. Later in this same child's school career, when reading is a source of information his relatively unmodularized reading skills would detract from the processing he would need in order to master the material he is reading. Thus, early truly linguistic differences might be expected to have a snowballing effect on a child's school performance[11]. Since language is like any cognitive achievement, such differences can theoretically be avoided by giving a young child practice in the constituent skills. There is every reason to do so, but that reason is not to prevent the child from "thinking differently" from other children.

To summarize, I have rejected differences in truly linguistic skills as a candidate for overall, basic, cognitive differences between social classes. Furthermore, I have shown that many "linguistic" differences that have been found between various groups of people are really examples of my second candidate for basic cognitive differences, overall competence in acquiring skill, to which we will now turn. Do people differ in their

---

[10] The extreme linguistic simplicity of first texts, written in language appropriate to the speech of much younger children, is an educational device based on these considerations. Just as when a child needs to paint with a brush, his grip of it regresses a few years, so when he must read language, it is best to provide him with language modularized for years, so the language itself makes no demands on his attention or efforts.

[11] I am indebted to Courtney Cazden for this argument.

ability to recognize problems, set cognitive goals for themselves, analyse, structure and modularize constituents? Are these higher order skills acquired more easily by some people than by others? I would argue that there are no differences between people in the process of acquiring skills (except perhaps in extreme pathological cases). Instead the differences that have been found reflect domain specific, local rather than global, developmental differences. Before I present this argument, I would like to give a made-up example taken from this volume to show the form of a very common and important mistake which I believe permeates the search for basic cognitive differences between people.

Elliott and Connolly described cross-sectional stages found in children's acquisition of a motor skill—the skill of manipulating two knobs which tilt a board along two axes to make a ball go diagonally across the board. They pointed out that in the early stages of task analysis, children often expressed their frustration by saying "*it* won't do it". In later stages, when the child understood the nature of the task (had analysed it in terms of the major constituents), failure was described as "*I* can't do it". New, this difference is consistent with the interpretation that the younger children have a great sense of their own powerlessness, while the older children have a sense of mastery of their environment. This difference (certainly a global one) is development—every child presumably goes through a stage of feeling powerless before feeling competent. This appears to be exactly the type of overall development hypothesis that I argued against in the first section of this paper. My position is that such a difference is task specific, it is not an overall stage in a child's development. That is, it reflects competence with respect of the particular task used by Elliott and Connolly. The child who says "it won't do it" does not have any of the constituents of the task—doesn't have a clue as to how the apparatus works. Thus the "sense of powerlessness" is an emotional factor caused by a local limitation of skill; it is not a general personality trait of young children. I am certain that I could find a related, slightly more complex, motor skill on which the older children would express their frustration in terms of "it won't do it". Furthermore, the problem becomes compounded. According to the theory of skills being proposed here, immature behaviour on a particular task results either from relatively limited processing space or relatively incomplete modularization of the constituent skills. One could assume that the children in lower class families are less comfortable with strange adults and this detracts from the processing space available to them in the Elliott and Connolly task. Or assume that they mature more slowly, or that they simply have had less experience with fine manipulatory toys, so they have less command of the constituent skills. All of these assumptions are reasonable. It follows that lower socio-economic status children will perform in a more immature way on this task than upper or middle socio-economic status children of the same age. Then, the former children will be more likely to say "It won't do it", than the latter, who will be more likely to say "I can't do it". From this, our made-up experimenter would conclude that the poor have a greater sense of powerlessness than do the comfortably well off. This inference is doubly flawed. It is flawed because the general developmental difference was not an overall stage difference and it is flawed because the very same lower socio-economic status children in a few months or a year would act exactly as the upper and middle socio-economic status children do on that same task. A general sense of powerlessness cannot be attributed to lower socio-economic status children on the basis of single task evidence of this sort—it is important to check first that the difference found is not part of the developmental stages all children go through with respect to that task[12]. I hope that the form of this argument is clear, because I believe that many so-called general differences between social class are of this type.

With this caveat in mind, reconsider the Turner and Pickvance results discussed above. The differences between *groups* of people that they inferred are paradigm examples of differences found in the stages which a single child goes through in solving a particular problem (see first section). Thus, their results may show no more than that middle socioeconomic status subjects were better at the particular tasks they used and not that the middle socio-economic status subjects were in general more aware of alternatives, better able to formulate problems, etc.

This point is the main burden of several related attacks on the thesis that blacks and the very poor have basic cognitive-linguistic differences from middle class whites (Labov, 1970; Moffett, 1968; Strandberg and Griffeth, 1968). These writers contend that the differences between the groups disappear if you control for the child's interest and involvement in the task. For instance, Moffett found that language complexity increases when the child writes or speaks about an event in which he himself has participated in a goal-seeking manner. He presents protocols comparing a child's description of a fight he himself was in and the same child's description of an episode of *A Man from UNCLE*. The latter is incoherent, composed mostly of simple declarative sentences; the former is full of syntactically complex multiply embedded forms and is fully coherent. Strandberg and Griffeth present a similar comparison

[12] I want to re-emphasize that this is a made-up example; Elliott and Connolly did not themselves draw any such inferences from their example. I am using this as a vehicle to draw attention to an important criticism.

of a child's description of a picture he took of his own tree house and his description of a picture somebody else took of a horse. Finally, Labov compares the monosyllabic speech of a ghetto youth brought into the laboratory for testing with the speech of the same child when the same tester came to his house, produced a snack, and began talking to the boy and some friends in street talk. The lesson is clear—the complexity of a child's speech is extremely task specific. It depends upon his command of the particular material he is talking about and his ease in the overall situation.

Hess and Shipman proved that maternal variables can directly affect the child's mastery of a particular skill. Although highly correlated with socio-economic status and maternal I.Q., the maternal teaching variables were the best predictors of success on the taught tasks, better than maternal socio-economic status or I.Q. But we are looking for overall cognitive differences between children resulting from such differences in mothering. Several studies suggest that there are such overall differences (Ainsworth and Bell, this volume; Schoggen, 1969). In all of these studies, broad cognitive developmental[13] differences are related to differences in the children's interactions with their mothers. However, such results are consistent with two quite different interpretations. One, the differences between children and the sums of differences in many particular, narrow skills in which the maternal variables account for the differences directly, as in Hess and Shipman. Two, the maternal variables account for overall cognitive differences in children, such as differences in the general competence in acquiring skills (setting goals, analysing problems, integrating constituents, etc.). Most of my reasons for favouring the first interpretation have already been presented. Briefly restated, the descriptions of overall differences between social classes are usually appropriate to descriptions of stages in an individual's solving of particular problems, and thus suspicions of the fallacy revealed in my "It won't do it", example arises. This suspicion is strengthened if the differences disappear when widely different tasks (in terms of the child's involvement in them[14]) are used. This is sometimes the case. Finally, I have one more reason for my preference for the first interpretation, although I realize that it is not a conclusive argument.

The model of skill acquisition presented in the first section is a very weak descriptive theory. It applies to motor and cognitive achievements

---

[13] I will discuss below the non-cognitive differences suggested by these studies.

[14] I do not see the child's involvement in the tasks as a motivational variable. The consequences of involvement are that the constituents of the task are better modularized, so the child shows higher level skills.

made by the developing child (and developed adult) minute by minute throughout his life. It simply seems unlikely to me that people can differ in functioning so fundamentally. I envisage the model of skill acquisition presented in the first section to be as basic to a cognitive theory as the concept "reinforcement" is to behaviourism. To postulate that people differ in this functioning is anathema to me, as the postulation that people differ in their susceptibility to the law of effect would be anathema to a behaviourist[15]. The skill of problem solving—that is, the skills of analysing problems, setting subgoals, making new combinations of practised constituents, etc.—is the wrong kind of theoretical construct in terms of which to expect differences among people. This is especially true because there is a perfectly sensible and simpler explanation for apparent differences in problem solving skills and that is differences in the battery of problems which have already been solved, differences in the battery of modularized skills. However, the practical consequences of both interpretations seem to me to be identical.

To summarize, I have argued against there being identifiable basic linguistic or cognitive skills which are learned early in life and which underlie differences in cognitive functioning among people. Instead, I have argued that whatever the cognitive differences are among people they can best be seen in terms of differences in their arsenal of modularized skills. There is not a small number of such skills, rather the number is staggeringly large—each piece of knowledge can be thought of in this way. These differences develop early in life and they are extremely important. Because each new skill depends upon the last, the effect of unmodularized skills is to detract from building new ones. This becomes cumulatively more disastrous in school, where a pace is set for mastering new material.

This view has clear implications for the educator interested in the cognitive development of the child. An analysis of the constituents of higher order skills deemed important is needed. Teaching procedures which allow the child to modularize the successive levels of constituents are needed. These procedures must give the child practice in using the constituents in as many contexts as possible since this is what is needed for their modularization. Thus, pre-school experiences should be designed to give a child practice in his arsenal of skills. It should concentrate on the explosion of knowledge which can be put to later use and which will not drain processing capacity when new skills are called for, involving that knowledge.

[15] A behaviourist would allow individual differences in the effect of a single reinforcer, but would require that all the behaviour of every person be some function of his past reinforcement history.

The above concerns the purely cognitive aspects of the child. Let us turn now to our third candidate for general differences between people which might be established early in life, I refer to personality factors. Perhaps there are general differences between social classes which are not basic differences in language or ways of problem solving, but personality factors which relate to cognitive functioning (Greenfield, 1969). It would seem probable, to some extent at least, that this hypothesis is correct. For instance, Coleman found that the self-concept and a feeling of control accounts for more variance in performance in grades 9–12 than any other family background, or school characteristic (Coleman *et al.*, 1966). Let us consider this hypothesis. There are at least three ways that "sense of efficacy" can be conceived, each with different practical implications.

1. There is a "sense of powerlessness" that the poor have which results from a correct analysis of their political and social situation. While this may lead to defeatism and ennui in some people, this is not a cognitive problem, nor is it going to be cured by giving the child a sense of efficacy in his early life. It will be cured as the political and social situation changes.

2. There is a "sense of powerlessness" or negative self image which is a deep personality variable that accounts for variance within a social group. For example, a study of which teenagers drop out of high school and which do not in a depressed black area in Boston revealed this personality difference (Weissburg, unpublished). Those with low self-images had a low tolerance of frustration, were unable to set realistic goals for themselves in life and were deeply hopeless. These personality variables have cognitive implications, but it would be naive to think that they were cognitive in origin, and could be prevented by giving the child more practice in solving problems early in life. Social work and therapeutic intervention seem called for in these cases.

3. There is a "sense of powerlessness" that is task specific, a frustration which follows from not having understood the nature of the task even at a primitive level (see the imaginary example based on Elliott and Connolly's work above). This is not an overall personality factor—it relates to an immediate assessment of local competence. This local sense of "powerlessness" can be minimized by good teaching of particular tasks, good general structuring of the environment, helping the child acquire the constituent skills he needs in order to master the skills appropriate to his developmental level. The pre-school experience the child needs to maximize this sort of "sense of efficacy" is that cognitive programme outlined above.

It is most important that the sense of "powerlessness" described in three different situations above should not be confused, since each is quite distinct from the others and requires a different analysis.

I have argued here that there are no basic linguistic or cognitive differences in people's problem solving or thinking. Much of the argument may have seemed of hair-splitting theoretical interest only, but I believe that it has important practical consequences. If one believes that the poor think differently from the rich because of some simple difference in linguistic or cognitive skills suitable for enshrining in a catchphrase such as Bernstein's restricted *v.* elaborated code, then one would set oneself the goal of preventing that difference in linguistic or cognitive skills from arising. I believe such approaches would prove fruitless. I have tried to show that the search for such fundamental differences in ways of problem solving is doomed to failure, at least in our present state of theorizing about cognitive functioning. We do know enough about the mechanisms involved in learning particular skills to design structured and supportive environments for the child's pre-school experiences; at present, this is where our efforts should be concentrated.

References

AINSWORTH, M. D. S. and BELL, S. M. 1974. Mother–infant interaction and the development of competence. This volume.

BEE, H. L., VAN EGEREN, L. F., STREISSGUTH, A. P., NYMAN, B. A. and LECKIE, M. S. 1969. Social class differences in maternal teaching strategies and speech patterns. *Develop. Psychol.*, **1**, 726–734.

BERNSTEIN, B. 1961. Social class and linguistic development: a theory of social learning. In A. H. Halsey, J. Floyd, and C. A. Anderson (Eds.), *Education economy and society*. Free Press, Glencoe, Illinois.

BERNSTEIN, N. 1967. *The co-ordination and regulation of movements.* Pergamon Press, Oxford.

BRUNER, J. S. 1969. Origins of problems solving strategies in skill acquisition. Presented at the XIX International Congress of Psychology, London, July 1969.

BRUNER, J. S. 1973. Nature and uses of immaturity. This volume.

BRUNER, J. S. and KOSLOWSKY, B. 1972. Visually preadapted constituents of manipulatory action. *Perception*, **1**, 3–14.

BRYANT, P. E. and TRABASSO, T. 1971. Transitive inferences and memory in young children. *Nature* (Lond). **232**, 456–458.

CAREY, S. E. 1971. Are children little scientists with false theories of the world? Unpublished Ph.D. thesis, Harvard University.

CAZDEN, C. 1974. Two paradoxes in the acquisition of language structure and function. This volume.

COLEMAN, J. S. *et al.* 1966. *Equality of educational opportunity.* U.S. Department of Health, Education and Welfare, Office of Education, Washington, D.C.

CONNOLLY, K. 1973. Factors influencing the learning of manual skills by young children. In R. A. Hinde and J. S. Hinde (Eds.), *Constraints on learning: limitations and predispositions.* Academic Press, London.

CONNOLLY, K. and ELLIOTT, J. 1972. The evolution and ontogeny of hand function. In N. Blurton Jones (Ed.), *Ethological studies of child behaviour.* Cambridge University Press, Cambridge.

CROMER, R. F. 1968. The development of temporal reference during the acquisition of language. Unpublished Ph.D. thesis, Harvard University.

ELLIOTT, J. and CONNOLLY, K. 1973. Hierarchical structure in skill development. This volume.

GREENFIELD, P. M. 1969. Goal as environmental variable in the development of intelligence. Presented at Conference of "Contributions to Intelligence", University of Illinois, Urbana.

HAGGSTROM, W. 1964. The power of the poor. In F. Fiessman, J. Cohen and A. Pearl (Eds.), *Mental health of the poor.* Free Press, Glencoe, Illinois.

HANSON, N. R. 1965. *Patterns of discovery.* Cambridge University Press, Cambridge.

HESS, R. D. and SHIPMAN, V. 1965. Early experience and socialization of cognitive modes in children. *Child Dev.*, **36**, 869–886.

KLAUS, R. and GRAY, S. 1968. The early training project for disadvantaged children: a report after five years. *Monog. Soc. Child Dev.*, **33**.

LABOV, W. 1970. The logic of non-standard English. In F. Williams (Ed.), *Language and poverty.* Markham, Chicago.

MCNEILL, D. 1973. How to resolve two paradoxes and escape a dilemma: comments on Dr. Cazden's paper. This volume.

MOFFETT, J. 1968. *Teaching the universe of discourse.* Houghton, Boston.

SCHOGGEN, M. 1969. *An ecological study of three-year-olds at home.* George Peabody College for Teachers, Nashville, Tennessee.

SINCLAIR-DE-ZWART, H. 1967. *Acquisition due langage et development de la pensee: sous-systemes linguistiques et operations concretes.* Dunod, Paris.

SMEDSLUND, J. 1961. The acquisition of conservation of substance and weight in children, III. Extinction of conservation of weight acquired "normally" and by means of empirical controls on a balance. *Scand. J. Psychol.*, **2**, 85–87.

STRANDBERG, T. E. and GRIFFETH, J. 1968. A study of the effects of training in visual literacy on verbal language behavior. Eastern Illinois University.

TOUGH, J. 1969. Language and environment: an interim report of a longitudinal study. University of Leeds, Institute of Education.

TURNER, G. J. and PICKVANCE, R. E. 1970. Social class differences in the expression of uncertainty in five-year-old children. Sociological Research Unit, University of London, Institute of Education.

WEISSBERG, C. Project pathways: Harvard University; Study of high school dropouts. Unpublished.

WELFORD, A. T. 1968. *Fundamentals of skill.* Methuen, London.

WILLIAMS, F. (Ed.). 1970. *Language and poverty.* Markham, Chicago.

Language Acquisition and Development

Two Paradoxes in the Acquisition of Language Structure and Functions[1]

COURTNEY B. CAZDEN

Harvard University

DISCUSSIONS OF SKILLED performance usually include speaking as one example—along with other behaviours as diverse as spelling, playing chess, swimming, bicycling, and playing the piano (see Miller *et al.*, 1960; and three philosophers: Polanyi, 1964; Ryle, 1949; Scheffler, 1965). Scheffler and Polanyi distinguish between two levels of skilled performance—levels in the sense of a set of nested hierarchies in which one level is a component of the next. Scheffler uses the terms "facilities" and "critical skills" to contrast them, and places speaking, or "grammatical talk" as he calls it, at the lower level:

> Grammatical talk, like observance of chess propriety, is an ingredient of intelligent performance. It is a bit of know-how nested within another, more complex, bit of know-how. None the less, it is not itself of the same order, being removed from the sphere of critical judgement, which focuses on the whole (Scheffler, 1965, p. 100).

Polanyi discusses the same distinction as two kinds of awareness: subsidiary and focal. When hammering in a nail, the nail is the focal object of our attention, while the hammer is the subsidiary instrument of it:

> Subsidiary awareness and focal awareness are mutually exclusive. If a pianist shifts his attention from the piece he is playing to the observation of what he is doing with his fingers while playing it, he gets confused and may have to stop. This happens generally if we switch our focal attention to particulars of which we had previously been aware only in their subsidiary role. . . . This scheme can be easily reformulated and expanded in

[1] An earlier version of part of this paper was presented at the New England Psychological Association, New Haven, 13 November 1971. Some of the research reported herein was supported by a grant from the Ford Foundation to Courtney B. Cazden.

terms of *meaning*. If we discredit the usefulness of a tool, its meaning as a tool is gone. All particulars become meaningless if we lose sight of the pattern which they jointly constitute.

The most pregnant carriers of meaning are of course the words of a language, and it is interesting to recall that when we use words in speech or writing we are aware of them only in a subsidiary manner. This fact is usually described as the *transparency* of language (Polanyi, 1964, pp. 56–57).

Everything we know about the language of adults and children justifies this distinction between "facility" and "critical skills". We can consider knowing how to speak and comprehend sentences as a facility, attended to only in a subsidiary way as it constitutes a part of some higher order unit of behaviour which can be called a critical skill and to which we give our focal attention. The more familiar terms for these two aspects of speech are language structure and language functions respectively, but we do not always realize the difference in our level of attention to them.

It is intuitively obvious to us as adult language users that when either speaking or listening, our attention is focused not on sounds or words of syntactic patterns, but on the meaning and intention of what we or someone else is trying to say. It is less obvious that, with the exception of self-initiated play with sounds and practice of syntactic patterns (Weir, 1962), the same is true of the child language learner.

Descriptions of spontaneous mother–child interaction can be summarized. First, adults simplify their speech to young children. Snow (1972) shows that women, whether or not they are mothers, simplify their speech in particular ways, and Drach's analysis of the speech of a lower-class black mother (Slobin, 1968) shows that such simplification is not confined to middle class adults. Martin Richards spoke at this conference about the special behaviour of mothers towards their infants. There may be special characteristics, as yet unidentified, of the speech of mothers to their own babies, but rules for simplifying speech to children seem to be a part of general adult communicative competence. Second, parental responses are fitted to the child's speech in the form of expansions and extensions (see Cazden, in press, for one recent discussion). Third, there is no deliberate sequencing of what the child hears or is asked to say, and no correction or reinforcement of his maturing syntax (Brown *et al.*, 1969). Whatever environmental assistance the child gets, it is clear that he never gets sequential tuition based on any deliberate analysis of component skills.

Psychologists may, after the fact, conjecture about the information on language structure conveyed in parent utterances. Snow proposes specific benefits for some of the simplifications in parent-initiated statements, for example, partial repetitions like *Put the red truck in the box now. The red truck*, may provide information on the boundaries of grammatical units and similarly with partial repetitions in new frames: *Pick up the red one, Find the red one, Not the green one, I want the red one*. Controversy over the effect of parental expansions continues.

Whatever the benefit to the child's language learning, the mother's attention is focused not on his learning of language structure but on her intended function of successfully guiding his actions. Bellugi's comments on the conversation of one mother–child pair fits all the families where spontaneous mother–child interaction has been studied (Brown *et al.*, 1969; Horner, 1968; Phillips, 1970; Slobin, 1968; Snow, 1972):

> The mother and child are concerned with daily activities, not grammatical instruction. Adam breaks something, looks for a nail to repair it with, finally throws pencils and nails around the room. He pulls his favorite animals in a tow wagon; fiddles with the television set; and tries to put together a puzzle. His mother is concerned primarily with modifying his behavior. She gives him information about the world around him and corrects facts. Neither of the two seems overtly concerned with the problems that we shall pursue so avidly: the acquisition of syntax (Bellugi, in press).

THE FIRST PARADOX: STRUCTURE VERSUS FUNCTION

The first paradox is that while the attention of neither parent nor child is focused on language structure, that is what all children learn well. In *Alice in Wonderland*, the Duchess says at one point, "And the moral of all *that* is—Take care of the sense, and the sounds will take care of themselves." A variant of the Duchess's moral also seems true: take care of the function and the structure will take care of itself. For, in Polanyi's terms, even if our attention is focused on critical skills, the facilities take care of themselves—in our own language and in the child's acquisition.

I am not claiming that individual differences do not exist in the rate at which children learn the language structure of their home community. Differences do exist in the mean length of utterance of young children of any given age. Figure 1 shows production differences for eighteen children that presumably indicate differences in their rate of acquisition of underlying knowledge of language structure. Moreover, it can be argued that individual differences in language comprehension are even greater. For instance, in her study of the relationship between organizational features of residential day nurseries in England and children's scores on the Reynell Language Development Scale, Barbara Tizard found significant relationships with the comprehension subscale but not with the expression subscale (Tizard *et al.*, 1972). Differences in language

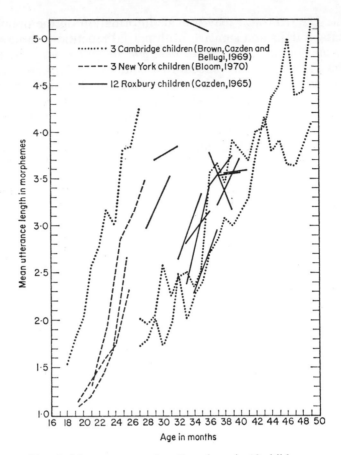

FIG. 1. Mean utterance length and age in 18 children.

comprehension probably become critical in later reading comprehension. In speech, however, both the presence of redundancy and supplementary non-linguistic context, and the absence of comprehension tests at critical points make it unlikely that differences in knowledge of language structure affect communication.

Consider the knowledge required for correct interpretation of such sentences as "Ask John what book to read", or "John asked Mary what to paint". To test Lenneberg's hypothesis that a critical period for language learning ends with the onset of adolescence, Kramer *et al.* (in press) tested people before and after the age of twelve for their comprehension of these structures, previously studied in younger children by Carol Chomsky (1969). Two years after the original experiment, they retested those subjects who had failed the first one to see if those from 8–12 years had learned more in the interim than those from 12–20 years. Lenneberg's hypothesis was not confirmed; there were subjects on both sides of Lenneberg's linguistic watershed who still had not learned how to interpret this construction correctly. Of more interest for the present discussion, Kramer *et al.* found that the high school and college students who did not understand it in pure test situations seemed at no loss in normal conversation.

> We have wondered how an adult fares without competence in these exceptional structures and have attended to real-life situations with adults who lacked some syntactic structure. It seems to us that adult speakers have enough redundancy in their everyday speech to cover up lack of competence. They may respond incorrectly but they often continue talking, thus providing the answer to the question posed. Adults rarely correct other adults' linguistic errors. Thus, once the information requested is given, the form of the response is rarely remarked upon. Language is for communication; the redundant answer "corrects" the linguistic error (Kramer *et al.*, in press).

I have argued elsewhere (Cazden, 1970) that differences in language effectiveness among children are concentrated in aspects of language use rather than in the relative size of a child's structural repertoire. This is admittedly a controversial point. It has received additional theoretical arguments from Cole and Bruner (1971), and assent without additional evidence from Ervin-Tripp (1971). Ervin-Tripp puts it this way:

> The evidence that we have suggests that the vast majority of linguistic rules are alike in the different varieties of English. But children might differ in the *rate* of mastery of shared rules. For such comparisons, test structures must use the dialect of the child's milieu, and [test] fundamental rules in the child's capacity, not his frequency of output which is subject to stylistic preference. ... The widespread belief that there are class and ethnic group differences in developmental rates, leading to "verbal deprivation" requiring compensatory linguistic training, seems extremely ill-founded. We simply do not know whether there are reliable differences in the rate of development of basic linguistic skills, in the emergence of fundamental milestones such as the ability to understand or imitate multi-word sentences, subject versus object, and imbedded sentences. The little evidence we have suggests no differences (Ervin-Tripp, 1971, pp. 31–32).

Two sets of observational data are now available in further support of that argument.

First, some observations of children's use of negatives. One of the goals of the Bereiter-Englemann (1966) pre-school curriculum is to

	NEG–IMP	NEG–MV	NEG–AUX	NEG–INDEF

Darnell (9)	D Don't take all of it.	D My name ain't Gail.
		D You don't know
		   how.
			D No, you can't do 3s.
			D Why can't we pull
			   this up?
			D I can't either.
			D You can't do like
			   this.
				N We don't have
				   nothing to cat with.
				R I don't want any
				   cheese.

Laura (15)	D Not over here, over
	   there.
		D You don't have no
		   badge on.
		D I don't like green
		   peppers.
		D I don't like J.
		D I don't like Mom.
		D That 8's not upside
		   down.
			D You can't do it.
			D I can't do this.
			D We can't dig it
			   cause snow's on the
			   ground.
			D I can't hear you.
			D I can't see you.
			D I'm not gonna do it
			   on the back.
			D I'm not gonna fall.
			D That girl don't
			   supposed to have no
			   dress on a rainy day.
				D I never seen green.

Aaron (36)	D Don't do that.
	D Don't mess up my
	   thing.
	D Don't mess up that.
	D Don't take them.
	D Don't put no little
	   ones there.
	D Don't bend it.
		D No, this 3 is not
		   lying down.
		D This string is not
		   straight.
		D I didn't.
		D We didn't talk about
		   that, right?
		D We don't eat it.
		D I don't eat green
		   peppers.
		D No, we didn't.
		D My mother don't
		   cook that.
		D I don't like green
		   peas.
		D We don't have them.
		D Not me.
		D He don't do his 8s
		   right.
		D Them are not 8s.
		D That's not a 8.
		D That's not a white
		   triangle.
		D You don't like it
		   like this?
		D No, I don't want to.
			D Lester won't stop.
			D You can't play.
			D Paul won't stop.
				D I never taste that.
				D Don't put no little
				   ones there.

FIG. 2. Negative utterances from three children (from Schrager, 1971).

teach children to make negative statements such as *That is not a pen.* It seemed likely to me that children in any group of four-year-olds could use these negative structures in their spontaneous speech. Last year, a research assistant, Tina Schrager, spent many hours in a Head Start programme which followed the Bereiter-Englemann curriculum, recording children's negative statements in all situations except the language lesson itself. She worked out a set of structural categories derived from Klima and Bellugi's (1966) longitudinal research; and she stayed on the job (for 14–16 hours in each of three groups) until she had examples of all but the negative indefinites from all the children, even those in their first term in this programme. Figure 2 gives utterances in all four structural categories for three of these beginning (B) children (Schrager, 1971).

Negative statements can also be categorized according to semantic intentions rather than structural characteristics. In her longitudinal research, Bloom (1970) uses three categories, and suggests the following order of acquisition: non-existence (N), rejection (R), and denial (D). Of the three children in Fig. 2, only Darnell used negative-utterances for rejection or denial while Schrager was listening. Overall, Schrager found that 360 out of 395 negatives from all three groups fit Bloom's definition of "denial": in which, "the negative utterance asserted that an actual (or supposed) predication was not the case" (Bloom, 1970, p. 173). Denial is the semantic category emphasized in the Bereiter-Englemann curriculum.

In reporting observations that structurally these children are capable of more complex utterances than are being requested in their lessons, I am not arguing that the Bereiter-Englemann curriculum is unnecessary or useless. The question remains as to what the children are learning about language use.

Second, Joan Tough, whose research at Leeds on the language of "favoured" and "less favoured" three-year-olds I have reported elsewhere (Cazden, 1971), now has data on seven-year-olds. While her analysis is not complete, she writes, "it seems to me that in fact our less-favoured children are capable of using a good deal of complexity of structure, but that its use is confined to a rather limited range of functions" (personal communication, 1971).

WHICH LANGUAGE FUNCTIONS ARE OF MOST WORTH?

If we are going to look for the developmental antecendents of effective language use, what should we focus on? Given the wide range of possible language functions, which are of most worth on some criteria? These questions become particularly important when we shift from describing development to planning the kind of deliberate environmental assistance that is called education. In a still unfinished paper, Kohlberg and Mayer suggest criteria for answering the question from the viewpoint of a "developmental philosophic strategy" that draws on both Piaget and Dewey. The following is a precis of a section of their paper subtitled, "Development as the aim of education".

Development defines a behavioral change of educational worth. Development is not just any behavior change, it is change in the direction of greater differentiation, integration and adaptation. While theories of specific learning have assumed that information and habit are learned for extrinsic motives, cognitive-development theory assumes that the child's present stage is rejected and the next one sought as preferred because of its greater intrinsic adequacy.

The cognitive-developmental position claims that to call a behavior change "development" implies that it meets the following criteria:

1. The change is irreversible.
2. The change is general over a field of responses and situations.
3. The change is a change in shape, pattern, or quality of response, not merely in the frequency of its correctness according to an external criterion.
4. The change is sequential: it occurs in an invariant series of steps.
5. The change is hierarchical, that is, the later forms of response dominate or integrate the earlier forms.

A specific area of behavior change like "fundamental arithmetic reasoning" may meet these criteria or it may not. Englemann claimed to have artificially taught children the "naturally developing" operation of conservation, but Kamii found that the children so taught met Englemann's criteria of conservation without meeting the criteria of development, e.g. the response could be later forgotten or unlearned, it was not generalized, etc. We have given an example in which a set of responses taught artificially do not meet the developmental criteria met by "natural development". This is not because an educational intervention is incompatible with developmental change, but it is because the intervention was found to mimic development rather than to stimulate it.

To call development natural is to call it universal, not to call it either independent of experience or inevitable . . . It is the universality of sequences of development which warrants them as educational goals.

It seems obvious that many changes or learnings are of value which are not universals in development. As an example, the capacity and motivation to read does not define a universal of development, yet it seems to be a basic educational objective. According to Dewey, the worth of any special form of learning must be judged in terms of its impact on and relevance to universal and general development. It seems plausible that increased capacity to read, though not itself a development, can contribute to cognitive, social and aesthetic development (quoted in abbreviated form from Lawrence Kohlberg and Rochelle Mayer, unfinished MS., 1972).

What changes in language would be considered developmental change according to Kohlberg and Mayer's criteria? In language structure the answer is clear because the sequence of development has been described in some detail in recent research. At least this is true for the first 4–5 years. Beyond that age, the picture is inevitably more fragmented because of the complexity of the whole syntactic system. But how do we think about language use in these terms?

Potentially, Kohlberg and Mayer's criteria provide a basis for evaluating the assertions that language functions highly developed in particular subcultural groups should be incorporated into the school curriculum. It does not devalue the importance of particular verbal skills in a group's cultural life to suggest that the education should focus on aspects of language use which cut across particular functions and show developmental change in all children. In saying this, I accept Cole and Bruner's admonition that the context and content for such education should vary from culture to culture and that, "relevant materials are those to which the child already applies skills the teacher seeks to have applied to his own content" (Cole and Bruner, 1971, pp. 874–875).

Three aspects of language use seem candidates for goals of education. First, coding ability, the term used by Brown (1966) for the ability to free language from dependence on its non-linguistic context and communicate ideas through words alone. Second, meta-linguistic awareness that makes it possible to focus on language as an object of attention as well as use it as a medium of communication (Elkonin, 1971). Third, the use of language in some form of inner speech that leads during the 5–7 year period to an ability to internalize directions given by another and stay with an imposed task, in tests or in real life, without visual or verbal support and reinforcement from another person. All three aspects of language use meet Kohlberg and Mayer's secondary criterion of being instrumental to other aspects of development, and may also meet their primary criteria as well.

In this paper I will discuss only coding ability, or the decontextualization of speech as it is sometimes called[2]. Because discussions of context-dependent versus context-free speech often centre around the writings of Basil Bernstein, it is important to confront the controversies over his work. Discussing one of Bernstein's more recent articles (Bernstein, in press), Hymes (in press) takes this position:

> Bernstein is of course noted for his concepts of *restricted* and *elaborated* codes. . . . In this paper the essential difference between "restricted" and "elaborated" codes is taken as the predominant use of particularistic, relatively context-specific, meanings in the former, and of universalistic, relatively context-free, meanings in the latter.
>
> It would be easy to conclude that the "elaborated" code with its universalistic meanings is simply superior to the "restricted" code which many of the children whom Bernstein has studied bring to school, and that the

---

[2] Just as "decontextualization" refers to the use of symbols outside of and *subsequent* to their use in contexts of concrete reference, so we might adopt the term "precontextualization" for playful practice with symbols outside of and *prior* to such use. An example of precontextualization would be the Anthony Weir's practice with sounds and syntactic patterns during his presleep monologues (Weir, 1962).

task of the school is to replace the one by the other. This conclusion would distort Bernstein's meaning. Context-dependent meanings are essential to many kinds of communication that make social life, a meaningful personal life, possible. All of us seek out people we can "talk to", with whom much can be taken for granted. It is in the nature of man to need symbolic interaction of this kind. One of the great dangers of modern society is the rapid encroachment of technocratic-bureaucratic modes of communication upon spheres formerly reserved for symbolic communication of the particularistic kind. A life in which all meanings had to be made explicit by the norms of some external rationality, where there was no one to whom one could say, "you know what I mean", would be intolerable.

Bernstein is in the complex, difficult position of both defending the value of the kind of communication he calls a "restricted code" and of insisting on its limitations. His position will please few. Those who defend children by placing all blame on the schools, and those who explain the failures of schools by blaming the language of the children, will be both offended. For Bernstein maintains that one must respect, understand and maintain the culture of the child, including its "restricted code", but that one must also give the child the essential elements of the "elaborated code" with its universalistic meanings. He maintains that the latter is not "compensatory eduction, it is eduction pure and simple".

Let me repeat. Bernstein is not talking about social acceptability—about negative concord, pronunciation, or other traits of language varieties, and he is not saying that some children lack language or cognitive skills. In demanding that all children have access to the universalistic meanings of the "elaborated code" he is arguing for a revolution in relationships of power. For in his conception it is the "elaborated code" which contains an elaboration of means for "talking about talk", a meta-language, in other words, for objectifying and analysing the forms, school, and society at large. Bernstein is saying that the purpose of teaching this mode of language use is not to preserve existing forms of social control and inequality (as it appears to many who see the schools as instruments of repression), but to aid those who are unequal to analyse and transform their situations (Hymes, in press).

I agree, and in the remaining two sections, I will describe experimental attempts to increase children's coding ability, and then discuss the second paradox: language acquisition versus language education.

CODING ABILITY

Differences in coding ability have been found in both observations of what children say in spontaneous speech and what they can say on tests, and among both age and social class groups (Table I). These differences cannot, therefore, be passed off either as an artifact of an

TABLE I. *Reports on differences in coding ability*

	Differences in spontaneous speech	Difference on tests
Differences among ages	Piaget (1926) Flavell *et al.* (1968)	Krauss and Glucksberg (1969)
Differences among social class groups	Tough (Cazden, 1971)	Heider (1971)

unnatural test situation to which some children adjust more easily, nor as merely a disposition or preference in ordinary conversational situations where minimal explicitness is adequate.

Five attempts to teach coding ability illuminate how knowledge of language use may depend on different kinds of environmental assistance rather than on a knowledge of language structure. The five attempts were made by Donald Moore (1971), Smothergill *et al.* (1971), Luria and Yudovich (1959), Vera John (1968) and Jean Berko Gleason (1971).

Moore designed, conducted and compared two pre-school language programmes aimed at fostering explicit language use in talking about selected materials and pictures. On specific days, syntactic patterns, vocabulary and concepts such as the following were the focus of attention:

> use of the copula: *This dog is black.*
> expression of part–whole relationships: *The dog has a tail.*
> expression of spatial relations: *The dog is behind the cage.*
> categorization: *This is an animal.*
> use of compound subjects: *The boy and girl are running.*
>
> (Moore, 1971, Appendix B)

The two programmes shared the language curriculum, but differed in mode of adult–child interaction. In what Moore called the "patterning" treatment, the adult tried to elicit descriptions from the child and even asked the child to repeat her more adequate model; in his terms, the child's language was contingent on the adult's. In what Moore called the "extension" treatment, the adult's language was contingent on the child's; she responded to the child and, in so doing, modelled for the child the particular aspect of language which was the focus of attention in both programmes that day. There was also a third "control" group in which adult and child talked with no particular linguistic intentions embodied in the adult utterances.

Thirty-six four-year-old black children were randomly assigned to these three groups. Three adult tutors talked with them in pairs, two pairs per adult from each of the three groups, during a three-hour pre-school held in two adjacent apartments in the large low-income project in which all the children lived. Moore used a set of tests which included a sentence-imitation test (the kind of test widely assumed to test syntactic maturity), the W.P.P.S.I., and a version of the two-person communication game.

For the communication game, arrays of abstract designs previously used by Krauss and others (e.g. Krauss and Rotter, 1968), and more realistic pictures of children (designed by Arthur McCaffrey in another research project at Harvard) were presented, and each child was asked to describe a target picture so that his partner could pick out the same picture from his differently arranged array. Moore scored the children's verbal descriptions for both complexity and accuracy. Complexity included the length of the noun phrase: *ball* v. *the big, round ball*. Accuracy can be scored in several ways. If the arrays of pictures are selected to separate criterion from non-criterion attributes, one can objectively determine whether the descriptions include all criterion attributes. Moore's arrays were too complex to make this determination possible. A second method is to invoke the functional criterion of whether the listening child guesses correctly. But then the listener's ability to process information contaminates the analysis. Moore used a third technique adapted from Krauss. Random subsets of all the children's pre- and post-test descriptions were presented, with the full array of pictures, to a group of adults in the child's home community—adults in the local Community Action Program (C.A.P.) office, etc. These adults were asked to guess which picture the child was describing. From these answers, one can work back to a communication accuracy score for each child.

Moore found no treatment effects on the sentence imitation test scores after correction for dialect differences, despite the fact that the patterning treatment included practice in imitating adult utterances. To retun to an earlier argument, this finding, together with the finding that on a factor analysis of pre-test scores the imitation test came out as a separate factor all by itself, provides further evidence that syntactic development is a separate aspect of communicative development. An aspect not only relatively less vulnerable to naturally recurring environmental differences but also less amenable to deliberate environmental intervention. The patterning treatment was more effective in raising scores on the W.P.P.S.I., especially for the children who started with an initial W.P.P.S.I. I.Q. score below 85. It was also more effective in improving the complexity and accuracy of the children's descriptions on the realistic pictures.

An important part of Moore's research was his investigation of the relationship between a child's gains from pre-test to post-test and characteristics of the interaction between that child and his tutor during the treatment sessions. Midway through the three-month treatment, Moore recorded two seven-minute segments of these sessions for each child and analysed them for the length and complexity of adult and child utterances. Table II gives this data on two measures: mean length of all utterances, and number of noun phrases which include nouns and therefore are "expandable" because nouns, unlike pronouns, can be modified. In general teachers modelled more complex language in the extension treatment whereas children used more complex language in the patterning treatment.

TABLE II. *Language measures from recorded treatment sessions (from Moore, 1971)*

Teacher language		Child language	
Mean length of utterance		Mean length of utterance	
Patterning	5·02	Patterning	4·36
Extension	5·18	Extension	3·48
Activity	4·84	Activity	3·11
Average	5·01	Average	3·65
Total expandable noun phrases		Total expandable noun phrases	
Patterning	101·4	Patterning	39·00
Extension	140·0	Extension	25·91
Activity	35·1	Activity	8·18
Average	92·1	Average	24·36

Moore then did a stepwise regression analysis to answer two questions. Starting with a set of pre-test scores for each child, how much is added to a prediction of that child's post-test scores by information on how his tutor talked to him during treatment? Then, how much additional predictive power is added by information on how the child himself talked during treatment. For the imitation test, neither added a significant increment. For the W.P.P.S.I., predictions were so high from the pre-test alone that neither teacher nor child speech data made any difference. But for the accuracy and complexity scores on the communication task, information on the tutor's language added nothing, while information on child language added significantly to the prediction of post-test scores. That is, across all treatments, on these particular verbal performance skills of explicit description, children learned what they had themselves practised, not what they had only heard.

Smothergill *et al.* (1971) compared the effect of two kinds of teacher talk on the speech and problem solving of twenty-four white nursery school children, all of whose mothers were on welfare. For seventeen days, each child was in a twenty-minute small group session of six children and one teacher. With twelve of the children, teachers used an "elaborative" style—both elaborating their own language beyond the minimum and deliberately eliciting verbal feedback from the children; with the other twelve children, the teachers maintained an equally warm but non-elaborative style of interaction. As in Moore's research, the treatment sessions were monitored to make sure that the treatments did in fact differ in the desired ways and to obtain records of child speech during the sessions. An analysis of variance of child verbalizations showed that children in the elaboratively taught group (E) did show a greater frequency of elaborated statements which conveyed more than the minimum information required for a task. Furthermore:

> As might be expected, the verbalizations of Group E were significantly more often teacher-elicited than was true for Group NE ($p < 0.01$). This finding indicates that children in this group probably were responsive to their teachers' attempts to elicit comments from them. In fact, inspection of the interaction effects indicates that teacher-elicitation is specifically responsible for the greater frequency of elaborative statements of Group E subjects since a markedly greater number of teacher-elicited elaborations characterized this group compared with Group NE ($p < 0.01$), while the number of spontaneous elaborations of the two groups was essentially identical (Smothergill *et al.*, 1971, p. 1235).

The hypothesis that the elaboratively taught group would produce more alternative solutions to problems was not confirmed.

Luria and Yudovich (1959) recount the story of a pair of twins who were retarded in speech development primarily because of the "twin situation which did not create an objective necessity for the development of speech as a special means of communication" (p. 55). The two children were finally placed in separate kindergarten groups, and the weaker twin, Yura, was given supplementary "special speech training":

> The lessons were as follows. The child was first encouraged to give answers to questions, then required actively to name objects, and finally actively to answer questions, to repeat complete phrases and to describe pictures. The instruction continued for three months, then there was a break of two months; afterwards instruction was renewed and continued for a further six months (Luria and Yudovich, 1959, p. 56).

Table III gives a comparative analysis for the functions of speech before separation and after three and ten months of treatment for Yura (A) and Liosha (B). For both twins, synpraxic speech tied to direct action decreased, and planning and narrative speech increased. The biggest difference between the two children, presumably due to the speech training, was in "speech transcending the bounds of a situation". After ten months, this constituted 52% of Yura's speech, but only 27·7% of Liosha's speech. From an all too rare combination of behavioural observations and tests, Luria and Yudovich conclude that both twins gained a great deal from the creation of an objective necessity for speech, but that in addition, Yura's special training produced greater initiative in verbal formulations of play projects, in comprehension of speech in test situations, and in what they call a "theoretical attitude" toward speech (what I called meta-linguistic awareness above) which enabled Yura to reflect on words in sentences and perform operations on them such as counting.

TABLE III. *Comparative analysis of the functions of speech before and after separation (from Luria and Yudovich, 1959, p. 63)*

Forms of speech Number of sentences recorded	Before separation		After ten months separation	
	A 69%	B 69%	A 45%	B 58%
1. Synpraxic speech (connected with direct action)	92·8	94·1	33·2	25·8
2. Planning speech	4·4	4·3	45·9	46·5
(a) within the bounds of a situation	4·4	4·3	10·5	24·1
(b) anticipatory	0	0	35·4	22·4
3. Narrative speech	2·8	1·6	20·9	27·7
(a) connected with a situation	0	0	4·3	22·4
(b) not connected with a situation	2·8	1·6	16·6	5·3
Speech transcending the bounds of a situation (2b; 3b)	2·8	1·6	52·0	27·7

Vera John's (1968) comparison of two treatments which she calls "verbal mediation training" and "story telling" is informative for what she did not find. The two treatments shared the same topics of conversation such as the concepts of same and different, growth, liquids and solids. In the verbal mediation training, the teacher played a directive and questioning role in eliciting from the children labels for attributes and functions, categorizations of the materials, and predictions of what would happen after certain actions were performed. In the story telling treatment, the same concepts were discussed as carefully selected stories were read in an atmosphere of child listening and talking, similar to bedtime story reading at home. Fifteen-minute treatment sessions were conducted individually and daily with each child for five weeks in several Head Start centres.

John predicted differential effects from the two treatments and got most of what she predicted, but not all. She used three tests: a concept sorting task, the Peabody Picture Vocabulary Test, and a story retelling task. As predicted, children in the verbal mediation training improved significantly on the concept sorting task but not on the Peabody Picture Vocabulary Test, whereas for children in the story telling treatment, the reverse was true (John, 1968). But of greatest interest for the present discussion was the one surprise.

> The surprising finding was that the story telling intervention did not produce significant gains in story-retelling skills among these children. Some small gains were made, but they did not correspond in any way to the more dramatic results of the Verbal Mediation method of intervention.
>
> Intervention appears to establish a highly specific link between performance during training and similar skills elicited on post-testing. Though motivationally children may show great involvement—story telling was an enormously popular time in these Head Start centres—gains are less likely when the method of post-testing is indirectly related to intervention. Though children were encouraged to tell stories, the pressure was low, and they were not asked to produce lengthy, well-connected stories. We assumed that the learning, while indirect, would show up on post-testing. It did not! (John, personal communication, 1971.)

Jean Gleason (1971) conducted a small-scale communication training in a nursery school, mixed in race and social class, which we shall call the Main Street School. In a two-child communication game, the children were asked to give descriptions of one of an array of pictures that had an M & M[3] under it. Descriptions varied through the following scale:

> Pointing only.
> Pointing plus *It's under there.*
> Pronouns with exophoric reference: *She's putting them under there.*
> Effective communication: *The M & M is under a picture of a lady who's saying goodnight to her children.*

After the pre-tests, Gleason trained half of the better communicators and half of the poorer communicators in fifteen-minute sessions once a week for four weeks.

---

[3] Smartie in English (Eds.).

The training was really more of the same game, except that each child who was being trained played with me instead of with another child, and I made every effort to provide a good model for him when it was my turn, and to ask questions of him when it was his turn, and generally steer him toward the kind of language we wanted (Gleason, 1971, p. 5).

Even in this short time, the trained children showed markedly greater improvement than the untrained children. When asked in the post-test to describe a picture they had never seen before, "All but one of the eight trained children were in the highest, least egocentric category in their ratings. Only one control child gave a description of this type" (p. 8). Gleason comments:

I cannot believe that in one hour of training, spread out over a period of weeks, we actually taught these children any new language. Instead, what we must have done was to indicate to them which, of a variety of descriptive styles they had the potential of producing, was the one we wanted them to use, and our training sessions facilitated their use of that style. The fact that they were able to learn our style so easily indicates that elaborated code can be acquired by young children, regardless of their background (Gleason, 1971, p. 10).

While the children were being trained by an adult, they were post-tested in child–child pairs, and Gleason (personal communication, 1971) believes there was some regression from the highest quality descriptions the children had given with her. In other words, their learning may have been too situation specific: namely, that certain kinds of statements are valued by a particular adult.

What can we conclude from these five studies about environmental assistance to the use of language we call coding ability? First, in the acquisition of language use as distinct from language structure, the child is aided by what he is encouraged to say, not by what he simply hears (John, 1968; Moore, 1971; Smothergill et al., 1971). Second, adults seem to be essential for such encouragement (Luria and Yudovich, 1959). Finally, there is a danger that specific training will produce learning which is too specific (John, 1968; Gleason, 1971) and we need more concurrent behavioural observations (Luria and Yudovich, 1959) in order to track the generality of what children learn. Only then will we know if any such training meets Kohlberg and Mayer's (1971) criteria.

SECOND PARADOX: LANGUAGE ACQUISITION VERSUS LANGUAGE EDUCATION

Let us assume that the children in the above five studies did make some short-term gains in coding ability. What I am calling the paradox of language acquisition versus language education has two versions: one general, one more specific. The general version can be stated very simply: whereas all children learn their native language with seeming ease and despite wide variations in environmental conditions, attempts at any kind of deliberate language education are rarely very successful, particularly if long-term effects are examined. The more specific version takes longer to describe; it contrasts descriptions of effective home environments for spontaneous language acquisition and descriptions of effective language education programmes which achieve short-term effects at least.

As part of his long-term research project on the development of educability, Burton White (1971) is making observations in the homes of one- and two-year-old children across the social class range whose older siblings have attained either a notably high or a notably low level of social and intellectual competence. On the basis of incomplete analysis of these observational data, White comments:

> Our most effective mothers do not devote the bulk of their day to rearing their children. . . . *What they seem to do*, often without knowing exactly why, is *to perform excellently the functions of designer and consultant*. By that I mean they design a physical world, mainly in the home, that is beautifully suited to nurturing the burgeoning curiosity of the one- to three-year-old. . . .
>
> In addition to being largely responsible for the type of environment the child has, this mother sets up guides for her child's behavior that seem to play a very important role in these processes. She is generally *permissive and indulgent*. The child is encouraged in the vast majority of his explorations. When the child confronts an interesting or difficult situation, he often turns to his mother for help. Though usually working on some chore, she is generally within earshot. He then goes to her and usually, but not always, is *responded to* by his mother with help or shared enthusiasm plus, occasionally, an interesting, naturally related idea. These ten to thirty second interchanges are usually oriented around the child's interest of the moment rather than toward some need or interest of the mother. . . .
>
> These mothers very rarely spend five, ten or twenty minutes teaching their one- or two-year-olds, but they get an enormous amount of teaching in "on the fly", and usually at the *child's* instigation. Though they do volunteer comments opportunistically they mostly act in response to overtures by the child (White, 1971, p. 87).

In White's research, verbal interaction is just one aspect of the child's life being studied. But his description fits the more focused analysis of mother–child speech carried out by Brown and his colleagues (Brown *et al.*, 1969). Here too, the responsive but generally non-didactic adult is highly effective.

A paradox arises when that responsive role is translated into deliberate educational practice. The teaching role of designer and consultant closest to White's description takes place in the best traditional nursery schools, or in "open education" schools which take English infant schools as their model. Yet comparisons of the impact of different kinds of pre-school programmes indicate that the more didactic programmes— seemingly farthest from White's mothers—are more effective. (See Bissell, in press, for a general discussion compatible with the comparison of techniques for teaching coding abilities above.)

In short, we seem to have reached an impasse. On the one hand, the more didactic educational treatments which do bring about short-term gains may produce such limited behavioural change that, in Kohlberg and Mayer's terms, development is mimicked rather than stimulated. On the other hand, those group environments which seem to be most like homes that are good for language development have not been proved effective even in the short run. Part of the lack of proven effect may be due to insensitive measures. But we should not rely completely on the excuse of poor measures to resolve the paradox.

Consider three aspects of group environments which do not exist at home and which therefore require special planning by teachers. First, teachers are inevitably less familiar with individual children than mothers are. Mothers may be superb interlocutors for their young children just because they know the child and his world so well. When children in their second year of life can utter only a few meaningful words, a mother is most likely to understand the child's idiosyncratic pronunciation and be able to make a meaningful response. If the child says, "Baa," his mother can respond, "Your blanket? It's in the kitchen. On your chair", whereas no one outside the family would understand. Later when the child's speech more closely approximates normal pronunciation and is therefore intelligible to a wider audience, idiosyncracies will remain in his vocabulary, and the child will speak egocentrically apparently assuming that his listener knows the referents for his words. When a boy not yet three told his father, "Betty and I played radio last night", his father understood that Betty Bryant, a graduate student, had been there with her tape recorder; but only the child's mother knew that Betty had actually come earlier that day rather than the previous night, and so only she could correct the child's encoding of past time. Someone outside the family could have said little more than, "Oh, that's nice", while wondering what had been going on.

In pre-schools, children will be speaking to adults (or peers) who are more familiar with his pronunciation, his vocabulary, and his world. In day care centres, the problem is magnified because more of the children will be under three years, each child will encounter a larger set of adults each week (changing shifts of staff, different volunteers each day, etc.) and the group environment will account for more of his speaking day. Under these conditions, unless teachers talk frequently with parents and visit children at home, meaningful conversation will necessarily be more limited to the momentary here and now of life in school. Structured language lessons are often limited in just this way, but then the child gets little help in clarifying concepts and their verbal formulations outside this limited world. Furthermore, new communication skills practised at school will be less likely to generalize to the child's non-school world if topics of conversation in the two settings rarely overlap. Consistency in adult–child relationships may be as important for language as for effective development during the early years, even though an opposite case can be made for the beneficial challenge to older children of communicating with strangers.

Secondly, one aspect of any group setting, in contrast to the one-to-one relationship that prevails for at least part of most children's home day, is that teachers must distribute their attention and their conversational initiatives among a group of children. In addition to the simple matter of a division of talking time, there is the more complex matter of an unequal division. A group environment can be twenty-four different environments for twenty-four children. Because teachers themselves respond to reinforcement, they may talk more to the children who talk most to them. Last year a student at Harvard, Anne Monaghan, provided empirical support for this hypothesis in the Main Street School where Gleason had worked the year before. Ignoring the heterogeneous age, race and social class of the children, Monaghan coded interactions according to who initiated the conversation and then computed the rank-order correlation between the list of children, ranked according to number of verbal contacts they initiated with any teacher, and the list of the same children ranked according to the number of verbal contacts any teacher initiated with them. The correlation was significant at $p = 0.05$ level in the fall and at $p = 0.001$ level in the spring. In Monaghan's words, over the course of the year:

> the teaching staff appears to be reinforcing and amplifying what already exists when children enter—those children who initiate a great deal get teacher initiations in return while those who initiate infrequently are not frequently sought out by teachers. By omission or commission, the general configuration of social abilities or deficits which a child brings with him to school will be strengthened as classroom policy now stands (Monaghan, 1971, p. 16).

Monaghan's findings fit the only comparable research I know of, Talbert's (1968) study of a black kindergarten. Talbert found that those children, mostly boys, who started out on the periphery of teacher attention and teacher-led activities became more isolated as the year went on. One positive factor explaining the effect of the more didactic programmes may be simply that they guarantee a more equal distribution of teacher attention.

A third characteristic of group environments is that they provide a variety of interactional settings which may be more or less congruent with those the child is familiar with from home. Another Harvard student, Helen Featherstone (in press), discovered some intriguing facts about the settings in which children choose to spend their time in the Main Street School. Here the kitchen is available as one setting for the children. Featherstone noticed that in twenty-five observations in the kitchen, certain children were there very often while others were rarely there. What was special about the kitchen? Not eating, as little tasting was done. She suggests that activity in the kitchen had several characteristics: it was the only place in the school that always had a stationary adult, and it had an activity structured in two ways—by teacher direction, telling children what to do to help prepare today's recipe, and a definite beginning, middle and end to the activity itself. In further observations, Mrs. Featherstone found that the children most often in the kitchen were also most often found in the one other school setting where an adult was sometimes stationary—a room for art projects. These children were among the top half of the entire group on a measure of seeking the occasional stationary adult in settings other than these two.

Featherstone then looked at the distribution of children in three settings which contrasted with the kitchen on these characteristics—the art table, block area and rug where table toys were used. There was not one child who scored highly for any of these more self-directed settings and for the kitchen. She comments:

Clearly different children are actively seeking different kinds of settings in a very consistent way. Furthermore the kinds of choices they make seem to be associated with ethnicity and economic class: of the eleven children scoring high for the kitchen all are either low-income or Black. For neither type of setting is there striking homogeneity along lines of age or sex.

This could be taken to suggest that the school was poorly integrated—that in one setting an observer would find only white middle-income children and in another only Black low-income children. That was not, in fact, the case. In all my observations of the school, I rarely saw groups of children which were homogeneous by race, economic class or age. Children worked and played constantly with children (and teachers) who were different from themselves. It was only when I observed particular settings over an extended period that I saw distinctive preferences in the use of that setting (Featherstone, in press).

In searching for interpretations of this data, one wishes immediately for transcriptions of those kitchen conversations. Unfortunately, the pattern of Featherstone's data became clear. Because Monaghan and Featherstone worked in the same school during the same year, we know a little about the children but not enough. We know that the children most often in the kitchen were distributed throughout Monaghan's ranking of frequency of interactions with teachers. Some of the children must have actively initiated conversations with teachers or been the recipients of adult initiatives, while others talked with peers or waited silently for initiatives, from the teacher which rarely came. One possible advantage of the more didactic programmes is that they guarantee the kind of settings which some children seem to seek for at least some time each day.

Because everything we know about language development suggests that it develops best, in functions as well as structure, when motivated by powerful communicative intent, and because we want to stimulate development and not just mimic it, it is important to try to make "natural", less didactic, group environments more effective. It should be possible to maximize consistency and thereby familiarity in child–adult relationships and guarantee that the children who need talking time with adults get it. Research by Tizard *et al.* (1972) on the organizational structure of residential nurseries indicates some of the structural qualities of a good language environment: low child–adult ratio in the actual face-to-face group (six to one is more effective than twelve to two); staff stability versus staff turnover; and staff autonomy on the job. The existence of various interaction patterns and children's differential response to them is harder to understand and to use. We do not know how children's preference for interactional settings relates to their own mother's teaching styles (for instance as studied by Hess *et al.*, 1968), and we don't know how to use these preferences for the development of communication skills.

REFERENCES

BELLUGI, U. *The acquisition of the system of negation in children's speech.* M.I.T. Press, Cambridge, Mass., in press.

BEREITER, C. and ENGLEMANN, S. 1966. *Teaching disadvantaged children in the preschool.* Prentice-Hall, Englewood Cliffs, New Jersey.

BERNSTEIN, B. A critique of the concept "compensatory education". In C. B. Cazden, D. Hymes and V. John (Eds.), *Functions of language in the classroom.* Teachers College Press, New York, in press.

BISSELL, J. S. The cognitive effects of pre-school programs for disadvantaged children. In J. L. Frost (Ed.), *Early childhood education rediscovered*, 2nd ed. Holt, Rinehart and Winston, New York, in press.

BLOOM, L. M. 1970. *Language development: form and function in emerging grammars.* M.I.T. Press, Cambridge, Mass.

BROWN, R. 1966. From codability to coding ability. In J. Bruner (Ed.), *Learning about learning: a conference report.* U.S. Department of Health, Education and Welfare, Washington, D.C.

BROWN, R., CAZDEN, C. B. and BELLUGI, U. 1969. The child's grammar from I to III. In J. P. Hill (Ed.), *1967 Minnesota symposium on child psychology.* University of Minnesota Press, Minneapolis.

CAZDEN, C. B. 1965. Environmental assistance to the child's acquisition of grammar. Unpublished doctoral dissertation, Harvard University.

CAZDEN, C. B. 1970. The situation: a neglected source of social class differences in language use. *Journal of Social Issues,* **26** (2), 35–60. Shorter version in F. Williams (Ed.), *Language and poverty: perspectives on a theme.* Markham, Chicago.

CAZDEN, C. B. 1971. Language programs for young children: notes from England and Wales. In C. S. Lavatelli (Ed.), *Language training in early childhood education.* University of Illinois Press for the ERIC Clearinghouse on Early Childhood Education, Urbana, Illinois.

CAZDEN, C. B. 1972. *Child language and education.* Holt, Rinehart and Winston, New York.

CHOMSKY, C. S. 1969. *The acquisition of syntax in children from 5 to 10.* M.I.T. Press, Cambridge, Mass.

COLE, M. and BRUNER, J. S. 1971. Cultural differences and inferences about psychological processes. *Amer. Psychol.,* **26**, 867–876.

ELKONIN, D. B. 1971. Development of speech. In A. V. Zaporozhets and D. B. Elkonin (Eds.), *The psychology of preschool children.* M.I.T. Press, Cambridge, Mass.

ERVIN-TRIPP, S. 1971. Social backgrounds and verbal skills. In R. Huxley and E. Ingram (Eds.), *Language acquisition: models and methods.* Academic Press, New York and London.

FEATHERSTONE, H. The use of settings in a heterogeneous pre-school. *Young Children,* in press.

FLAVELL, J. J., BODKIN, P. T., FRY, C. L., WRIGHT, J. W. and JARVIS, P. E. 1968. *The development of role-taking and communication skills in children.* Wiley, New York.

GLEASON, J. B. 1971. An experimental approach to improving children's communicative ability. Unpublished manuscript, Cambridge, Mass.

HEIDER, E. R. 1971. Style and accuracy of verbal communications within and between social classes. *J. Pers. Soc. Psychol.,* **18**, 33–47.

HESS, R. D., SHIPMAN, V. C., BROPHY, J. E. and BEAR, R. M. 1968. *The cognitive environments of urban preschool children.* The University of Chicago Graduate School of Education, Chicago.

HORNER, V. N. 1968. The verbal world of the lower-class three-year-old: a pilot study in linguistic ecology. Unpublished doctoral dissertation, University of Rochester.

HYMES, D. Introduction. In C. B. Cazden, D. Hymes and V. P. John (Eds.), *Functions of language in the classroom*. Teachers College Press, New York, in press.

JOHN, V. P. 1968. A study of language change in integrated and homogeneous classrooms. Progress Report No. 2, February 15.

KLIMA, E. S. and BELLUGI, U. 1966. Syntactic regularities in the speech of children, In J. Lyons and R. J. Wales (Eds.), *Psycholinguistics papers*. University Press. Edinburgh.

KOHLBERG, L. and MAYER, R. S. 1972. Early education: a cognitive-developmental view; II. The developmental-philosophic strategy for defining educational aims. Unpublished manuscript, Harvard Graduate School of Education, Cambridge, Mass.

KRAMER, P., KOFF, E. and LURIA, Z. 1972. The development of competence in an exceptional structure of English in children and young adults. *Child Dev.*, **43**, 121–130.

KRAUSS, R. M. and GLUKSBERG, S. 1969. The development of communication: competence as a function of age. *Child Dev.*, **40**, 255–266.

KRAUSS, R. M. and ROTTER, G. S. 1968. Communication abilities of children as a function of status and age. *Merrill-Palmer Q. Behav. Develop.*, **14**, 161–173.

LURIA, A. R. and YUDOVICH, F. 1959. *Speech and the development of mental processes in the child*. Reprinted by Penguin Books, 1971.

MILLER, G. A., GALANTER, E. and PRIBRAM, K. H. 1960. *Plans and the structure of behavior*. Holt, Rinehart and Winston, New York.

MONAGHAN, A. C. 1971. Children's contacts: some preliminary findings. Unpublished term paper, Harvard Graduate School of Education.

MOORE, D. 1971. A comparison of two methods of teaching specific language skills to lower-class pre-school children. Unpublished doctoral dissertation, Harvard University.

PHILLIPS, J. R. 1970. Formal characteristics of speech which mothers address to their young children. Unpublished doctoral dissertation, The Johns Hopkins University.

PIAGET, J. 1926. *The language and thought of the child*. World, Cleveland, Ohio.

POLANYI, M. 1964. *Personal knowledge: towards a post-critical philosophy*. Harper Torchbooks, New York.

RYLE, G. 1949. *The concept of mind*. Barnes and Noble, New York.

SCHEFFLER, I. 1965. *Conditions of knowledge*. Scott, Foresman, Chicago.

SCHRAGER, T. 1971. "Aint" didn't never hurt no one. Unpublished research paper, Harvard Graduate School of Education.

SLOBIN, D. I. 1968. Questions of language development in cross-cultural perspective. Paper prepared for symposium on "Language learning in cross-cultural perspective", Michigan State University.

SMOTHERGILL, N. L., OLSON, F. and MOORE, S. G. 1971. The effects of manipulation of teacher communication style in the preschool. *Child Dev.*, **42**, 1229–1239.

SNOW, C. E. 1972. Mothers' speech to children learning language. *Child Dev.*, **43**, 549–565.

TALBERT, C. S. 1968. Interaction and adaptation in a Negro kindergarten. St. Louis: Washington University Department of Anthropology. Paper presented at meeting of the American Anthropological Association, Seattle, November.

TIZARD, B., COOPERMAN, O., JOSEPH, A. and TIZARD, J. 1972. Environmental effects on language development: a study of young children in long-stay residential nurseries. *Child Dev.*, **43**, 337–358.

WEIR, H. 1962. *Language in the crib*. Mouton, The Hague.

WHITE, B. 1971. An analysis of excellent early educational practices: preliminary report. *Interchange* (Ontario Institute for Studies in Education, Toronto), **2** (2), 71–88.

How to Resolve Two Paradoxes and Escape a Dilemma: Comments on Dr. Cazden's Paper[1]

DAVID MCNEILL

University of Chicago

THERE ARE MANY points that one might discuss in Dr. Cazden's paper. Selectivity becomes inevitable. I have chosen two, the two paradoxes, one of which is actually a dilemma. These are, in a certain way, related to each other and the relationship suggests a rationale for escaping the dilemma of the second paradox.

The two paradoxes are, first, that young children and their mothers have all their attention focused on meaning and language use, none on structure, yet all children acquire knowledge of language structure, and so quickly and so well. The second paradox is that, among training programmes, those which are didactic have demonstrable short-term effects of limited scope, whereas those which are most like homes have no apparent effects, even in the short run. The combined effect of the two paradoxes is distressing for educational practice. No way has been found to reproduce the largely unconscious acquisition of language that takes place naturally with young children who are leading normal home lives.

Cazden discusses the first paradox in relation to linguistic "transparency". That is, in relation to the curious fact that while individuals who use language are constantly making use of a large number of phonetic and syntactic details, they are rarely aware of any of these, and certainly are never aware of all of them. The phonetic and syntactic details are "transparent". It is exactly these transparent details in normal language use that children paradoxically acquire. Thus, linguistic transparency seems to hold from the earliest stages of language use.

[1] Preparation of this paper was supported by grants from the N.S.F. to David McNeill.

Cazden quotes two philosophers, Scheffler (1965) and Polanyi (1964), who view the question in terms of a kind of hierarchy of awareness. Meaning is at the top of this hierarchy and it is in the focus of attention. On the sidelines are the "transparent" details. These carry meanings but cannot be made the focus of attention without losing this meaning bearing capacity (Polanyi, 1964).

Both Scheffler and Polanyi contrast meaning, which is "opaque", with form, which is "transparent". Without attempting to explain the nature of this contrast, which is a traditional puzzle, I will argue that it is, merely one of several such contrasts that can be shown to exist in language. Consider the following experiment. I tell you a sentence: *mind is more than a four letter word*. You are to listen for this sentence in a random series of spoken sentences, and press a button that stops a clock the instant you hear this target. You will have a certain reaction time. According to an experiment by Savin, Bever and Hurtig (reported in Foss, 1971), this reaction time will on average be *shorter* than if you had heard exactly the same series of sentences but had been searching for a single word (e.g. *four*) instead. In this case, searching for an opaque sentence takes less time than searching for the transparent word. One can explain this result with the hypothesis that the word, being transparent, is sought either through a derivative process (passing through the sentence) or through some special process used in searching for transparent elements. In either case, search time is greater than when a direct, normal process can be used.

Now, consider another version of the same experiment (Savin and Bever, 1970). In this case you are given a nonsense syllable target (*barj*) and hear a series of spoken nonsense syllables. Your reaction time when you hear the target will be on average shorter than if you heard the same series of syllables but were searching for a single phone (*b*) instead. By the same reasoning as before we can conclude that, among syllables, the syllable is opaque and the phone is transparent. Clearly, however, opacity is not a fixed property of syllables. Among words, for example, syllables are transparent, and words, which before were transparent, are opaque.

The principle thus seems to be as follows: whatever is last (or largest) to be processed in speech perception is opaque, and is in the focus of attention, and everything preliminary (or smaller) is transparent. The processing of language can be stopped anywhere, of course, simply by selecting the forms of the material to be presented, where phones, syllables, words, sentences, sentence-groups, etc. Hence, rather than a dichotomy between opaque meaning and transparent syntax or phonology, there is a series of opaque–transparent oppositions, depending on how far linguistic processing has advanced before it is stopped.

The traditional opposition of opaque meaning to transparent syntax or phonology reflects the way language is usually used. The final, hence opaque, step is ordinarily some meaningful state of affairs. That does not mean, however, that one does not ordinarily engage in phonetic, syllabic, word, or syntactic processing. On the contrary, one usually does these things (although not necessarily in the order mentioned) but cannot be made aware of the transparent, intermediate stages. The proof of this is the sudden opacity of such usually transparent elements as words or syllables when processing is brought to an early halt. Thus, in mature speakers, much linguistic processing can take place without conscious awareness of what is being done developing. And, apparently, a similar statement is true of linguistic development. Much of language can be acquired without the processing that we assume must be occurring ever being the focus of conscious awareness. This is Cazden's first paradox. I think it is more of a paradox for theories of conscious awareness that it is for the theories of language. For it means that one can process (acquire) many linguistic details without this having an impact on conscious awareness.

Phonetic and syntactic details are not always transparent. For phoneticians phones are opaque and for syntacticians syntax is—these are specialists who have undertaken often extensive training in order to see *their* level as opaque even when it is buried under one or more higher levels. They seem to do this by mastering the technique of stopping normal linguistic processing at peculiar points, e.g. where all phonetic information is available but word information is not.

The phenomenon of specialized linguistic training is of interest to us for the light it sheds on Cazden's second paradox. Language change on a large scale probably requires something akin to the training of linguistics. Not training as systematic or as preoccupied with theory and notation, but like linguistics training in that it has as one of its goals the capacity of stopping normal processing at peculiar points. Once this trick is learned, a child can introduce changes into the stream of processing, he can compare different linguistic forms, and in general he can deal consciously and deliberately with what he is attempting to accomplish.

Such deliberate control may be necessary to achieve much lasting linguistic change. Whatever makes initial acquisition take place unconsciously also makes the details of language transparent and hence largely immune to further change, once established. A major reason that schools which are most like homes have no effect on language, must be that normal linguistic processing simply precludes further acquisition. Some way must be found to overcome the inevitable transparency of linguistic structure.

It is obvious that a way to escape the second paradox lies in a combination of didactic instruction with a home-like atmosphere in which development, once it becomes possible, can naturally occur. The critical point, which seems to have been overlooked, is that didactic instruction should be given on only certain skills, namely, those that must be made opaque. The defect with many didactic programmes which currently exist appears to be that they teach skills that do *not* have to be opaque.

This is not to say that children should be little linguists, although the example Cazden cites of Yura suggests that even this might be a good idea. It is only to say that it may be necessary to teach (for example) what the middles of words are, in order to teach what verb inflections are (which in turn govern auxiliaries, etc.). It is also true that not all language change requires conscious control by the learner. An occasional visitor to England notices this in his former American friends who have taken up residence here, many of whom (contrary to American speech) unconsciously have begun to elevate vowels and to aspirate final stop consonants. The mechanism in this case may be close if not identical to that in primary language acquisition. However, it is not known how widespread such changes are in mature speakers. Lenneberg's (1967) theory of a critical period for language acquisition implies that they are not widespread. In this case, there is some point in contemplating how the didactic and spontaneous modes of instruction can be put together intelligently.

REFERENCES

Foss, D. J. 1971. On the time-course of sentence comprehension. Paper presented at a CNRS symposium on current problems in psycholinguistics, Paris, 13–17 December 1971.

Lenneberg, E. H. 1967. *Biological foundations of language.* Wiley, New York.

Polanyi, M. 1964. *Personal knowledge: towards a post-critical philosophy.* Harper Torchbooks, New York.

Savin, H. J. and Bever, T. G. 1970. The nonperceptual reality of the phenome. *J. verb. Learn. verb. Behav.*, **9**, 295–302.

Scheffler, I. 1965. *Conditions of knowledge.* Scott Foresman, Chicago.

Do Social Relationships Affect Language Development?

BARBARA TIZARD

University of London

FOR A VARIETY of reasons pre-school educationalists, especially in the United States, have lately lost much of their faith in maturation and addressed themselves to active intervention, particularly in the field of language development. Working on the belief (for which there is surprisingly little direct evidence) that the talk in working-class families is deficient both in quality and quantity, pre-school centres have increasingly stepped in to remedy this presumed deficiency. This has been done by attempting to ensure that each child is regularly and progressively exposed to certain concepts or grammatical constructions, either through a structured language programme, or by appropriate staff initiated discussions of his spontaneous play activity. The results of most of these efforts have been disappointing in terms of test score gains. Even when gains have been noted there is little evidence to show that the children's habitual speech habits have changed.

However, ten to twenty minutes a day for a year or two, which is the longest period of individual attention which even the most generously staffed unit can usually afford, compares poorly with the continuous verbal education in the middle-class family. Hopes have turned in some quarters, therefore, to the primary educator, the working-class mother, in the belief that by persuasion and example she can be induced to talk to her children in much the same way as a middle-class mother. With a little encouragement and regular demonstrations from a visiting "playlady" she could surely be induced to spend more time playing with her children, explaining casual connexions, pointing out similarities and differences, encouraging questions, defining words, and so on.

Such a hope would appear to be naive in so far as it fails to analyse the factors which determine the nature of verbal communication within the family (or elsewhere). After all, the vocabulary, syntax, and conceptual understanding which one might wish to impart to five-year-olds is within the capacity of almost every adult. Why then does the "working-class mother" fail to play with her children, give explanations with her commands, answer children's questions fully and so on? According to Bernstein the answer involves a whole complex of factors relating to her perceptions of her role as mother, her place and her child's future place in society, and the value she places on language in communication and socialization (Bernstein, 1971). Bernstein summarized his argument in a phrase: speech codes symbolize the form of social relationships. The characteristic of working-class speech habits, which appears to educators as a verbal deficiency, is a tendency to be confined to a restricted code. This, Bernstein related both to the type of authority structure within the family, and to the nature of the occupational role of the adult members. If his theory is correct, one would expect speech habits to be relatively resistant to advice and example, but to respond to structural changes in the family and society.

Such a theory is very difficult to test, and is perhaps of most value for highlighting certain issues. It suggests, for example, that a study of language usage within a rapidly changing society would be of great interest.

A less ambitious approach to the question of how social structure affects speech habits can be made by comparing residential children's institutions which differ in organizational structure. It is easier to draw conclusions from comparative studies of institutions than from studies of families of different social class, since one can select for comparison staff of similar social class background, education and training, carrying out the same task, but in differently structured institutions. At the same time the development of the children in the different institutions can be compared without contamination from genetic variables. Moreover, the disrupting effect of an observer is much less in an institution, which is more open to public scrutiny, than is a private family.

This approach was used by J. Tizard and colleagues in a study of institutions for retarded children (King et al., 1971). Comparisons were made between large mental subnormality hospitals and small hostels, all caring for severely or profoundly retarded children. Child care practices in the hospitals tended to be institution orientated, that is the children were treated as a group, individual differences were not catered for, and the daily programme was very routine. This was much less true of the more child-orientated hostels, where in addition the staff interacted more often with the children. Retarded children in the child-orientated units were significantly more advanced in feeding and dressing skills and in speech development than in the hospitals.

The authors presented evidence that the principal reason for the differences in child care practice between hospitals and hostels was not the size of the institution but its organizational structure. In the hospital the nurse in charge of each unit (ward sister or charge nurse) had very little authority to make decisions about matters affecting most aspects of the unit's functioning, and the more junior staff had virtually none. In the hostels the supervisors had considerable autonomy, and tended to share decision making with their junior colleagues. There were also corresponding differences in social distance between grades of staff, and in role differentiation. In the hospitals the senior staff tended to keep aloof from their junior colleagues, and also from the children. They were less often engaged in child care, and more often with office work, than were their counterparts in hostels. The children were therefore taken care of by staff who had virtually no autonomy or responsibility.

Mental deficiency institutions are faced with special problems' and present gross differences of a kind no longer to be found in England amongst institutions for normal children. Nevertheless differences in the autonomy of the basic unit in such institutions can be found, especially in residential nurseries. If these differences have an important effect on the behaviour of the staff, then an effect on the development of the children in residence should also be apparent, since the children's environment is almost entirely circumscribed by the institution. A study of long-stay residential nurseries for normal children was therefore undertaken by the author and colleagues (Tizard et al., 1972). Most of the children in the nurseries we studied had been admitted as infants, and had remained there ever since without a break and without contact with their families. The majority were illegitimate children who had not been found adoptive homes either because of their colour or family background, e.g. a family history of epilepsy, psychopathy or depression. About a quarter of the children were regularly visited by their mothers, who, it was thought, would probably take them home eventually.

Apart from the difference in the autonomy of the basic unit the nurseries we studied were quite similar, and offered in many respects a high standard of care. The majority contained 15–25 children, and were organized into a baby unit and two or three mixed age groups of six children, ranging in age from about twelve months to the upper age limit of the nursery, which varied from four and a half to seven years. Each group had its own suite of bedroom, bathroom and living room, with its own nurse and assistant nurse. The nurse in charge of the group was usually a qualified nursery nurse, and the assistant was a student trainee. Two or more staff were on duty with the group each day. Each living room was plentifully supplied with toys and books:

outside was a large garden containing further play equipment. In all the nurseries children over three years old attended a play group, where sand, paint, water, etc., were available.

The children were always read to at least once a day. Most of the nurseries made considerable efforts to broaden the children's experiences by organizing shopping expeditions, excursions, car and bus rides, and occasional weekend visits to the homes of staff members. The nurseries were rarely short of staff, and indeed had a long waiting list of applicants. This is probably because the job of nursery nurse, which involves obtaining a certificate at the end of two years practical and college training, has a relatively high status in England. Moreover, since each student on entering had to agree to remain for three years, staff turnover in all the nurseries was relatively low.

Despite these similarities, there were important differences between the nurseries in social organization. We distinguished three groups which differed markedly in the autonomy of the basic unit. Those in the first group were run very much like hospitals, decisions being made on an entirely routine basis or else referred to the matron. Each day was strictly timetabled, the matron would make frequent inspections of each group, and the freedom of both nurse and child was very limited. Child care practices were institution-orientated; the children were moved through the day *en bloc*, e.g. the group had to be kept together in the living room, or in the garden, all were taken to the toilet together, the children were not allowed in the bedrooms except when all were taken there at night. The nurse had little more autonomy than the children, e.g. she would have to ask permission to take the children for a walk or to turn on the television set. Very often the intellectual and emotional energy of the nurse appeared to be invested elsewhere, and her responses to the children appeared mechanical and superficial.

In an organization of this kind the nurse's tasks are so well defined that someone else can easily take her place. Such an arrangement is administratively convenient, because staff become interchangeable, and inexperienced staff can be put in charge of a group, but it results in very restricted role-playing by the staff, whose function is reduced to maintaining order and "minding" the children on behalf of matron. Because the staff were given little autonomy they could not offer it to the children. More important, perhaps, the ethos of an institution where decisions are made at the top and each grade knows its position in the hierarchy favours the inculcation of child obedience and conformity rather than child autonomy. The staff's primary concern often seemed to be the maintenance of order and the imposition of rather high standards of behaviour in certain spheres, e.g. cleanliness, tidiness, and good table manners. Even during play the children were often assigned a passive role, e.g. they might be pushed on a swing, or expected to sit quietly whilst a book was read.

Social relationships of this kind have consequences in terms of verbal interchange; the expectation of group conformity was so pervasive that it was rare to hear a child offered a choice of any kind, or given an explanation for any request. A large part of the staff talk appeared to be made up of commands, and of a category of remarks which we called "supervisory". These are the kind of remarks which adults make to children when they want to show goodwill but have no real communication to make—e.g. ritual verbal accompaniments to certain actions, "Here you are", "Off we go"; ritualistic comments, "Aren't you clever", "Lucky boy", "That's nice", "Did you"; repetitions of what the child said; and "social oil" remarks such as "Thank you" and "Hullo". Both commands and "supervisory" comments have certain characteristics in common: they tend to involve the use of short simple sentences and a restricted, repetitive vocabulary, and they tend not to elicit responses.

In a second group of nurseries the organization was somewhat less centralized. The nurse in charge of the group might be given responsibility for allocating domestic work, or she might be allowed to organize expeditions outside the nursery. In other respects, however, she took little part in day to day decision making.

In the most decentralized institutions, which make up the third group of nurseries, each nursery group was separately housed in a cottage or self-contained flat, and the staff were responsible for shopping, cooking, and arranging their own day. The children could move freely about the house and garden and the staff rarely referred a decision to the matron. Their role, in fact, approximated more closely to that of a foster mother. Since they could plan their own day and were not under constant surveillance they could treat the children more flexibly, and there appeared to be corresponding differences in their speech. Discussion became possible on such topics as the day's menu, how to spend the afternoon, or which television programme to watch, and explanations were sometimes given with requests. The nurse's talk was therefore more varied and interesting, and children appeared both to address and answer her more often.

It should be noted that even in the most autonomous groups the social structure differed from that of the hostels for retarded children. A hospital-type hierarchy prevailed within all the nursery groups; the junior staff were students or untrained assistants who spent only a limited time with each group, and did not share in decision making. Social distance was marked: junior staff wore special uniforms and had separate living quarters. Role differentiation was universal: because the junior staff were transitory the nurse-in-charge tended to give them a larger share of the domestic chores, assuming more of the child care functions herself. Less difference could therefore be expected in the behaviour of the junior staff in different nurseries.

As in the mental subnormality studies, it was decided to examine the relationships between three sets of data. The first set, obtained from records and by interview, was concerned with the organizational structure of the nurseries, the second, obtained through direct observation using time-sampling techniques, measured the "verbal environment" of the children; the third, obtained through formal psychological testing, comprised measures of both verbal and non-verbal development of the children. It was expected that the more autonomous the group, the more often the staff would converse and play with the children, rather than passively "mind" them, the more often both staff and children would answer each other's remarks, and the more often children would address remarks to the staff. When the staff were playing with the children, or reading to them, it was predicted that the more autonomous the group, the more the child would be assigned an active role in the play or reading situation. Further, it was predicted that these differences in staff–child interaction would result in superior language development in the children in the more autonomous groups. The autonomy of the nursery group was measured by a score based on the number of day to day decisions the nurse in charge of the group and the children could make for themselves.

A large number of nurseries were visited in order to establish the autonomy of their nursery groups. Finally thirteen nursery groups were chosen, which included the extremes of social organization found. Five days were spent by an observer in each group, time-sampling the way in which the staff used their time and the remarks which they made to the children. The frequency with which the children in each group answered the staff and talked to each other and to the staff was also time-sampled. Subsequently a clinical psychologist, who was not part of the research team and not informed about the predictions, tested all the healthy 2–5 year old children (N = 85) in the nurseries studied, with the Reynell developmental Language Scales and the non-verbal scale of the Minnesota Pre-School Scale.

Unfortunately, sufficient nursery groups could not be found which differed only in autonomy and it was considered necessary to measure differences in three associated organizational variables which might affect staff behaviour and/or language development. Thus there was a tendency for low autonomy to be associated with low staff stability. By staff stability is meant not staff turnover, which as explained above was everywhere relatively low, but the length of time staff worked with a particular group of children. In some nurseries both students and trained staff did night duty for one or two weeks every two months, and at these times the regular staff were replaced by "floating staff". In other nurseries greater stability was achieved by employing special night staff, and by appointing two permanent trained nurses to each group, so that when one was off duty the other was on. It seemed likely that low stability would affect staff behaviour in much the same way as low autonomy, since staff who only stayed for a short time with the children would tend to "mind" them, and the children would tend to ·talk to them and answer them less often.

Secondly, in some nurseries the children were moved on to all-age homes at the age of four plus, so that half or more of each group were under the age of three. In others, children could remain until they were seven, and each group had one or two children aged five or older. Because of the burden of physical care and the more restricted vocabulary and syntax likely to be used with a young group it seemed likely that the lower the mean age of the children in the group, the lower the level of language development of the children.

Finally, although all the nurseries were generously staffed by most standards, some were better staffed than others; e.g. in the best staffed nurseries there were always at least two staff present with each group of six children, some of whom were away for part of the day at school, whilst in the worst staffed nurseries only one staff member would be on duty with the group during most of the morning and afternoon. It seemed likely that the better the staff–child ratio, the more often would the staff be able to converse and play with the children, and the better would be the language development of the children.

Since all but one of the intercorrelations between the scores of these four nursery organization variables were significant, with only thirteen groups the effect of each variable could not be examined separately. Each group was therefore given a single composite score, derived by a principal component analysis from the correlation matrix. Differences in composite score were found to be strongly associated with differences in patterns of staff–child interaction. In the highest scoring groups (henceforth referred to as the most autonomous groups) the staff spent more time talking, reading and playing with the children, and doing things with them in which the children were rated as "active" rather than passive. There was no significant difference between nurseries in the *amount* the staff talked, but there were very significant differences in the quality of talk. Staff in nursery groups which had most autonomy spoke in longer and more complex sentences, made more "informative" remarks (e.g. telling or asking the child something about present, past, or future activities, naming objects, asking for or giving opinions and explanations), gave more explanations with their commands, gave fewer negative commands, answered the children more often, and were more often answered by the children. Thus the linguistic as well as the social environment differed markedly between the nurseries.

These differences were associated with significant differences in the children's attainments. In non-verbal intelligence the mean scores of children in nurseries with differing autonomy did not differ: the overall mean non-verbal I.Q. was 104·9. In verbal attainments however there were marked differences. The mean verbal comprehension score of the three nursery groups which had the highest autonomy was 114·9, 1·5 standard deviations higher than those in the three most institutionally orientated groups—a difference in mean scores equivalent to that found between the verbal comprehension scores of children of professional families growing up in their own homes, and children of manual workers. The mean language expression score in the three most autonomous nurseries was 100·0, 0·6 standard deviations higher than those in the most institutionally orientated.

Significant relationships were also found between test scores and observational data. As predicted, there were significant correlations between the mean language comprehension score of the nursery and the frequency of "informative" staff talk, the frequency with which staff read to and played with the children, and the frequency with which the staff answered children's remarks. There were no significant correlations between the mean Minnesota non-verbal scores of the nurseries and any of the observational data.

The conclusion that both staff behaviour and the children's language development are significantly related to the social organization of the nursery rests on the assumption that children and staff were randomly allocated to different nurseries. As far as could be ascertained there is no evidence to suggest that allocation was related to intelligence. All the nurseries were managed by one or other of three national voluntary societies, and both intending students and infants entering care were sent to whichever nursery had a vacancy. No I.Q.s of the children's parents were available, but there was no significant difference between the social class distribution of the mothers of the children in the three most and the three least autonomous nurseries. It will be remembered that there were no significant differences in the non-verbal intelligence test scores of the different groups. The staff in all the nurseries were studying for, or had achieved, the same diploma (N.N.E.B.). All were the daughters of skilled workers or small shopkeepers or farmers and all had left school at the age of fifteen or sixteen with from 0–4 "O" levels. There was no significant correlation between their educational level (defined as number of "O" levels obtained) and the composite score of the nursery. However, there was a significant tendency for more autonomous groups to be staffed by more experienced nurses. Probably only inexperienced staff would accept a very low level of autonomy, whilst only experienced staff would be given the responsibility of an autonomous group.

An unsatisfactory feature of the study was the inability to isolate autonomy as the crucial organizational variable because in the more autonomous groups the children tended to be older, there was a higher staff–child ratio and the staff were moved less often. However, a variety of evidence suggests that the crucial variable in determining the quality of staff talk was the authority relationship within and outside the group. If the staff–child ratio was the crucial variable then one would expect that on occasions when two staff were present with 3–6 children (as happened much more often in the more autonomous groups) the children would benefit by a much greater output of play, talk and "informative" talk than if only one nurse had been present. In fact, analysis of these occasions showed that although the amount of staff talk increased, it by no means doubled, and the amount of "informative" talk remained the same. This was because of the marked staff hierarchy, when two staff were present, it was always understood that one of them was in charge. The attribute of being "in charge" was not a fixed one, but varied on a minute-to-minute basis. Thus a trained nurse in charge of a group was no longer in charge if joined by a more senior nurse; a student or untrained assistant, normally not in charge of a group, would be placed in charge when the trained staff were off duty or even left the room. All but the most senior staff could therefore be observed on different occasions in two authority positions. The difference between staff behaviour when "in charge" and "not in charge" was similar to, but even more marked than, the difference between the behaviour of the nurses in charge of the most and least autonomous groups. That is, staff on duty but not in charge functioned in a notably restricted way, talking much less and using less "informative" talk than the nurse in charge.

These effects of staff hierarchy also override the effects of training. Regardless of training, whoever was in charge talked more, used more informative talk, and played more with the children than the nurse not in charge. The only significant difference between the behaviour of trained and untrained staff in charge was a slight tendency for the untrained staff to play more with the children and allow them to be more active. The original prediction that the behaviour of junior staff would be similar in all nurseries, was therefore not confirmed. It was the nurse at that time in charge, whether trained or not, who was affected by the organization of the nursery. There were no significant differences between the behaviour of the staff not in charge in the various nurseries, except for their tendency to use more negative commands in the least autonomous nurseries.

It is by no means the author's intention to suggest that the staff–child ratio and staff training are factors of no significance, or that the only important variable in an institution is staff autonomy. Children's institutions could well exist where staff autonomy was high and there was little staff hierarchy, but interactions with the children were minimal or punitive. The evidence of the study suggests, however, that given staff of a certain social class, education, training, and goodwill, the social framework in which they are placed has an important effect in determining their behaviour. If given a limited role to perform, they will behave in a limited way. The nurses in the least autonomous nurseries, whose mean sentence length to the children when on duty was four words, could be heard in their own homes talking and playing in a very different way with their young brothers or sisters.

Injunctions to "Talk more" or to "Improve your talk" when on duty are thus likely to be of little avail if, as suggested, the nature of their talk depends on their perception of their role in relation to their superiors and to the children.

Again, whilst improvements in staff–child ratio are likely to be valuable, the size of the contribution of extra staff members depends on the role to which they are assigned, and the benefit to the children of additional staff may be more limited than would appear at first sight. This is often the case with volunteer help; unless assigned specific tasks or responsibilities the contribution of those who are "generally helping" a nurse in charge of the group may be slight and unsatisfactory to all.

In conclusion, the two studies referred to in this chapter would appear to offer direct evidence both that the level of children's language development is significantly related to their verbal environment, and that the way in which adults talk to children may be significantly affected by the social framework in which they find themselves.

REFERENCES

BERNSTEIN, B. 1971. *Social class, language and socialisation: class codes and control.* Routledge and Kegan Paul, London.

KING, R. D., RAYNES, N. V. and TIZARD, J. 1971. *Patterns of residential care: sociological studies in institutions for handicapped children.* Routledge and Kegan Paul, London.

TIZARD, B., COOPERMAN, O., JOSEPH, A. and TIZARD, J. 1972. Environmental effects on language development: a study of young children in long-stay residential nurseries *Child Dev.*, **43**, 337–359.

Personality and Social Competence

Competence and the Growth of Personality[1]

WANDA C. BRONSON

University of California

THE CENTRAL CONCERN of this paper is the relationship between a problem and the methods brought to bear upon its resolution. Human beings develop as babies not in conditions which systematically isolate and control the nature of stimuli, rewards and responses but in a real world of their own. In recent years there has been an increasing demand from many quarters for more research directed to uncovering what factors affect a child's development rather than to the analysis of responses in whatever conditions the investigator finds experimentally elegant. To criticize, however wisely, is one thing; to implement the programmatic statements with which one whole-heartedly agrees is another. How to deal with issues which many believe it is our mandate to address without compromising either the integrity of the issue or the integrity of the methods which permit the achievement of knowledge, rather than mere opinion leads to uncharted territories. Preliminary though my work is at this stage I feel justified in presenting it for common scrutiny.

THEORETICAL FRAMEWORK

Competence and the growth of personality, what are these words to signify?

In the sense that White (1959) has used the term, competence refers to the exercise of behaviours which lead to a feeling of efficacy and thus to a source of gratification that is universally and spontaneously sought by all members of our species. That the exercise of certain functions should

[1] The research reported in this paper is supported by the National Institute of Mental Health under grant MH 17312.

occur spontaneously, that the feedback contingent upon their exercise is not random within the environment natural to the species, and that the experience of such feedback is of itself rewarding to the organism, are ideas no longer revolutionary. Conceptions as to the nature of predispositions that may support the emergence of adaptive behavioural systems and the nature of stimuli appropriate for their activation and progressive integration into hierarchically organized structures still vary widely. With the current dearth of appropriate factual information, differences in emphasis cannot be resolved. Nevertheless, such conceptions open up new fields of thought and serve as powerful sources of provisionally held working hypotheses.

One such hypothesis emerges from the work of Watson (1967) who focuses on the contingency-seeking properties of the human organism. It is his view that the infant arrives predisposed to scan recent memory under the guide-lines of a "learning instruction" which reads: "Find and repeat the response which preceded the reception of the rewarding stimulus". Recently Watson (1970) has shown how his notions apply to the development of early social behaviour. The mother's responsiveness to the baby, manifest in her readiness to play social "contingency games" of smiles or vocalization with him, is adapted to the contingency-seeking properties of the infant. Hence, in an insightful reversal of common assumptions Watson suggests that "The game is *not* important to the infant because people play it; people are important to the infant because they play the game".

The contingency-seeking hypothesis establishes a powerful source for the activation and exercise of diverse behavioural systems. It paves the way for the development of competence, in the sense that linguists and some cognitive theorists have come to use the term, and it is shown in the baby's increasing capacity to form ever less rudimentary representations of various facets of the world in which he lives. The unavoidable search for contingent effects results, to borrow Piaget's (1970, p. 703) words, in "the establishment of cognitive or, more generally, epistemological relations which consist neither of a simple copy of external objects nor a mere unfolding of structures performed inside the subject, but rather involve a set of structures progressively constructed by continuous interaction between the subject and the external world".

The relationship between competence used in this specialized sense and competence in its common meaning of a prevalence of behaviours that are adapted to cope with environmental demands in a growth-enhancing manner is by no means direct. To possess a capacity and to act according to it are two very different things, a fact which has come to be recognized in the distinction between competence and performance models. However powerful contingency-seeking and exercise of functions may be, they are not the only forces to shape the infant's development. Avoiding that which is too discrepant from existing schemata and on which no response can be brought to bear; seeking to maintain proximity to objects of attachment; striving to maintain the individually proper balance between arousal and satiation: I need hardly enumerate the goals of the various systems which interact to determine how a baby will behave and what experience he will achieve in any given situation. As the child grows older, with increasing cognitive and voluntary control over behaviours within his repertoire, the areas in which he chooses to exercise his competence and the domains in which he may find himself required to act *in*competent, so as to be able to maintain a sense of control over his own fate, become an ever more complex product of the expectations he has developed. This is the process of personality development in which, under the right circumstance, a "sense of competence" becomes part of the image that the individual has of himself and which leads him to expect that, under most conditions he is likely to encounter, he will be able to cope with whatever demands he meets, and to derive joy from the encounter.

ISSUES OF RESEARCH STRATEGY

If the development of competence within the growth of personality follows along the lines I have sketched, then it is a process whose roots lie in the infant's early experiences and which extends over many years. Whatever facet of the process is under study, at whatever developmental stage, its full temporal range should not be lost from sight. From its inception, the process is developmental, multivariate and transformational in nature. It is one within which diverse parameters will interact to compensate, enhance, or interfere with both the development and the behavioural expression of other parameters. It therefore presents questions we are unlikely to resolve by the conventional method of isolating some construct, defining a number of behaviours as indicative of its operations, and proceeding to relate it to similarly derived indices of other constructs. I am not suggesting that this conventional method is not powerful, or indeed the only way eventually to allow the making of definitive statements. However, I am suggesting that its application to the issue at hand is premature. And therefore, it is unlikely to advance a solution to the problem and may even trap us into making misleading statements, which if transformed into action will give rise to programmes detrimental to the children with whose development we are concerned.

A far less elegant and I fear, far more difficult strategy appears to

be required. If the issue concerns the child's ability to make transformations; that is the emission of different behaviours in the service of the
same function, depending upon the age of the child and the context in
which he finds himself, then the likelihood of such transformations
and their limits must be determined before construct measures relying
on behavioural indices can be reasonably applied. As soon as this issue
is raised the sad realization follows, that despite numerous studies on the
behaviour of young children reliance upon the strict hypothesis testing
approach has failed to provide adequate information about the quality
and frequency of various types of behaviours which characterize
children at different ages or in different environments. Without some
normative, well-documented information as to what a twelve-month-old
baby will typically do under a variety of circumstances, and just how his
behaviours will differ from those typically shown by a child six months
older, I do not see how the critical questions surrounding the issue of
behavioural transformations can be adequately approached.

What a given child will do under a *variety* of circumstances is to my
mind as important and as little understood as are the changes that
typically occur with maturation or experience. We have very justly
focused a lot of attention on the reliability of our measures and observations: because of the requirements for proper experimental procedures
this has generally meant repetitions of the identical situation in the hope
of finding the baby responding in the same manner on all occasions.
However, this method has nothing to say about generality—the extent
to which, given different variants of a situation, the baby will nevertheless respond in a similar fashion. The overemphasis of a narrow view of
reliability has contributed to limit the possibility of achieving insight
into the full nexus of functions from within which the baby operates.
The most obvious of all facts continues to elude our method: at no
time is the baby actually operating at the level of only *one* behavioural
system. In a laboratory we appear able to isolate one system from the
others and to vary systematically the conditions that should affect it
(whether we actually succeed in being as convincing to the baby as we
are to our colleagues is another matter). But the laboratory is not an end
in itself and to the extent that laboratory conditions may distort a
fundamental aspect of the child's life it is necessary that the nuances
affecting the child be first delineated.

I have been focusing on the problems that follow the proposition that
behavioural transformations are central issues in development; positing
that the identification of the major domains in which they occur and
understanding the rules they obey, is a prerequisite to defining the
functioning of a system at any given time, and to the study of its develop-

ment over time. It is through inquiry about such systems, defined by sets of second-order constructs, that we seek to achieve knowledge of development which transcends inter-individual differences and thus can be meaningfully applied to all members of the species. In studying the very young, the difficulty lies in the translation of the properties of a system into appropriate second-order constructs. What *is* a competent twelve-month-old? What behavioural dimensions should fill out the principle of contingency-seeking so as to give rise to constructs appropriate to a given developmental stage and powerful enough to demonstrate the manner in which this principle operates, or fails, within the real life situation of the baby? The most frequent approach is to look to theory for rules of derivation, with that elusive quality of research judgement (which is probably neither more nor less than the accumulated experiences and intuitions of the individual investigator) coming in to make the difference between a pedestrian and a brilliant research strategy. A more powerful aid to such a translation process is used but rarely—an intimate acquaintance with the variety of behaviours which characterize the organism under natural circumstances, logically the best source to suggest meaningful and realistic constructs—is not part of the usual armoury of the investigator. I whole-heartedly agree with Sullivan's dictum that "people are more human than otherwise"; however, I also believe, that though profoundly human, the nature of babies' behaviour will often be seriously misconstrued if the narrow adult experience is the principal framework from which it is examined and through which it is given structure.

These are the main points in my case for the need of a research strategy which, directed by an urgent sense of what needs to be accomplished, aims at ambitious goals, focuses on asking what *is* rather than on what theoretically should be, and survives in the ambiguities of a bootstrap operation without ever losing the commitment to the methods and aims of science. Having thus stated my own position, let me return to reality and discuss some delights and frustrations to which this position has led me in preliminary attempts at implementing it in a study of development in the second year of life.

THE STUDY OF DEVELOPMENT IN THE SECOND YEAR OF LIFE

The full project is a short-term longitudinal study of forty babies between the ages of twelve and twenty-four months, followed by observations of their behaviour in a nursery school programme at $3\frac{1}{2}$ years of age. Observations of development in the second year were completed between January 1970 and May 1971; the follow-up assessment takes place in the summer of 1972. The infants and their mothers were observed in their own homes on six occasions spaced throughout the second year. Each trimester the babies were given a developmental test and were observed in structured situations designed to offer systematic information on attachment behaviours, fear, curiosity, and problem-solving strategies. They were observed in informal playgroups constituted from the participating mother–infant pairs first at four-week then at six-week intervals. It is to these playgroup observations (recorded on videotape, as were all observations other than those made in the home) that I turned my initial attempts at grappling with the problems which follow from the position I have described.

The choice of method was almost inevitable. Recording the behaviour on videotape provided an opportunity to repeatedly observe the baby operating in what is (at least for Berkeley babies) a very common situation in a context which simultaneously presents him with the mother, strange adults, a number of toys, and a few peers. It is a chaotic slice of life at its most natural and therefore, in terms of the research model I chose to follow, the most appropriate arena for working out a "language" adequate for describing what is, rather than what should be.

I have stressed my conviction that lack of sound normative observations, coupled with a premature narrowing of the problem to consider only such questions as are dictated by armchair theory serve to severely limit the growth of our understanding. Consequently, long before the question of individual differences in the matrix of factors which may impede or enhance the development of competence could be tackled, I felt obliged to provide myself with such normative information about development in the second year as would subsequently allow identification of what behavioural transformations in fact occur, and what constructs may most validly serve to organize diverse observations.

The strategy for processing the play session observations evolved from a view of development as a process in which repeated experience with particular contingencies leads to a progressive learning of the expectancies appropriate to the environment in which the baby has been operating. Four different types of potential respondents are present in each playgroup setting: the mother, strange female adults, peers, and inanimate objects. Due to their different nature, each provides different contingency experiences to the baby and may therefore lead him to develop different types of predictive expectancies, achieved at different rates. Although, as we shall see, babies often use objects to mediate their interpersonal behaviour, and their mothers to mediate all types of experiences (thus blurring all neat divisions) the inquiry nevertheless can focus on each domain of respondents separately, thus highlighting both that which is unique to the domain and that which serves to enmesh it with the others.

Peer Behaviour

The currently available data are preliminary and incomplete. I must emphasize that they are present here only to illustrate the kinds of problems and insights which follow from the research strategy I am using. They are *not* as a statement of findings about behaviour in the second year.

The rationale for focusing on peer behaviour in the context of studying the development of competence is quite simple. The world of peers will surround every individual throughout his life and will be a significant source of experiences which will become incorporated into his image. To achieve a sense of competence almost certainly requires that one be effective in implementing plans involving conspecifics. In order to reach the potential for such effectiveness the child must learn (a) that what he does can affect the actions of the other; (b) what the probabilities are that certain of his actions will produce particular types of reaction from the peer, and (c) how to link interpersonal action–reaction patterns in accordance with, or at least not in violation of, his ongoing plans. The purpose of the preliminary work in this area was to determine the nature of social acts that are directed by babies to their peers during the second year, focusing on the emergence of whatever chainings may occur in the development of interpersonal action–reaction patterns.

I will discuss the preliminary findings in terms of quite gross categories noting merely the nature of the data they reflect. A social contact (the basic unit in descriptions of different types of social behaviour) is a cluster of a minimum of two *bits*[1] from different component behaviour categories directed by a baby to his peer either concurrently or in close temporal contiguity. *Bits* are specific action patterns—a glance, a gaze, a look, are all examples of *bits* within the category of visual behaviour. There are five such component behaviour categories from which *bits* are selected by the coder to describe a contact, an action–reaction arc, or a chain composed of a series of such arcs: gross motor movements, visual behaviour, vocalizations, gestural action patterns, and facial expressions. On every occasion that a baby clustered two *bits* and directed them toward a peer, a contact was said to occur and, irrespective of the nature of the peer's response it was timed and described in code language. The description of each contact or action–reaction chain is

The term *bit* is used here to denote a specific action pattern, it is not a measure of information—the binary digit (Eds.).

highly detailed so as to allow for subsequent soundly based differentia-
tions among apparently similar behaviours emitted in the service of
different functions. However, for present purposes I limit myself mainly
to gestural patterns in describing what this initial analysis suggests.

TABLE I. *Composition of playgroups in which pilot babies' peer behaviour was sampled: indicated. (*= absent during segment; mths = months)*

Subject baby	Peers		Segment 1	2	3	Peers		Segment 1	2	3	Peers	
			Play session 1 12½ mths; 5 playgroups					*Play session 3* 14½ mths; 8 playgroups			*P* 17 mth.	
Ben	F	(1) An	1	0	0	F	(3) An	*	2	1	M	(3)
(Bn)	M	(1) Mo	2	1	1	F	(2) Li	0	2	1	F	(3)
	M	(1) Em	*	0	1						M	(2)
Mort	M	(1) Bn	*	1	2	F	(2) Re	*	0	0	F	(5)
(Mo)	F	(1) An	1	1	1	M	(1) Ir	0	2	0	F	(3)
	M	(1) Em	*	2	0	F	(1) Ga	0	0	1	M	(2)
Kurt	F	(1) Re	3	0	0	F	(2) Co	*	0	2	F	(5)
(Ku)	M	(1) Gr	*	0	0	M	(1) Dk	1	0	1	F	(4)
	F	(1) Ki	*	1	0						M	(3)
Grant	F	(2) An	3	2	0	F	(3) Di	*	1	1	M	(3)
(Gr)	M	(2) Mo	*	3	1	M	(1) Pl	0	4	0	F	(3)
	M	(2) Ku	*	1	0						M	(2)
Sean	F	(2) Ki	*	*	0	M	(4) Mo	1	3	0	F	(6)
(Sn)	M	(2) Se	0	1	1	F	(4) Di	0	0	0	F	(6)
						F	(1) Be	0	1	1	M	(5)
Anne	M	(1) Bn	*	1	0	M	(3) Bn	1	1	1	M	(5)
(An)	M	(1) Mo	1	1	1	F	(2) Li	1	1	1	F	(3)
	M	(1) Em	*	1	0						M	(2)
Diana	F	(1) Ma	*	12	4	M	(3) Gr	0	3	4	F	(5)
(Di)	F	(1) No	2	4	0	M	(1) Pl	2	1	0	M	(4)
											F	(3)
Norah	F	(1) Ma	*	*	3	F	(3) Ma	2	3	0	M	(5)
(No)	F	(1) Di	2	1	2	M	(2) Sn	*	1	0	F	(4)
											M	(3)
Renee	M	(1) Ku	3	0	0	M	(3) Mo	0	0	1	M	(4)
(Re)	M	(1) Gr	*	0	0	M	(1) Ir	0	3	1	M	(3)
	F	(1) Ki	*	3	2	F	(1) Ga	1	0	0	F	(3)
Kim	M	(1) Ku	1	0	0	M	(2) Se	4	0	0	M	(3)
(Ki)	F	(1) Re	0	1	1	F	(2) Ey	2	3	0	F	(3)
	M	(1) Gr	0	0	0						M	(3)

The preliminary work focused exclusively on a pilot group of ten babies and employed a time sampling technique. The three time segments from a play session cover five minutes of behaviour each; the first segment beginning immediately upon the baby's entry into the room,

d play session status of peer; number of interactions with each peer in each segment are

sion 5 ygroups		Play session 7 20 mths; 7 playgroups				Play session 9 22½ mths; 8 playgroups			
gment 2	3	Peers	Segment 1	2	3	Peers	Segment 1	2	3
*	0	F (5) Co	0	1	1	M (9) *Mo*	1	3	3
2	0	M (4) Mx	0	2	2	F (8) Li	0	1	0
0	2					M (7) Ir	0	0	1
0	0	M (6) *Sn*	5	3	1	M (9) *Bn*	1	2	6
0	0					F (8) Li	2	0	0
2	5					M (7) Ir	*	0	0
1	0	F (7) *Di*	0	1	0	F (9) *Ki*	1	0	1
0	0	M (5) Mi	0	1	0	M (7) Mi	1	1	1
1	0	F (5) Ro	0	0	1	F (7) Be	1	0	1
3	1	F (7) Ma	3	0	3	F (9) Ma	0	0	0
1	0	F (7) *Re*	3	1	0	M (7) Ra	2	1	1
0	0	F (6) Ga	0	2	2	M (7) Pl	1	0	0
4	2	F (8) *No*	0	1	1	F (9) Li	0	3	0
0	1	F (8) *Di*	0	2	1	F (8) Co	0	1	1
1	1	F (8) *Ki*	1	0	2	F (7) Lo	*	3	1
0	1	M (7) Em	1	2	0	M (8) *Sn*	1	0	0
0	1	M (6) Mk	0	0	0	M (8) Ni	0	0	1
1	0	M (4) Ab	0	2	0				
0	0	M (7) *Ku*	*	1	0	M (8) Se	2	0	1
1	0	M (5) Mi	3	0	2	M (7) Ja	*	1	1
0	0	F (5) Ro	1	1	0	F (6) Le	0	0	0
2	0	F (7) *Ki*	*	1	2	F (9) Dn	*	0	0
0	0	F (6) Ey	2	2	0	F (8) Ey	0	0	0
0	0	M (5) Dk	0	3	1	F (7) Ro	*	0	0
0	1	M (7) *Gr*	2	0	1	F (8) Ga	1	5	2
1	1	F (7) Ma	3	2	1				
0	0	F (6) Ga	1	0	0				
2	0	F (7) *Re*	2	0	1	M (9) *Ku*	1	0	1
0	0	F (6) Ey	1	0	0	M (7) Mi	2	0	0
0	0	M (5) Dk	1	0	1	F (7) Be	1	0	2

the second chosen from about the middle, and the last from about the end of the approximately forty-five-minute play session. The play-groups always met in the same room, measuring about 12×14 ft and furnished with a variety of toys. Videorecording was always done from behind a large one-way vision mirror. The mothers were of course aware of our recording procedures and realized that we were interested in seeing how babies play with toys and with one another. The extent to which any mother may have wished to shape her child's behaviour was left up to her, with an introductory statement to the effect that anything that was all right with her was all right with us. The current data reflect codings of time-sampled observations made in play sessions 1, 3, 5, 7 and 9. The conditions of observation are described in Table I.

In every time segment the experiences of a single child were followed by the observer who coded these in the manner indicated above. The baby was used to pinpoint the occurrence of social events, and all contacts, whether emitted by him or to him and irrespective of his response, were coded with equal concern for his and the other partici-pant's behaviour. As is apparent from Table I, more than one pilot baby was occasionally present in the same playgroup. In a few instances overlap of observation could not be avoided, and nineteen of the interactions specified in the table are repeats of each other. However, such duplications have been eliminated for statements concerning the number of interactions or the percentages of various patterns. Note, finally, that the interactions sometimes occurred between babies of the same age and sometimes between babies of different ages and play session experience. I do not have enough data yet to evaluate what effect same versus different age, same versus opposite sex, or partici-pation in a four-, three- or occasional two-member group may have had upon the occurrence and nature of peer interactions. Inspection of such data as are now available does not suggest any striking effects. The three five-minute time samples for each of the ten babies add up to a total of $2\frac{1}{2}$ hours of observation coded for each of five successive age levels.

I have made no full-scale attempts to assess all facets of observer agreement since I am as yet not certain which of the many judgements required in coding a single interaction will be retained beyond the pilot stage. For eight of the play sessions two independent observations were made of all interactions occurring in the three time samplings. Agree-ment on the presence of a contact was usually exact when the interaction involved some gestural action pattern, a behaviour defining a large majority of the social contacts. Occasions of contacts defined only by mutual looking (visual regards plus postural orientation or gross movements towards) were sometimes missed by one of the observers, and there were occasional disagreements on whether parallel activities in a shared toy complex included enough contact behaviour to be coded within some type of "play" interaction. The distinction between initiator and target of an interaction reached complete agreement. A few differences on whether two short, or one long interaction should be specified could be settled by clarification of endpoint criteria. Differences in codings of gestural action patterns were minor, extending only over adjacent patterns: a *show* or an *offer*, a *reach for* or a *point to*. In general, a very good agreement could be assured on those aspects of behaviour on which I focused—the presence, general nature, and duration of the various interactions.

What do these preliminary data suggest? The number and duration of peer interactions observed for the ten pilot babies are plotted in Fig. 1. Clearly, neither the number of interactions nor their duration varied much from age to age. The vast majority of interactions observed at

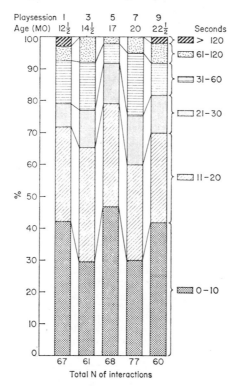

FIG. 1. Incidence of peer interactions of different durations coded in successive play sessions.

any age level were very brief, at least three-quarters of them spanning less than thirty seconds. Considering that this time period reflects the approach movement of one baby to another, the time it takes him to direct some cluster of social behaviour to the peer, the duration of the peer's reaction if any, and some terminal period during which both babies ignore one another (allowing the observer to conclude that the interaction is completed) then one realizes how brief were most of the social interactions observed. Contrary to expectation, the duration of interaction time does not suggest any developmental pattern of increase.

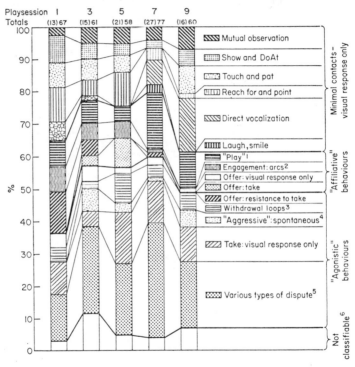

FIG. 2. Incidence of various types of peer interactions occurring in successive play sessions. Numbers within bar areas representing the number of interactions coded in the first five minutes are entered in parentheses.

[1] All occasions in which participants maintain proximity while sharing a common toy complex.

[2] A brief contact responded to by another brief contact; touch/touch, for instance.

[3] Movement away (from touch and reach for; once from a direct vocalization).

[4] Occurring not in context of a dispute: hit, shove, punch, yank hair, etc.

[5] Takes protested and protested strongly; attempted takes defended, or defended strongly; tugs-of-war; verbal disputes over possessions.

[6] Either completely directed by mothers or composed of appearingly unrelated action-reaction patterns.

From the data on the first ten babies, there is little apparent change in the capacity or willingness to sustain a social contact with a peer throughout the second year.

What of the tone of these interactions? These data are summarized in Fig. 2. First, it appears that at all ages a large proportion of what was observed are not true "interactions" but rather occasions in which social contact behaviours shown by one child were met with no response beyond visual regard by the other. Here again there is no suggestion of an orderly progression in the frequency of such minimal contacts. What then of the quality of such action–reaction patterns as do occur? Grossly lumped categories of action–reaction patterns indicate that the most frequent type of interactions were various kinds of disputes over possession. Dividing even more grossly into what can be seen as "affiliative" and "agonistic" types of interactions we find that the frequency of the latter far outweighs that of the former. To the extent that the ten pilot babies did affect one another, they did so more frequently in a manner suggesting an unsatisfactory experience for one or both participants rather than an experience which would tend to increase their pleasure in social behaviour. Let me emphasize immediately, however, that I am speaking of what appears as agonistic and affiliative *behaviour* with no suggestion as to the babies' *intent*. Despite the frequency of dispute and non-affiliative behaviours, it would be highly misleading to take these data as indicating that the children we observed were mostly aggressive little beasts. To give just one instance of the observations that lead me to stress this point: in Play session 5, a seventeen-month-old boy turns to the $18\frac{1}{2}$-month-old girl, hits her shoulder, and then proceeds to repeatedly hit her on the back in a series lasting for fourteen seconds. She turns and looks at him. He follows by another smack and a yank of hair. She again turns and gazes at him, while one of the mothers present touches the boy in restraint, another admonishes him to be gentle, and he is physically directed away. In less than a minute the little girl turns to the little boy and offers him a toy. He accepts it, and both children separate to engage in other activities. In this sequence of two interactions, the adults' reaction clearly differs from the response achieved from the peer: the question of the nature of the initiator's intent and the recipient's interpretation of a behaviour is obviously an important one. Whether the feedback contingent upon a baby's action is congruent with his expectations or not, must depend on the intent of the baby emitting the behaviour. Further, we observed that adults who attempt to shape the infant's behaviour into channels appropriate to their social mores will often act more in accordance with their perception of his intent, than as a function of the behaviour itself. In the vast majority of the many disputes we observed, I believe there was no trace of what we commonly think of as "aggressive" intent but merely a desire to possess the toy—the fact of its being in another child's hand appearing totally irrelevant from the baby's perspective. There are indications that it may be possible to isolate specific cues suggestive of different intent in otherwise identical action patterns. Direction of gaze promises to be one such fruitful cue. Although the evidence to date is merely suggestive, it appears that gazing at the participant's face while engaged in a tug-of-war, or approaching to take with regard on the face rather than the toy to be taken, is more characteristic of babies who seem to be exploring the effect of their actions upon the peer than it is among those children whose concern is with the toy, and not with the peer to whom it is attached.

The first segment sampled for observation purposes covers the first five minutes of behaviour after entry into the room. We can look for

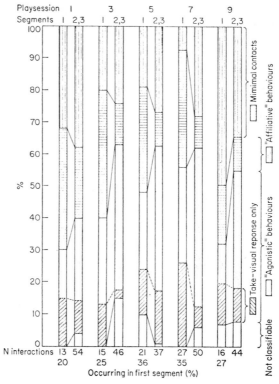

FIG. 3. Quality of peer interactions occurring in the first five minutes upon entry and in subsequent segments of each play session.

some understanding of the experience of the play session by contrasting
social peer behaviour occurring in this initial period with that which
occurs later in the session. Detailed information on Segment 1 behaviour
is included in Fig. 2. Drawn in grosser terms, the contrast between the
first and the two subsequent five-minute samples of a session is plotted
in Fig. 3. To me these data came as a surprise. With the exception of the
initial five minutes of the first play session (the first introduction these
children ever had to the playroom, as well as to the playgroup) the
number of peer interactions occurring in the period immediately after
entry does not depart by much from the 33% expected on the basis of
the proportion of total time represented by the first segment. Minimal
contacts do not decrease with increased exposure to playgroup participants. Most curiously, the gross category of "affiliative" behaviours
tends consistently to be somewhat more frequent during the first five
minutes than later, while conversely, the gross grouping of "agonistic"
behaviours shows a consistently higher incidence in the latter
segments.

Does familiarity breed contempt? Partly, we may be seeing the results
of fatigue, made perhaps more likely by the often considerable degree
of noise and commotion within the playroom. Partly, disputes increased
as individual babies became involved in their own activities with toys,
and became less willing to accede to a *take* without protest or defence.
And partly, these, and the other data, reflect what has become my
current working hypothesis, namely, that the learning of interpersonal
contingencies is very difficult to achieve within the age span with which I
am concerned. The feedback given by peers is too variable and often
too delayed to allow the baby to develop firm predictive expectancies
of links between his behaviour and the actions of a peer. The maintenance of intentional affiliative action and reaction patterns requires for
its existence an understanding of interpersonal contingencies. Not having
built up enough predictive expectancies as to the signal value of their
own action patterns or that of their peers, and being placed in a situation
in which inter-personal variability predominates while intra-personal
consistency is difficult to assess, combine to turn the baby's efforts to
engage away from peers and towards toys. Thus making the prevalence
of apparently agonistic behaviours inevitable. Let me add immediately
that I am speaking here of peers in general, not of long-term playmates.
It is most important to remember that these data reflect interactions
among babies who are strangers to one another. We know from observing even younger infants' behaviour with adults or their mothers that
they are capable of social interactive behaviour given a participant
whose responses bear a predictable relationship to the actions of the

child. There is no reason to suppose that with consistent exposure to one particular child the baby may not learn the contingencies appropriate with this given individual as well, if not as easily, as when the participant in the interaction is an adult. Indeed, the mothers who participated in the study commented on a number of occasions how surprised they were at seeing their child play so little with other children in the playgroup situation. Many had anecdotal evidence about some "little friend" with whom their child engaged in a great deal of mutual interactive play. I respect this anecdotal evidence and suggest that we should do some systematic work on the effects of consistent exposure to one specific child on the dyad's interactive behaviour. Concurrently, however, I think it is most important to assess the extent to which learning of inter-personal contingencies appropriate to one particular peer can be generalized at this age, to behaviour with other peers; and whether it leads in any way to enhanced interpersonal competence in a broader arena.

One more comment before leaving the data on peer interactions. I have focused on the ways in which they suggest a relative lack of developmental change in the effectiveness of interpersonal peer behaviour, partly out of my own surprise and partly in reaction to the assertion often heard nowadays, that being with children of their own age is good for everybody, at all stages of development. As preliminary as they are, I think these data strongly indicate that some caution should be exercised before the validity of such assertions be accepted wholesale. However, I do not wish to leave the impression that the social behaviour of the babies did not undergo some degree of change in the twelve-month period. Reverting to Fig. 2, you will note that the incidence of what I have called "play", although not frequent, nevertheless does increase in the seventh and ninth play sessions. Moreover, while the so-called "play" interactions in the early sessions were never more than an acceptance of a peer's presence within the confines of the baby's toy-complex activities or a simple reflection of the peer's actions with minimal, intermittent, one-sided or mutual regards, the seventh and nine play sessions saw the emergence of more truly interactive play behaviour. We have an instance of one child rocking another in the teetertotter while the peer smiles (one of the only eight occasions in the total of 323 coded inter-actions in which a smile towards the peer was noted). There is a twenty-one second period in one of the ninth play sessions in which two girls —here again with one of the rare instances of smiles and laughter— mimic each other's spitting sounds. And, most complex of all, for over two minutes we see two boys attempt to work out what appears to be a joint plan for one of them, riding on a giraffe, to pull the other who is seated in a connected wagon. Repeated attempts on the part of one of the two girls who joined in the spit-play to re-engage her peer in repetition of the game were ignored throughout the subsequent four minutes; and the two boys' attempt succeeded for only a few brief seconds in a period taken up by a series of intense and involved miscommunications and miscoordinations. The moments of interpersonal connections in these late sessions are brief and very rare but they do occasionally appear where previously there were none.

Behaviour with Inanimate Objects

Let us turn now for a brief look at behaviour with objects. The rationale for this facet of the study was essentially the same as that proposed for investigating behaviour with peers. To learn about the rules which govern the physical world and his position in it, the baby must discover that his actions on objects have consequences and that the nature of such consequences, being predictable, may be brought under control. In elaborating on this discovery the infant will continue to broaden his range of effectiveness, increase his knowledge, and become progressively more capable of constructing plans that work in accordance with reality yet in the service of his personal goals. The function of the preliminary work was again, to seek what normative patterns could suggest as meaningful ways to pursue the study of this developmental process in the context of emerging competence.

Observations of the same ten pilot babies' actions with toys during the same ten segments but only in the first, third, seventh and ninth play sessions represent the material I shall discuss. Every object that the child touched during each time segment was specified and the durations of all such contacts were noted. In all instances when the baby maintained physical contact with a toy for more than five seconds, his actions with the object were observed and coded.

The coding system for behaviour with objects distinguishes between investigation and play in terms identical to those used by Hutt (1970). Investigation is said to occur when the child's actions show him to be asking "What is this object?" while in play, the focus of the behaviour shifts to asking, "What is it that I can do with this object?" The difference between these two by no means mutually exclusive categories calls for a different descriptive system to capture adequately the qualities of each.

The quality of investigatory behaviour was described in terms of two independent dimensions; intensity of visual regard, and extensiveness or complexity of physical actions exerted upon the object. The three-point scale of intensity or regard summarizes the amount of time that the baby spends in looking at the object he is holding or otherwise acting upon. Of the three categories of physical action the first subsumes the most passive ones; holds, carries, fingers. The second group's somewhat more active behaviours; turns over in hands, pats, squeezes, waves. To be placed in the third category, the behaviour needs to be either intense—shakes vigorously, bounces up and down, hits repeatedly, pulls apart—or, at a more moderate degree of intensity, include a variety of action patterns being brought to bear on the same object.

Play can occur within what is nevertheless behaviour orientated primarily to asking what the object is. At its most rudimentary level, it consists in exerting (whether coincidentally or not) simple action patterns that seem adapted to some salient characteristic of the object.

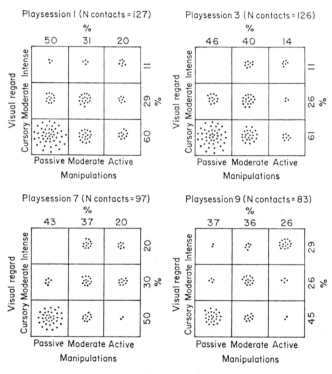

FIG. 4. Intensity of visual regard and complexity of manipulation in investigatory contacts with inanimate objects. The dots represent the number of contacts coded in each cell at successive play sessions. The percentage of contacts falling within each of the three categories of visual behaviour and each of the three categories of manipulative behaviour are given in the margins. (The individual investigatory contacts are of varying durations; there is no systematic relation between duration and either age of quality of contact.)

Shaking a rattle in the context of other investigatory behaviours would, in this coding system, be assigned an "elicited play behaviour" coding in addition to an investigatory behaviour classification. At the next level of play is behaviour which, although still primarily investigatory, contains within it a brief period of clear functional use of the object. A period of turning the pages of a book embedded amongst other uses made of it would thus qualify for a "part functional use" code. When the baby picks up the book and spends the entire period turning pages, perhaps naming pictures or making some other vocal responses, his behaviour would be judged to have passed from the "What is it?"stage to a full utilization of what he knows the object can offer. No longer investigatory, his behaviour would be coded as "functional play". Finally, when the baby begins to mix his own imagination with the functions of the object, we observe the emergence of "imaginative play". Giving a ride to various toys, all carefully seated on the giraffe, is an instance of what was considered as such an imaginative game.

Consider what this method of structuring observations yields when applied to behaviour in the second year. Figure 4 shows the distribution of investigatory behaviour codes assigned to all contacts with objects that the ten babies made at the four successive age levels. The number of such categorizations declines sharply in the seventh and ninth play sessions since, although the number of object contacts that were coded at each age level remained remarkably constant (varying between 128 and 139), the incidence of primarily investigatory behaviour became less frequent. The main point made by Fig. 4 is that, unlike the data on peer behaviour, a progressive developmental pattern can be discerned. The frequency with which intense visual regard is brought to bear on the process of investigation increases. Bestowing no more than a cursory glance at an object one has elected to obtain becomes less characteristic as the babies grow older. Although even as late as play session 9 more than a third of investigatory manipulations involve no more than holding or carrying, this period also sees an increase in the frequency of more extensive or more complex physical manipulations. Moreover, the relationship between the two dimensions becomes stronger with increased development, suggesting an increasing coordination among modalities and resulting in a potentially more powerful and effective system of information gathering and processing.

Figure 5 shows a complementary aspect of this developmental process by portraying the changes in the different levels of play behaviour. As was noted earlier, pure investigation although it remains the most frequent type of object contact, drops sharply by the ninth play session. In the first play session all but a few of the 130 contacts are either pure

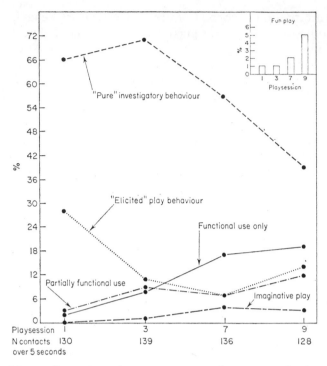

Fig. 5. Incidence of pure investigatory contacts and contacts reflecting different levels of play behaviour coded at successive play sessions.

investigation or investigation with occasional actions adapted to the salient characteristics of the object. Using toys solely in the manner dictated by their function begins to emerge in the third play session, and from then on this becomes a progressively more prominent characteristic of the baby's behaviour with the toys within the playroom. What I have called "imaginative play" was very rare among the ten babies and occurred mainly in the seventh and ninth play sessions.

A three-stage developmental progression suggests itself. After an initial period of working at discovering what objects are and what properties they possess, the baby begins to return over and over again to make use of what the particular toy best enables him to do. This is a period of what appears to be a kind of "functional fixity" during which the baby, adapting his behaviour fully in compliance with the toy's most obvious potential, reaffirms his grasp of the consequences of his actions. After certainty has been achieved through exercise and repetition, the baby progresses further and begins to look beyond the obvious, seeking to adapt to his own imagination whatever properties the object

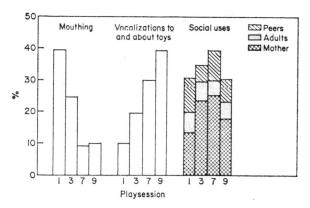

FIG. 6. Mouthings, vocalizations, and social uses of object. Incidence of mouthing of objects; of vocalizations to and about objects; and of uses of objects for social contacts in play sessions *1* (12½ months), *3* (14½ months), *7* (20 months), and *9* (22½ months).

has which will aid him to achieve his goal. It was striking to all who observed behaviour with objects how much intense work was reflected on occasions when a baby's investigatory or play behaviour was deeply aroused. The category of "fun play" plotted at the far end of the figure had been designed to accommodate the gay, lighthearted, incongruous qualities of behaviour I had conventionally thought of as playful. "Singing while swinging the stuffed rat by its tail" is a prime example of one of the rare occasions when this category was appropriate in describing the often more serious and even effortful play behaviour of the babies.

Before leaving these data, and to fill out the developmental picture a little more, consider the age changes portrayed in Fig. 6. As was to be expected, but was nevertheless pleasing to find, the incidence of mouthing toys in the process of investigation decreased over the second year. Vocalizing in the course of dealing with an object—naming the toy, talking to it, imitating the sounds it should make, or simple shouting in response to its presence—became more frequent with each successive play session. As language becomes better developed, it too becomes increasingly a part of the focused, functional and complex behaviour with objects. Finally, toys are used for social purposes—to show, to give, to ask about—in about a third of the object contacts at all play sessions. Such uses occur primarily in relationship to the mother and, consonant with the suggestions derived from data on peer behaviour, the discrepancy in the frequency with which mother and peers are thus invitationally approached with toys becomes more marked after the initial play session.

THE PROBLEM AND THE RESEARCH STRATEGY

I have discussed the intentions of my research and I have described some of the realities of the data I am generating: what can be learned from the juxtaposition of the two? Extended beyond the pilot study, further observations made along the same lines will establish the credibility, and bring into sharper focus, such normative and developmental patterns as are presently emerging. In this, at least three purposes will be served. First, a detailed knowledge about what babies actually do will prevent translating their actions into dimensions which may be salient at later ages but not properly applicable to the realities of early behaviour. To speak of a child as being "friendly", for instance, conjures a host of interrelated, intentional behaviour patterns and implies a definable orientation towards conspecifics. Looking at the peer behaviour data, I do not see the applicability of the term to these babies, or the sense in expecting that the incidence of such behaviours as, for instance, the offer gesture, should relate to an affiliative orientation to peers at later ages. Second, the emergence of developmental patterns in certain domains and the absence of developmental change in others is at the least suggestive of the operation of principles which govern certain processes and which should be further explored. It is my working assumption that the difference in the degree of change in behaviour with peers and with inanimate objects is, in part at least, a function of the different contingency experiences afforded by each. In accordance with this assumption, the development of capacities for mutual regulation should be most accelerated in the baby's relationship with his own mother, to appear at successively later stages in behaviour with other adults, with inanimate objects, and finally with peers. Third, increased delineation of the nuances in behaviour patterns shown by different babies, to which I have only alluded in this paper, may become a critical factor in allowing some resolution to the problem of behavioural transformations.

I say may because it is to just this problem, which I have specified at the outset as being of central importance, that the data generated by my preliminary approach cannot be directly applied. Transformations of behaviour can only be studied by means of firm longitudinal material. The method of time sampling facilitates delineation of normative patterns but does not facilitate the emergence of clear longitudinal information. Observation of sequences within units set by standard chronological time often violates the reality of the individual's phenomenological time; seen outside of its full sequence, the intent of a behaviour can remain obscure or be misconstrued to the detriment of any meaningful evaluation of its function and hence potential equivalence to other behaviours.

Finally, the current emphasis on detailed observations of specifics fails to capture the configurations of patterns wherein, intuitively, the burden of transformational continuities reside. Given some leeway, suggestive consistencies in individual differences can be outlined. For instance, out of the twenty-five so-called "aggressive" social behaviours coded over all play sessions (hits, beats, yanks hair, etc.), thirteen were initiated by one of the ten consistently observed babies, the remaining twelve instances being distributed among all other children who were observed. The baby who contributed the two strongest withdrawal loops (in one of them responding by crying at the mere approach and touch of a smaller peer) did not initiate a single direct take on any occasion and was unique in responding to an offer gesture by looking away while extending a foot towards the offerer. In addition of all the subject babies observed he spent the least time in peer interactive behaviour, which was just over six minutes out of the total $1\frac{1}{4}$ hours observation period. In the domain of behaviour with objects, seven of the eleven instances of "fun play" were contributed by only one little girl; the boy who gave us half of all occasions of imaginative games showed early evidence of consistent extensive physical investigation with concurrently intensive visual regard.

Notice that in each instance I focus on different domains, and perhaps different systems, to capture the flavour of the individual's consistency; in a number of cases I would have to delineate networks of apparently compensating or equivalent ways of functioning to make my point. This is the stuff of observations, but not the stuff of systematic inquiry. The leap from sound delineations of normative patterns of development to equally sound process and structure constructs requires more sophisticated analyses of longitudinal transformations than have as yet been undertaken. A stepwise series of successive approximations such as the one described here may have to intervene before the issues we care about can successfully be resolved.

ADDENDUM

The work which has followed since the preparation of this report has shown the effectiveness of two modifications in the approach to the analysis of the behavioural domains which were discussed here. In the area of social behaviour, a shift from reliance on clusterings of *bits* to emphasis on *interactive themes* (defined with equally detailed behavioural care but focused on the *issue* which temporarily joins a dyad) deflects the danger of becoming trapped in sterile taxonomies and results in a much more coherent view of developmental patterns in interpersonal communication. In the study of behaviour with inanimate objects, careful analyses of how attention is deployed and of what co-occurs with shifts in its focus have proved to be indispensable adjuncts in defining developmental transformations in activities with toys.

REFERENCES

HUTT, C. 1970. Specific and diversive exploration. In H. Reese and L. Lipsitt (Eds)., *Advances in child development and behavior*, Vol. 5. Academic Press, New York and London.

PIAGET, J. 1970. Piaget's theory. In P. Mussen (Ed.), *Carmichael's manual of child psychology*, 3rd ed. John Wiley, New York.

WATSON, J. S. 1967. Memory and "contingency analysis" in infant learning. *Merrill-Palmer Quart.*, **13**, 55–76.

WATSON, J. S. 1970. Smiling, cooing, and "The Game". Paper presented at the meeting of the American Psychological Association, Miami Beach, Florida.

WHITE, R. W. 1959. Motivation reconsidered: the concept of competence. *Psychol. Rev.*, **66**, 297–333.

Interpersonal Spacing of Pre-school Children[1]

WILLIAM C. MCGREW

Gombe Stream Research Centre, Tanzania

INTRODUCTION

THIS PAPER WILL deal with a neglected aspect of children's social interaction: the phenomenon of interpersonal spacing behaviour. It will summarize and inter-relate several studies of three- and four-year-old children observed during free play in a nursery school. This is part of a continuing research programme in ethological studies of pre-school children's behaviour being conducted in the Department of Psychology, University of Edinburgh.

Ethologists recognized some time ago the significance of both intra- and interspecific spacing behaviour in lower animals (e.g. Hediger, 1955). They realized that social dispersion and proximity are social behaviour in the same way that fighting, clinging and smiling are. Their studies have revealed a wide variety of forms of spacing behaviour, from the complex rituals of territorial confrontation to the subtle but consistent maintenance of inter-individual distance.

Various workers (Goffman, 1963; Hall, 1966) have speculated about the existence of spacing behaviour in human beings, and the label of *proxemics* has been attached to this area of inquiry. Other workers, primarily social psychologists, have attempted empirical studies of human spacing behaviour using adults in small groups (Argyle and

[1] Much of the data and ideas contained herein are those of P. L. McGrew, to whom the author is grateful. The following sources generously made financial support available to the author for the studies: The Population Council (1968–69); U.S. Public Health Service, National Institute of Mental Health (1969–70); Social Science Research Council (1970–71). The Department of Psychology, University of Edinburgh, kindly provided facilities and equipment. The author is indebted to Professor D. M. Vowles, who supervised the research, Dr. M. Manning, who helped with advice and inter-observer reliability testing; L. Bruce, who directed the nursery school; and C. E. G. Tutin, who aided with data analysis.

Dean, 1965; Sommer, 1969). A few studies of children's interpersonal spacing have recently appeared (Aiello and Jones, 1971; Bass and Weinstein, 1971; Baxter, 1970; Castell, 1970; Guardo, 1969; King, 1966; Meisels and Guardo, 1969). However, in most cases, these studies exhibit a number of limiting drawbacks. They utilize artificial and sometimes highly contrived experimental situations rather than real-life or naturalistic situations. Rather than study ongoing behaviour on a firsthand basis, they use indirect or projective techniques. Their categories of measurement are usually inferential and their validity untested. The result is that such studies, however methodologically elegant and statistically flawless, tell us nothing about what children actually do. Sometimes these methods produce highly dubious results; in one study (Bass and Weinstein, 1971) children were asked to place paper silhouette figures on to various test scenes, and the distances between the silhouette figure and figures in the scenes constituted the spacing measurements. Twenty-five per cent of the young subjects (5–7 year olds) produced "inappropriate placements", e.g. placed the silhouette figure on top of one of the test figures. Thus, even if the standard approaches did reflect children's real-life behaviour (an untested assumption), they would be of doubtful operational value with even younger children.

On the other hand, primatologists working on the social behaviour of nonhuman primates have been studying spacing behaviour for some time. They have used a variety of species of both Old and New World primates (Bernstein, 1964, 1965) and have compared spacing behaviour in closely related species housed similarly (Rosenblum et al., 1964), in wild-living and captive populations of the same species (Quiatt, 1966), in normally and deprivation reared individuals (Mason, 1961), and in different conditions of group composition and modification (Bernstein, 1969). This body of scientific literature has proved to be useful in supplying: (1) methods of recording spacing behaviour, (2) analogous and/or homologous measures of spacing behaviour, (3) important parameters to be explored, e.g. kinship relations, and (4) clues to the function of interpersonal spacing in social groupings.

NEAREST NEIGHBOURS

The first question to be considered is obvious: do pre-school children exhibit interpersonal spacing behaviour? Or, restated operationally, given an area of known dimensions occupied by a group of known size, are the individuals of the group dispersed in any nonrandom fashion over time or are they merely randomly scattered? In examining the question and succeeding ones in this paper, the area involved was the playroom of the Epworth Halls Nursery School, Edinburgh. It is a rectangular room (6·7 × 11·0 m) containing the usual nursery school toys and equipment. The group concerned was composed of up to twenty children three and four years old who attended the nursery school five weekday mornings per week. They were Caucasian, English-speaking, mostly of Scottish national background, physically healthy, and of average intelligence. They came from middle-class socio-economic backgrounds and had a median of one sibling each. All observations were conducted during the children's free play, i.e. when they had unrestricted access to all toys and other children under minimal adult supervision.

The measure chosen was the *nearest neighbour* technique. This has previously been used by plant ecologists (Clark and Evans, 1954) and by students of animal behaviour working with domestic fowl (McBride *et al.*, 1963) and rhesus macaques (Quiatt, 1966). The technique involved recording for each of the twenty children in the nursery school the three other children nearest him in space at one time. This was done in random order six times a day for a period of twelve days, which, accounting for absences, meant that each child was measured approximately seventy times. Note that this means that the results are not actual distances but ordinal data. Because this technique involved making relative distance judgements, it was felt necessary to conduct inter-observer reliability testing of the recording method. Two observers carried out two days of simultaneous recording. This produced an overall reliability coefficient of 0·82 for the first nearest neighbour, with most disagreements coming from cases of apparently equidistant neighbours or slight but cumulative discrepancies in timing between the observers. The results for second and third nearest neighbours are not discussed here.

The resulting data can be used to produce a 20 × 20 matrix, with the subject children cast in rows and the first nearest neighbours cast in columns. Each time a nearest neighbour dyad occurred, this was scored once in the appropriate cell. Excluding the twenty impossible cases where a child cannot be a nearest neighbour to himself, this leaves 380 cells. However, since the interest is only in dyads, the matrix can be reduced by "folding" it at the diagonal, thus combining cases where A-is-the-nearest-neighbour-to-B with cases where B-is-the-nearest-neighbour-to-A. This is justified by the highly correlated rank orders of the mirror-image cell frequencies on either side of the diagonal (Spearman rank correlation coefficient, $N = 190$, $r_s = 0·69$, $p < 0·001$). The combined 190-cell matrix is given in Fig. 1.

The number of nearest neighbour dyads recorded was 1317. Randomly dispersed throughout the 190 cells this would produce an expected

WILLIAM C. MCGREW

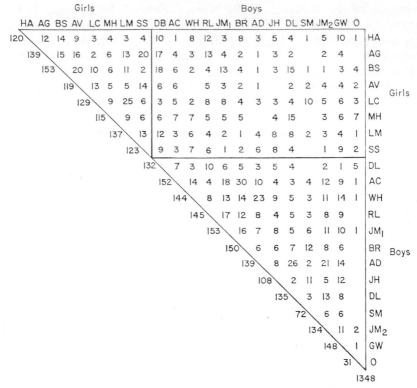

Fig. 1. Matrix of 190 possible combinations of nearest neighbour dyads for a group of twenty children. The figure in each cell is the observed frequency of that dyad. The two lighter internal lines delineate the sex subgroupings.

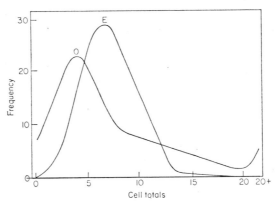

Fig. 2. Distribution of frequencies of nearest neighbour dyad cell totals, observed versus expected Poisson distributions.

TABLE I. *Sex composition of children's nearest neighbour dyads, observed versus expect frequencies*

	Boy/Boy	Boy/Girl	Girl/Girl
Expected	457	666	194
Observed	577	464	276

mean of just under seven occurrences per cell. The observed cell totals range from 0–30, with seven cells empty and sixteen cells containing fifteen or more occurrences. To test for nonrandom dispersal of the dyads, the data were fitted to a Poisson distribution (Snedecor and Cochran, 1956). The results (see Fig. 2) show it to be highly nonrandom ($\chi^2 = 1092$, $df = 14$, $p < 0.001$).

It is possible to learn more by examining subsections of the matrix. By subdividing the matrix along sex lines into two smaller triangles and a rectangle, one can determine whether or not nearest neighbour dyads tend to be of the same sex (see Table I). The results show significant concentrations of occurrences in the two smaller triangles, indicating a predominance of same-sex pairings ($\chi^2 = 125.7$, $df = 2$, $p < 0.001$). By further subdividing the two triangles and rectangle, one can determine whether or not nearest neighbour pairs tend to be of similar ages. This is accomplished by subdividing the eight girls and twelve boys into equal-sized subgroups according to age. These subgroups correspond almost exactly to three- and four-year-olds (see Table II). The results show that both older and, to a lesser extent, younger boys associate more often in same-sex nearest-neighbour dyads, while mixed-age associations are significantly less common ($\chi^2 = 50.1$, $df = 2$, $p < 0.001$). An identical pattern emerges in the older and younger girls ($\chi^2 = 22.1$, $df = 2$, $p < 0.001$).

The results from quartering the mixed-sex rectangle are more confus-

TABLE II. *Age composition of all-male and all-female nearest neighbour dyads, observed versus expected frequencies*

		Older/Older	Older/Younger	Younger/Younger
Boys	Expected	131	314	131
	Observed	177	251	148
Girls	Expected	59	157	59
	Observed	86	121	68

TABLE III. *Age composition of mixed-sex nearest neighbour dyads, observed versus expected frequencies*

	Older boy/ Older girl	Younger boy/ Older girl	Older boy/ Younger girl	Younger boy/ Younger girl
Expected	116	116	116	116
Observed	154	77	117	116

ing (see Table III). The older boy/younger girl and younger boy/younger girl combinations occur at precisely chance levels of frequency. The older-boy/older girl combination is at least partially inflated by DB's anomalous behaviour. He behaves as though he were a girl; his three nearest neighbours most frequently noted are the three oldest girls in the nursery (HA, AG, BS). The scarcity of younger boy/older girl nearest neighbour pairs is at present inexplicable. The overall results, that nearest neighbour pairs tend to be of alike sex and similar age, are not surprising, but they offer the first empirical demonstration of this in human infants.

TABLE IV. *Relationship of nearest neighbour status to other variables in nursery school children*

	Sex	Socio-economic status	Birth order	Number of siblings	Height	Weight	I.Q.	Nursery experience	Age	
χ^2	12·41	2·66	0·28	1·47	0·00	0·14	0·08	0·26	0·46	r_s
df		1	3	1	20	20	19	20	206	N
p	0·001	n.s.	n.s.	n.s.	n.s.	n.s.	n.s.	n.s.	0·05	p

χ^2 one-sample test.   Spearman rank correlation coefficient.

In addition to age and sex, other characteristics of "nearest neighbour-liness" can be investigated using the summed totals for the number of times each individual appears as a nearest neighbour. Table IV gives the results. Of the seven other variables examined (socio-economic status, birth order, number of siblings, height, weight, I.Q., and amount of nursery experience) none reveal significant relationships.

GROUP FORMATION

Having confirmed that nursery school children exhibit interpersonal spacing behaviour, what of its ontogeny? This brings us to the theme of the symposium *competence*. Performance of efficient spacing is presumably like any other social behaviour pattern, in that its deployment is sharpened and made more appropriate by suitable experience. This process of increasingly skilful performance of a behaviour is another way of saying that competence develops. No previous published work has examined the interpersonal spacing in three- and four-year-olds. Both the projective and observational studies cited earlier have asserted its existence in children of five years and older; whilst Castell (1970) has indicated its limited existence in $1\frac{1}{2}$–3-year-olds at home.

One way to examine this problem empirically is to look at the spacing behaviour of children who have different amounts of social experience as they interact in the same situation (McGrew and McGrew, 1971b). The approach was through nursery school group formation, i.e. assemblage of the children over the first seven days of the autumn term after the summer holiday. The differential social experience is provided by two subgroupings: (1) Five older, experienced (E) children were returning to the nursery school after the summer vacation. The three boys and two girls ranged in age from 55–59 months, with a mean age of fifty-seven months, and all had attended Epworth Halls for at least twelve months. (2) Eight younger, inexperienced (I) children were being simultaneously introduced into the nursery school for the first time. The four boys and four girls ranged in age from 39–49 months, with a mean age of forty-five months. None had ever been previously exposed to any long-term, large-sized peer group. Note that two variables, age and nursery experience, co-vary.

The next question was how best to measure interpersonal spacing behaviour? The nearest neighbour method was of proven usefulness, but it focuses on only one child at a time, and the resulting data are only on an ordinal scale. The ideal data would be on an interval scale, providing all inter-individual distances between all individuals at any one moment in time. Firsthand recording of this information, seventy-eight items in this case, from a group of highly mobile and unpredictable subjects was patently impossible. In theory, this could be done retrospectively from photographs. Given overhead still cameras pointing downwards to photograph children wearing initialled beanies, one might measure distances from the enlarged prints and convert to real distances. Unfortunately such facilities were not available.

A compromise method was devised which involved the recordings of data on a nominal scale which could at least be partially converted to an interval scale, and which could supply both individual and group data at the same time. This entailed marking the playroom floor with carpet tape in a 3×5 grid of approximately 2·2 m squares. The observer systematically scanned the room approximately every minute, recording

TABLE V. *Definitions of eleven categories of interpersonal spacing behaviour, listed in order of decreasing proximity*

Peer Contact (PC): In physical contact with another child.
Adult Contact (AC): In physical contact with an adult.
Peer Proximity (PP): Within "touching distance" of another child (1 m).
Peer Proximity' (PP'): Number of children in *PP*.
Per cent Peer Proximity (%PP): Percentage of children present with which a child was in *PP* daily.
Adult Proximity: Within "touching distance" of an adult (1 m).
Intermediate Proximity (IP): More than 1 m from another child but within same floor square (maximum distance: 2·5 m).
Intermediate Proximity' (IP'): Number of children in *IP*.
Solitary (Sy): Alone within floor space.
Solitary Peripheral (SP): *Sy* within 1 m of the room's walls.
Mobility (My): Ratio of number of floor square boundary crossings to number of observations per day.

the location of each individual present. This produced a scaled-down spacing map, and along with supplementary notes, provided up to eleven measures of spacing behaviour (see Table V). Figure 3 shows a sample data sheet.

If some form of specific competence in interpersonal spacing is contingent upon individual experience in a particular situation, then one would expect to find differences between the subgroups. The older

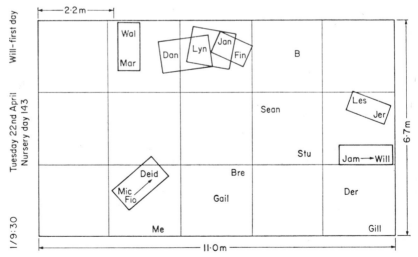

FIG. 3. Sample data sheet portraying schematic diagram of 3 × 5 floor grid. Abbreviations denote locations of individuals. Encircled individuals are within 1 m of each other. Individuals connected by arrows are in physical contact.

returning children are only resuming familiar activity in a very familiar situation after a brief absence. The newcomers have no acquaintance with nursery school and no sustained experience with large peer groups of any kind. On the other hand, one would expect to find no differences between the subgroups if they had already developed a general competence at social spacing in another situation which was more or less immediately transferable to this novel context. Or, one might expect no differences between the two subgroups if interpersonal spacing behaviour is a skill which is largely pre-programmed in young children and requires little individual practice.

TABLE VI. *Comparison of interpersonal spacing behaviour of nursery-experienced (E) and inexperienced (I) children during group formation. Figures represent mean frequency (or number) per child per observation*

	PC	AC	PP	PP′	AP	IP	IP′	Sy
E	0·04	0·001	0·70	1·11	0·05	0·38	0·65	0·15
I	0·02	0·007	0·52	0·86	0·07	0·40	0·60	0·26
p^1	0·02	0·05	0·02	0·05	n.s.	n.s.	n.s.	0·02

[1] Wilcoxon matched pairs signed-ranks test, two-tailed.

Table VI gives the results. The older, experienced children showed more *Peer Contact*, more *Peer Proximity*, and *Peer Proximity* with more children. The younger, inexperienced children showed more *Adult Contact* and were more frequently *Solitary*. On the other spacing measure the two subgroups were indistinguishable.

Not only do differences exist between the subgroups, but they do so in a coherent fashion. The older children show the more intimate proximity patterns more frequently: physical contact and maintenance within touching distance. This intimacy is also likely to be manifested in larger groups by these children. Presumably such intimacy is encouraged (or only allowed?) by prerequisite familiarity. The categories of intermediate, and presumably less threatening, dispersion show no differences between the subgroups. The category most indicative of avoidance of social proximity, *Solitary*, is exhibited much more often by the naive and possibly frightened newcomers. No differences exist in *Adult Proximity*, but *Adult Contact*, perhaps for comfort, is seven times more common in the inexperienced children. In summary, the older, nursery-experienced children were more social toward their peers, while the younger, nursery-inexperienced children tended to avoid their new peers and seek adult solace.

TABLE VII. *Composition of Peer Proximity dyads during group formation, comparing nursery-experienced (E) and -inexperienced (I) children*

	E–E (%)	E–I (%)	I–I (%)
Expected	13	51	36
Observed	51	29	20

Other differences in interpersonal spacing emerged between the experienced and inexperienced children. One way to pursue this was to examine the make-up of *Peer Proximity* dyads, i.e. pairs of children within 1 m of each other. If the children randomly paired themselves, one would expect the distributions of the observed pairings to conform approximately to the frequencies expected by chance. This does not occur, as the results in Table VII show. The older, nursery-experienced children significantly preferred each others' company in close proximity while the younger, inexperienced children avoided both the older children and each other ($\chi^2 = 479 \cdot 1$, $df = 2$, $p < 0 \cdot 001$).

The study also provides an opportunity to demonstrate an example of the possible heuristic value of nonhuman primate studies. Kawai (1960) reported of his group formation study of Japanese macaques in an open enclosure that "... the newcomers were centrifuged to the periphery, irrespective of their sex ..." This finding prompted us to look for evidence of similar behaviour in the nursery school, and the spacing category *Solitary Peripheral* was devised. Although they constituted 62% of the group, the new children provided 82% of the examples of solitary children found within 1 m of the playroom's boundary. This was significant statistically ($\chi^2 = 77 \cdot 3$, $df = 1$, $p < 0 \cdot 001$). It is not a surprising finding in retrospect nor is it an earthshaking one. But it demonstrates two points: (1) that hitherto ignored sources may be capable of producing stimulating and sometimes productive ideas for investigation, and (2) that the value of nonhuman primate studies for investigators of human behaviour lies not in the sometimes injudicious extrapolation of results by speculators. Rather, such studies may provide fresh viewpoints which we might co-opt in devising empirical studies of human behaviour.

INDIVIDUAL INTRODUCTION

The group formation findings are derived from cross-sectional data and give little insight into the longitudinal development of spacing behaviour. They do not provide information on how soon the nursery-inexperienced newcomer adjusts his interpersonal spacing sufficiently to become integrated with other group members. Another study (McGrew and McGrew, 1971a) examined this by following the progress of young, inexperienced children introduced singly into the established nursery group. Fourteen newcomers entered the nursery school group, which ranged in size from 13–19, at successive intervals of not less than a week. The eight girls and six boys had a mean age of thirty-nine months (range 36–56 months) at entry. Ten of the previously defined spacing behaviour categories were used (see Table V). Data were recorded for most children over three five-day periods; days 1–5, 6–10 and approximately 30–35.

TABLE VIII. *Comparisons of interpersonal spacing behaviour of introduced individuals over three five-day periods and results from another study. Figures represent mean frequency (or number) per child per observation*

	PC	AC	PP	PP′	%PP	AP	IP	Sy	SP	My
Days 1–5	0·04	0·01	0·66	1·19	0·71	0·11	0·14	0·18	0·07	0·40
Days 6–10	0·04	0·01	0·64	1·11	0·71	0·10	0·16	0·17	0·07	0·40
Days 30–35	0·03	0·01	0·66	1·12	0·69	0·11	0·15	0·17	0·10	0·41
McGrew (1970)	0·06	0·01	0·60	—	—	0·13	0·12	0·12	—	—

The results indicate that under certain conditions, competence in interpersonal spacing can develop very rapidly. As Table VIII shows, the children's mean frequency levels over the first five days of nursery experience were virtually indistinguishable from the later levels. The results also show that the children in Epworth Halls exhibit very stable interpersonal spacing behaviour. Comparisons between the three observation periods of this study and the normal condition of the density experiment which is discussed below show virtually no differences. This presumably means that under certain favourable social conditions, naive children are able to adjust their spacing very quickly to fall into line with group practices.

Detailed examination of the two conditions—group formation v. individual introduction—gives plausible explanations for the differential rates of adjustment found. In group formation, the majority of untutored newcomers presumably "swamp" any spacing norms presented by the minority of returning children, and this unsettled state must persist for some time. It may result in a protracted integration process, so that both subgroupings show aberrations even after seven days, from the more uniform frequencies of the other two studies. As would be expected, the nursery-inexperienced children show greater aberration. In contrast, the individual introduction situation would appear to be optimal for rapid integration. The newcomer, a minority of one amidst an established group, is surrounded by consistency in interpersonal spacing and presumably causes little disruption to the group's social affairs. It is not surprising that the individual newcomer appears to achieve proxemic compatibility almost immediately. That a process of adjustment does take place rather than the newcomer being proficient from the first is shown by comparisons within five-day periods. Significant inter-day changes in the frequencies of several of the categories occur during days 1–5 but not during days 6–10 or 30–35.

GROUP DENSITY

On the basis of the studies reported above a general conclusion is that children's competence in interpersonal spacing is a dynamic product of social experience and the particular social context. But other factors are also bound to affect the expression of spacing behaviour. One of the more obvious of these, group density, was experimentally manipulated in another study (a preliminary report is made in McGrew, 1970). Density is operationally defined as the amount of available floor space per child. However, density in itself is not a unilateral variable; instead, it is the interaction of two variables, in this case room size and group size. Thus, one may vary *spatial density* by holding group size constant and changing the size of the room. Or, one may vary *social density* by holding room size constant and varying the size of the group. The object of this study was to see if group density variations of either type had any effects on children's spacing behaviour.

Twenty children (eleven girls, nine boys) participated in the study. Their ages ranged from 38–59 months, with a mean age of forty-eight months, and all had attended the nursery school for at least six months. To vary the spatial factor, two conditions were devised: (1) 100% space, the normal room size, and (2) 80% space, in which the room's contents were moved into four-fifths of the area. The contents kept their same relative locations but the space between objects decreased. A naturalistic barrier of chairs was created, cutting off the now empty one-fifth, and the children were given a bogus but plausible explanation which they readily accepted. To vary the social factor, two conditions were devised: (1) 100% group, the entire nursery school group, and (2) 50% group, in which half the class were randomly chosen by a lottery game to play outside during the early morning observation session. The other half played indoors and were observed. After "milk time", the two subgroups exchanged places, so that each child got equal daily experience and observation time in both locations. The result was a 2×2 matrix of four group density conditions given in Table IX. The most crowded condition, A, easily exceeded minimal space requirements laid down by national nursery school regulations. Twelve thirty-minute observation periods were conducted under each of the four density conditions, and these were counterbalanced.

TABLE IX. *Four group density conditions (A, B, C, D) generated by two room sizes and two group sizes. Density figures adjusted for fluctuations in attendance*

		Room size	
		80% (56·2 m²)	100% (73·7 m²)
Group size	100% (14–19 children)	A 3·5 m²/child	B 4·9 m²/child
	80% (8–10 children)	C 7·0 m²/child	D 8·2 m²/child

Before presenting the results, it might be useful to consider the simple gas model from elementary physics as an aid to visualizing the situation. For the spatial density comparisons, consider a given volume containing a given number of gas molecules, if the volume is decreased by 20%, then one would expect the mean inter-molecular distances at any instant in time to be reduced on average by 20%. For the social density comparisons, consider that if the number of molecules in a given container is doubled, then one would expect the mean inter-molecular distances at any instant in time to be halved.

Tables X and XI present the results for the three most common

TABLE X. *Spatial density effects on children's interpersonal spacing behaviour. Two low : high comparisons (D : C and B : A) when group size is held constant. Figures represent mean frequency per child per observation*

Experimental condition	D 50% group 100% space	C 50% group 80% space	p[1]	B 100% group 100% space	A 100% group 80% space	p[1]
PC	0·06	0·09	—	0·06	0·07	—
PP	0·57	0·65	0·025	0·60	0·65	0·05
Sy	0·23	0·19	—	0·12		0·01

[1] Mann-Whitney U test, one-tailed.

TABLE XI. *Social density effects on children's interpersonal spacing behaviour. Two low : high comparisons (D : B and C : A) when room size is held constant. Figures represent mean frequency per child per observation*

Experimental condition	D 50% group 100% space	B 100% group 100% space	p^1	C 50% group 80% space	A 100% group 80% space	p^1
PP	0·06	0·06	—	0·09	0·07	—
PP	0·57	0·60	—	0·65	0·65	—
Sy	0·23	0·12	0·001	0·19	0·08	0·001

[1] Mann-Whitney U test, one-tailed.

measures of interpersonal peer spacing recorded (see Table V). The spatial density comparisons in Table X all show differences in the expected direction. *Peer Contact* is slightly more frequent at the higher densities, *Peer Proximity* is significantly more frequent at the higher densities, and *Solitary* is significantly less frequent at the higher densities. Thus, the gas model so far retains its predictive utility. The social density comparisons in Table XI present a different picture, however. Again, *Solitary* shows the predicted differences with its mean frequencies being significantly halved in both cases. However, in neither *Peer Contact* nor *Peer Proximity* does anything approaching a doubling in frequency occur, and in one case, a slightly lower frequency emerges. So, doubling the number of children does not halve the inter-child distances, instead these remain the same.

This unexpected result caused us to look at other data from social behaviour patterns which were recorded simultaneously with the spacing data by another observer. This research is reported in McGrew (1972). Twelve representative behaviour patterns selected from earlier studies were noted, e.g. *Hit*, *Push* (aggressive behaviour); *Digit Suck*, *Weep* (fearful behaviour); *Laugh*, *Passive Physical Contact* (nonagonistic behaviour). Again, returning to the gas model, one would expect more frequent inter-molecular collisions (or child–child interactions) at higher spatial and social densities. The overall results were in agreement with those found for the spacing measures; in the spatial density comparisons the expected increases occurred, while in the social density comparisons they did not.

What do these results mean? First, they mean that children do not behave like gas molecules. More specifically, they indicate that children apparently are able to adjust temporarily their interpersonal spacing behaviour under certain conditions. At certain high densities, they avoid each other by maintaining greater inter-individual distances than would occur by chance. Second, is it possible to say anything about differential effects of the social and spatial density manipulations on the children's spacing behaviour? Here, a serious but unavoidable flaw in experimental design weakens any conclusions. Space and group size were varied by different degrees in this study. Group size is easily variable over a wide range, i.e. one could have anything from one to twenty children in a room. But the manipulation of space is limited by the room's furnishings and other contents; anything more than a 20% reduction leaves little space for activities. However, the results suggest that social density changes may be more potent than spatial ones. If this is so, the explanation may lie in a double-barrelled stressful effect present in the social density comparisons. Higher densities, whether of spatial or social origin, produce general limitations of free movement, specific difficulties related to performance of specific activities, and frustrations related to decreased concentration and privacy. In addition, with higher social but not spatial densities, there are more individuals present to deal with and more possible social combinations which must be coped with. A more extensive experimental design, e.g. a 3×3 or 4×4 matrix of group size and space conditions, might enable one to elucidate this suggestion.

SOCIOMETRY

Finally, how does interpersonal spacing behaviour relate to more orthodox psychological methods of measurement? The only previous efforts in this area have involved projective measures of personal space (Dosey and Meisels, 1969; Meisels and Dosey, 1971). In this study, the standard measure chosen for comparison with the results from the nearest neighbour observations was sociometric testing. It should be noted that some disagreement exists in the developmental psychology literature over what sociometric tests actually measure in pre-school children. It is generally assumed that they reflect differential social attraction to and preference for individual peers.

Subjects were asked three questions and they responded three times to each by pointing to photographs of their classmates. The questions were: "Who do you like most to play with in the nursery?", "Who do you like most to sit next to when you do a puzzle?", and "Who do you think is the nicest child in the nursery?". The results from the fourteen usable records (of primarily older children) showed that children who appear most often as nearest neighbours also tend to be chosen often in response to sociometric questioning ($r_s = 0.40$, $N = 20$, $p < 0.05$). This is what one would expect if children are spatially attracted to other children whom they like.

Many more studies will have to be done before the ontogeny and organization of interpersonal spacing behaviour in young children is understood, but it is hoped that this preliminary contribution has indicated its significance as an integral part of the socialization process. By emphasizing naturalistic observation, the author hopes that other research workers in this area will be encouraged to look at what children actually do in day-to-day social situations.

REFERENCES

AIELLO, J. R. and JONES, S. E. 1971. Field study of the proxemic behavior of young school children in three subcultural groups. *J. Pers. soc. Psychol.*, **19**, 351–356.

ARGYLE, M. and DEAN, J. 1965. Eye-contact, distance, and affiliation. *Sociometry*, **28**, 289–304.

BASS, M. H. and WEINSTEIN, M. S. 1971. Early development of interpersonal distance in children. *Canad. J. Behav. Sci.*, **3**, 368–376.

BAXTER, J. C. 1970. Interpersonal spacing in natural settings. *Sociometry*, **33**, 444–456.

BERNSTEIN, I. S. 1964. The integration of rhesus monkeys introduced to a group. *Folia Primat.*, **2**, 50–63.

BERNSTEIN, I. S. 1965. Activity patterns in a cebus monkey group. *Folia Primat.*, **3**, 211–224.

BERNSTEIN, I. S. 1969. Introductory techniques in the formation of pigtail monkey groups. *Folia Primat.*, **10**, 1–10.

CASTELL, R. 1970. Effects of familiar and unfamiliar environments on proximity behavior of young children. *J. exp. Child Psychol.*, **9**, 342–347.

CLARK, P. J. and EVANS, F. C. 1954. Distance to nearest neighbour as a measure of spatial relationships in populations. *Ecology*, **34**, 445–453.

DOSEY, M. A. and MEISELS, M. 1969. Personal space and self-protection. *J. Pers. soc. Psychol.*, **2**, 93–97.

GOFFMAN, E. 1963. *The presentation of self in everyday life.* Free Press, New York.

GUARDO, C. J. 1969. Personal space in children. *Child Dev.*, **40**, 143–151.

HALL, E. T. 1966. *The hidden dimension.* Doubleday, Garden City, New York.

HEDIGER, H. 1955. *The psychology and behavior of captive animals in zoos and circuses.* Criterion Books, New York.

KAWAI, M. 1960. A field experiment on the process of group formation in the Japanese monkey (*Macaca fuscata*), and the releasing of the group at Ohirayama. *Primates*, **2**, 181–253.

KING, M. G. 1966. Interpersonal relations in preschool children and average approach distance. *J. Genet. Psychol.*, **109**, 109–116.

MASON, W. A. 1961. The effects of social restriction on the behavior of rhesus monkeys: II. Tests of gregariousness. *J. comp. physiol. Psychol.*, **54**, 287–290.

MCBRIDE, G., JAMES, J. W. and SHOFFNER, R. N. 1963. Social forces determining spacing and head orientation in a flock of domestic hens. *Nature, Lond.*, **197**, 1272–1273.

McGrew, P. L. 1970. Social and spatial density effects on spacing behaviour in preschool children. *J. child Psychol. Psychiat.*, **11**, 197–205.

McGrew, P. L. and McGrew, W. C. 1971a. Changes in children's spacing behaviour with nursery school experience. Unpublished manuscript.

McGrew, P. L. and McGrew, W. C. 1971b. Interpersonal spacing behaviour during children's group formation: a comparative study. Unpublished manuscript.

McGrew, W. C. 1972. *An ethological study of children's behavior*. Academic Press, New York and London.

Meisels, M. and Dosey, M. A. 1971. Personal space, anger-arousal, and psychological defense. *J. Pers.*, **39**, 333–344.

Meisels, M. and Guardo, C. J. 1969. Development of personal space schemata. *Child Dev.*, **40**, 1167–1178.

Quiatt, D. 1966. Social dynamics of rhesus monkey groups. Unpublished Ph.D. thesis, University of Colorado.

Rosenblum, L. A., Kaufman, I. C. and Stynes, A. J. 1964. Individual distance in two species of macaque. *Anim. Behav.*, **12**, 338–342.

Snedecor, G. W. and Cochran, W. G. 1956. *Statistical methods applied to experiments in agriculture and biology*. Iowa State University Press, Ames, Iowa.

Sommer, R. 1969. *Personal space*. Prentice-Hall, Englewood Cliffs, New Jersey.

Social Competence and the Educational Process[1]

ROBERT D. HESS

Stanford University

In this paper, the term *social competence* refers to behaviour which relates individuals to the institutions of the society in which they live. In psychological and educational literature, social competence has traditionally referred to acts and feelings through which persons are related as individuals to one another and to small groups—patterns of interaction which might be called *person-relevant* behaviour. There is another category of social activity which, following Dennis (1968), might be called *system-relevant* behaviour. This refers to attitudes and beliefs, feelings and acts which relate individuals to institutions and to political and social systems.

The latter category is not easily or specifically described. It includes a range of diffuse social behaviours, feelings and beliefs. These may be illustrated by political acts which express concern with social problems and conflict (protesting, picketing); by supporting political candidates; by behaviour which challenges, changes, or supports authority, tradition, and confidence in major institutions of the society—the family, the school, the church, the police, the courts and other agencies of government.

As psychologists and social scientists interested in the education and socialization of the young, we have concentrated attention upon the socializing process that transfers to the young, patterns of behaviour which represent the behavioural priorities of the adult society. The focus

[1] Some parts of this paper are drawn from a paper presented at the 1971 Invitational Conference on Testing Problems, Educational Testing Service, October 1971, New York City.

I wish to acknowledge the collaboration of Tom Fox and the assistance of William McKenzie, Joseph McGeehan, Lynn Curry and Paige Porter in the analysis of the materials.

283

of this paper is upon the reciprocal part of the cycle—the extent to which the behaviour that is acquired by the young operates subsequently to maintain or change social institutions, organizations and national political systems. So long as socialization functions effectively, there is little need to examine the processes through which child rearing and education help support the stability of social and political units. The stresses which have been created in institutions and within American society suggest, however, that an analysis of the ways in which socialization may sustain, modify or destroy institutions is urgently needed.

From this perspective, the current emphasis on humanistic experience, encounters and inner feelings in the United States has not been paralleled with an emphasis upon the care and feeding of social institutions. There seems to be little awareness of the essential functions that institutions serve in a society. Rather it has become fashionable, at least in the United States, to attack schools and other social organizations and to blame them for many of the problems that the society now faces. This discussion then, is orientated towards the development of social competence in the young which has long-term relevance for the effectiveness and vigour of socio-political structures.

SIGNIFICANCE OF SYSTEM-RELEVANT BEHAVIOUR

The consideration of social competence in this system-relevant sense draws its significance from some contemporary conditions in the United States and perhaps in several other highly industrialized countries. Major socializing institutions of the society are under severe pressures which makes it difficult for them to maintain their integrity and their functions. The obvious examples of this are the church, the family and the school, all three of which have been undergoing change and have been under attack from a number of sources.

There are many reasons why these institutions are less effective and why the attacks upon them have been so intense. I find the comments of Geoffrey Vickers in *Freedom in a rocking boat* (1970) especially applicable to an understanding of the complex processes that affect institutional growth and decay. An elaboration of the pressures on the institutions and the reasons why they have intensified in recent years is beyond the scope of this paper. It is widely assumed, however that they include several factors. First are the changes brought about by increased population density, its effect upon environmental resources and its social morphological revolution, to use Hauser's (1969) term. This has produced an enormously expanded number of opportunities for social contacts and interaction, many of which are not governed by the traditions of social controls of institutions; these encourage challenges to existing social values.

A second mediating influence is the rapid expansion of communication devices. This expansion has opened a flow of information and exposure to alternative models of divergent values and action across age groups (e.g. the publicity given to rock concerts at Woodstock); between institutions within a nation (a college protest or riot is flashed over television networks within hours across the entire nation); and across nations (an American tourist cannot but be struck by how widespread certain parts of his native culture have become throughout the world).

A third factor is the awareness, articulateness and open hostility among ethnic groups and the poor with respect to their relative disadvantage *vis-à-vis* a more affluent white society and the apparent failure of educational institutions to offer them a useful education.

Perhaps a fourth more significant factor for the United States is the disillusionment that has accumulated from the long and fruitless war in South-east Asia in which we have been engaged. In short, there are more people with whom to interact, they know more about each other and their patterns of behaviour and values, many of them feel powerless and disadvantaged and they mistrust national foreign policy and the corporate exploitation of national resources. These conditions encourage the emergence of subcultures and "deviant" reference groups.

These and other influences have led to a counter-culture (Roszak, 1969) which, whatever its substance, has created a spirit of anti-institutionalism, anti-authority, and anti-tradition which takes many forms.

One consequence of these changes has been an increase in the number and variety of sources of socializing influence on the young. These new sources include political youth movements, militant ethnic groups, rock groups and other forms of music transmitted by the youth culture, television, community organizations orientated towards reforms in the schools, and other reference groups of a transitory nature. These groups have both values and rewards to offer their members and are in many cases not directly linked (in the sense of being accountable to) with the major traditional institutions of the society. These emerging socializing influences have created a number of alternative reference groups for pre-adults, which offer quite divergent sets of values.

In the familiar model of socialization, much of the social competence the child needs to help sustain the institutions and systems of which he is a part, is acquired from adults through observation, imitation, modelling, identification and direct instruction. In periods of rapid social and cultural change, however, traditional values may not suffice either to equip him to deal with his own interactions with institutions or to help modify and improve the efficiency and usefulness of institutions which need to be adapted to new social and political conditions. Thus, typical modes of socialization ill prepares the child for system-sustaining behaviou r in times of social turmoil.

Although the traditional model of socialization is one of system maintenance, our task is to understand how to socialize the young in a society in which the system is not being very well maintained and in which there is increasing discontent with its priorities, its structure and its function.

THE ROLE OF THE SCHOOL IN SOCIALIZATION AND IN DEVELOPING POLITICAL ORIENTATIONS

The public schools in the United States serve a major function as socializing agents in addition to their more strictly educational activities. Supported by public funds, planned and controlled by persons and groups deeply identified with the values of the nation, vulnerable to political and community pressures, the schools necessarily pattern experiences for the young children in ways that are presumably consistent with the dominant values and norms of the society. They are in turn supported and sustained by the values and behaviour they transmit.

This classical model of socialization is a cycle of system maintenance that operates by instilling in the young the values and behavioural tendencies which perpetuate the adult social institutions. The form these institutions take and the particular values that are inculcated, vary from one society to the next. They appear to be related to the subsistence economy and other features of the environment in many instances (Barry et al., 1959; McKinley, 1964). This relationship between economic environment and child-rearing is sufficiently loose, however, to accommodate influences of other types that have little to do with the ways in which a given kind of child rearing is useful in adapting a people to their physical environment.

It is implicit in this classical concept of socialization that institutions of the society filter, arrange, and reinforce the stimuli to which the young child is exposed. Of the massive array of stimuli available in the world around him, the child learns to recognize some as more salient than others, to respond to patterns of sound, of light, of movement which come to have meaning because of the regularity with which they occur and the events in adult life to which they are related. It is this selective emphasis of filtering, of patterning positive and negative reinforcements that makes the child aware of what is good and what is bad, what is to be sought and to be avoided, what is to be monitored and what is to be ignored. This information about the way the world is viewed by the adults and institutions around him interacts, of course, with his own experience and developing comprehension of the world. These mediating and filtering functions are governed by tradition and cultural integrity as often as by logical analysis of the future relevance of a particular form of behaviour for the child's career. Their purpose is to establish expectations and internalize norms of conduct.

In the United States as well as in other countries (Bronfenbrenner, 1970; Counts and Lodge, 1947; Hess and Torney, 1967; Ridley et al., 1971; Weiler, 1968), schools actively induct the young child into political attitudes and behaviour. Initially, these are of a type to produce feelings of attachment and nationalism, positive affect and regard for the school, the state, the nation and its officials. This is done ritualistically and in incidental and subtle ways. The diffuse socialization input to which the young are exposed may include the salute to the flag and recitation of the pledge of allegiance; pictures of Washington, Lincoln, and other national heroes on the walls; and observance of special holidays to honour national leaders and military victories.

The intensity of national concern about such matters is indicated by the 1940 Supreme Court decision that students could be required to salute the flag, a decision reversed in 1943 (Oregon State Bar, 1968), firing of teachers thought to hold subversive ideologies, and community opposition to in-school activities thought to be openly opposed to our present form of government. Thus, the schools have been given a responsibility for shaping and producing system-maintaining behaviour in children.

Some of the issues inherent in teaching system-relevant materials appear in the schools in the way some contemporary social studies tests deal with socio-political education and indoctrination. In their efforts to help establish national loyalty, the schools present a positive image of the society. This is scarcely surprising and probably typical of most socializing agents. It is of special interest, then, to examine how they deal with social defects and problems.

How does a child become aware of the stresses and difficulties which he will encounter and try to solve as an adult? I would like to report some data on this point. Last spring, a graduate student, Tom Fox, and I began a study of the images that textbooks present of certain problems in American society. We selected four areas in which stress or defects in the United States are evident and examined texts to see how they were described and presented. The four categories of potentially stress-producing social interaction were defined as follows:

1. Race and ethnic relations, which involve the social relationships that exist between the majority white population and groups that are distinguished by their culture or by their race. An example would be a discussion of the problems American Indians might encounter in moving from a rural reservation to a large city.

2. Distribution of income, goods, and services, which involve access to the wealth and resources within our society. An example might be a discussion of the income and living conditions of migrant farm workers.

3. Political negotiations and processes, which involve the interaction between groups of people, institutions, public officials, and decisions which affect the allocation of resources or selection of political leaders. An example would be a discussion of the tactics students or minority groups have used to secure certain political rights and benefits.

4. Ecological practices, which involve the utilization of resources and the preservation of the natural pattern of relations between man and his environment. An example is a discussion of problems created when chemicals and sewage are dumped into waterways.

At the third grade level we identified eighteen textbooks adopted for 1970–71 by at least two states on a statewide basis. Eight states were included. Twenty textbooks from the same states at the ninth-grade level were also examined. We read and categorized 17 286 paragraphs at the third grade and 29,244 paragraphs in ninth-grade texts.

For each paragraph, we asked these questions: First, are any of these four topics mentioned in any way? The tally for this was a simple yes/no. A second question was applied when the answer to the first question was, yes: Is this topic presented in a way that indicates there is a conflict or problem involved? For example, if a Japanese gardener or art shopkeeper was mentioned with reference only to his business success as a member of an ethnic group but no reference made to discrimination, this was scored as a no-conflict mention. Third, for paragraphs that included allusion to conflict or to the existence of a problem—poverty, dissent, pollution, etc.—the relevant question was: Does the author of the text present the conflict or problem as one that was severe or one that was mild?

The final question was: To what degree was a conflict or problem presented as resolved or resolvable? If there was, for example, an incident of exploitation of workers by an industry, a complaint heard and a settlement agreeable to both worked out, the issue was considered resolved. If the author commented that there should be greater effort on the part of the community to help ethnic groups deal with their ghetto conditions, this was rated as resolvable but not resolved. A four-point scale was used to indicate the extent to which the reader was given the impression that the normal processes of the system were capable of resolving the difficulties described in the paragraph.

We thus had a *frequency count of mentions* for each category; a *frequency count of events described as involving conflict* or difficulty; *an intensity index* of the severity of the problem; and a *resolvability index*, reflecting the impression of the system's adequacy for handling and resolving stress.

A summary of this simple counting and rating approach shows that the appearance of social conflict in these texts is relatively infrequent. Roughly speaking, at the third grade, only 18% of the 17 000 paragraphs referred to these topics in some way, an average of about 4% per category. There was some variation among the four topics—economic and conservation topics were mentioned most often, political negotiation and processes least often. Although on the face of it, this frequency seems low, it is one of the interesting features of our state of theory and knowledge that we have no criteria for judging whether these topics received adequate coverage. At the ninth-grade level, 45% of the paragraphs discussed one of these four issues in some significant

TABLE I. *Percentage of paragraphs devoted to four social issues*

Categories of social interaction	Reference to social issues		Reference to related conflict	
	Grade 3	Grade 9	Grade 3	Grade 9
Race and ethnic	3·93[1]	2·75	0·56	0·42
relations	(680)	(804)	(97)	(122)
Distribution of				
income, goods	7·18	16·59	0·54	0·88
and services	(1 241)	(4 850)	(93)	(258)
Political				
negotiations	1·82	23·99	0·89	0·64
and processes	(315)	(7 014)	(154)	(187)
Ecological	5·25	2·11	2·58	0·006
practices	(908)	(616)	(447)	(2)
	18·18	45·44	4·27	1·946
Total mentions	(3 144)	(13 284)	(791)	(569)
Total paragraphs	17 286	29 244		

Total books coded = 18 (Grade 3) and 20 (Grade 9)

[1] *n*'s in parentheses.

way. These mentions were concentrated in two categories, those dealing with distribution or resources and those dealing with political negotiations (Table I).

More clearly significant is the way these topics were handled when they did appear. Of those paragraphs in third-grade texts which dealt with these four sensitive issues, only 25% included any suggestions that conflict and stress might be involved. In some categories allusions to conflict were even less frequent (Table II). Moreover, the frequency of mention of conflict appears to be inversely related to the intensity of the problem. Over half of the references dealing with conservation practices involved a suggestion of conflict or difficulty but only 12% of the references to race relations gave an impression that problems needed to be solved. To put it in more dramatic form, less than 1% of the 17 000 paragraphs gave the reader the impression that race and ethnic relations in this country involve conflict and stress. Less than 1% discussed distribution of income in any way that suggested economic inequality or exploitation. There are references to credit buying, savings accounts and pay rises, but few to poverty, unemployment, welfare, or hunger.

TABLE II. *Severity of conflict as presented by authors of social studies tests (all issues combined for mentions of conflict)*

Severity of conflict Cooperation	Grade 3	Grade 9
1. (+3)	56·64 (448)	0
2. (+2)	9·99 (79)	0
3. (+1)	4·30 (34)	1·05 (6)
4. (0)	23·64 (187)	31·64 (180)
5. (−1)	0·63 (5)	28·12 (160)
6. (−2)	4·55 (36)	35·85 (204)
7. (−3)	0·25 (2)	3·34 (19)
Hostility		
	100·00	100·00
Total mentions	(791)	(569)
Total paragraphs	17 286	29 244

At the ninth-grade level the contrasts are even greater. While a much larger percentage of total paragraphs discussed one or more of the four issues, the proportion of paragraphs that described conflict was roughly comparable or perhaps smaller. It appears that the extent of coverage of social issues is not related to the candour with which they are presented.

This general impression that we live in a benign society is extended in other ways. Not only are few problems presented; those that do exist are depicted as not severe. Most of the examples of conflict in the books we analysed, regardless of which issue was involved, tended to be presented either as neutral (24%) or as being carried out in a spirit of cooperation (combination of first three categories, 71%), as shown in Table II. There is little hint of the sort of conflict that leads to bus burning and school boycotts in the following examples: "groups will often campaign against a politician they disagree with", or "people disagree about school integration". The image of polite exchange that is offered is more suited to a tennis club than to the contemporary American scene.

At the ninth grade there is the first sign that discussions are related to the age of the students. Severity of conflict is appreciably greater across all categories than at the earlier level. More than a third of the references describe events in the two most extreme categories. Virtually none are presented in a context of cooperation. The larger part, however, still falls in the neutral or mildly negative zone (Table II).

Whatever the intensity of conflict, disagreement was usually handled in a fashion that led to a resolution of the problems. On our four-point scale from "Resolved" to "Not Resolvable", 92% were rated as

TABLE III. *Degree of resolution of conflict in reference to four social issues (percentages of mentions on all four issues)*

Degree of resolution	Grade 3	Grade 9
1. Resolved	48·30	35·3
	(382)	(201)
2. Near resolution	44·37	17·22
	(351)	(98)
3. Far from resolution	5·81	20·21
	(46)	(115)
4. Not resolvable	0	0·40
	(0)	(2)
5. Not discussed	1·52	26·87
	(12)	(153)
	100·00	100·00
Total mentions with reference to conflict	(791)	(569)

Total books coded = 18 (Grade 3) and 20 (Grade 9)
Total paragraphs coded = 17 286 (Grade 3) and 29 244 (Grade 9)

"Resolved" or "Near Resolution". Not a single instance was described as not resolvable. At the ninth-grade level, even with the increased intensity of the conflict described, roughly half of the incidents are presented as resolved or near resolution. Only 20% seem unresponsive to normal societal processes. It is perhaps of interest that in one-quarter of the incidents or conditions, the question of whether the conflict was to be resolved was ignored (Table III).

In summary, these major issues and sources of national tension were rarely presented as occasions of conflict or difficulty, were often seen as relatively mild in intensity, and were largely capable of resolution by the processes of our social and political system. This type of socialization is orientated towards maintaining the *status quo*; it fails to recognize defects, much less attempt to deal with them[2].

Such a summary is obviously only a partial statement of the problem. It is easy to point an accusing research finger at what seems to be a distortion in textbooks; it is much more difficult to identify theories or evidence which would give reason to argue that they should be changed. Why should not the initial impression that a child gets of his country be that it is benign and that problems can be solved? What are the consequences to the child of a more complete disclosure at an early age of our malignancies? At this time we do not know.

The task of socialization is relatively simple in a society where the purpose is to persuade the young to accept the values and behaviour of adults. In a society which has severe conflict and stress, however, this simplistic process is not feasible as an educational policy. To maintain the *status quo* will also be to maintain and probably accentuate the internal stresses. What is needed, perhaps, is much more difficult—to help the young develop attachment to the institutions and political systems of the society, tolerate the ambiguities of dissent and disagreement (Weiler, 1972) and yet be able to help institutions change sufficiently to deal with or adapt to severe internal conflict.

Such an orientation requires a knowledge base to assist curricular

---

[2] This general picture of social studies materials is consistent with other research findings, and there has been some pressure from political scientists and specialists in social studies curricula for more realistic portrayals of both historic and contemporary problems of the United States (*Harvard Educational Review*, 1968; American Political Science Association, 1971). The principal arguments behind this viewpoint are; first, that the young become disillusioned when they discover that all is not as benign and ideal as the textbooks suggest, and second, that the present teaching often does not give the young citizen effective skills with which to deal with social problems. There is an additional argument with respect to the history of ethnic groups which deals with the nationalism, prejudice, and discrimination written into many representations of ethnic history and the treatment ethnic groups have received in the United States. This is a related problem, but the rationale is different and carries its own justification.

planning. At the present time, our information about the development of system-sustaining behaviour in children is grossly incomplete. We have some heuristic theories about how socialization functions to perpetuate existing systems but few about how the young can be taught to maintain and yet change a complex social order.

RESEARCH ISSUES IN DEVELOPING SOCIAL COMPETENCE

Much of the research on system-relevant behaviour which is now available has emerged in the last decade primarily through studies of political socialization (Easton and Dennis, 1969; Greenstein, 1965; Hess and Torney, 1967; Weiler, 1968). Most of these studies, many of which were conducted by political scientists and sociologists, have dealt with the emergence of norms and attitudes in political learning and the impact of socializing agents, such as the family and the school upon the emergence of attitudes toward political objects. Not only have these studies been concerned with normative data, they have for the most part been interpreted in sociological and political science terms. There has been insufficient attention paid to developmental patterns and to the processes by which behaviour is acquired.

Thus, in spite of the recent dramatic growth in the amount of research on political socialization, we know relatively little about children's attitudes toward social problems and defects of the society. In addition, many of the studies of political socialization were planned and conducted before the effects of the counter-culture, with its sensitivity to social issues and its attack on the establishment, became a significant movement in the United States. The growth of political protest movements in America and the popularity of openly anti-traditional and anti-authority figures are only indications of the extent to which political learning in pre-adults can no longer be explained by traditional models of socialization and indoctrination of the young into the values of the adult world.

Perhaps what is needed now to make this field more useful in the formulation of educational policy is a more systematic body of knowledge relevant to two questions. First, what processes are involved in the acquisition of system-relevant social behaviour? It is important to learn more about the age at which concepts about social issues are attainable and the sequences in which they develop. It is also essential to understand more about the ways in which social behaviour is acquired and what relationship, if any, social competence has to the growth of social concepts.

The processes by which orientation towards institutions and political systems is acquired is apparently related to developmental phases. On the basis of present knowledge, for example, children apparently become attached to social and political units long before they have a conceptual grasp of either the process or the objects of identification (Easton and Dennis, 1969; Hess and Torney, 1967; Zellman and Sears, 1971). In the United States, for example, regard for the flag, respect for country, response to the pledge of allegiance appear before clear concepts of government are present. That is, the process of national affiliation or attachment seems to be essentially non-cognitive or at least non-conceptual, in the usual sense of the term. It is an affective reaction, mediated largely by symbols rather than by understanding, informed choice or other processes in which the school presumably specializes. This type of early emergence of nationalism is obviously not confined to the United States (Tajfel, 1969).

Similarly, compliance with rules and laws appears to be learned in large part through conditioning, modelling, and other non-conceptual mediating operations (Brown, 1965). Thus, two of the most basic system-relevant behaviours—national loyalty and compliance with authority—are apparently acquired in extra-conceptual ways.

The selectiveness with which institutions filter the range and pattern of experience for the child also argues that transmission of social values is not essentially logical and that socialization is in many ways a non-conceptual and non-logical process. The ways in which the child learns attitudes towards the political system early in life are not educational so much as they are affectively indoctrinating and are thus not unlike the strategies described in *The making of a model citizen in communist China* (Ridley *et al.*, 1971). This makes the educational process in the early grades much more a mingling of ideas and information with affective value orientations than is commonly supposed, at least in American education, where the ability to make a decision, to reflect, to set objectives, to see all sides of a problem, seem to be encouraged not only in high school, but at earlier levels in the educational career.

The capability to comprehend the need for change, to make decisions and to work with others to take effective action, however, requires a more conceptual grasp of problems and an understanding of the different consequences of alternative solutions. In short, the need to be critical and to examine institutions and their faults calls upon different teaching and learning processes than those of earlier stages[3].

---

[3] Even these are not necessarily restricted to conceptual experience. There is perhaps a need to experience (ethnic) discrimination to understand it fully, and to know what it means to be a minority in some situation, in order to understand the social logic of the concept of minority rights. The processes, then, appear to include both affective and cerebral functions and experiences.

It is on these theoretical problems of cognitive readiness, sequence, and trainability that research is now needed. It may be, for example, that currently popular attempts to teach social science concepts in the early grades are not a productive use of time and may even interfere with the development of effective citizens.

A second research question grows out of the character of socializing networks. What are the special transactional features of socialization in a fractionated society?

If the stability of familiar institutions is threatened and they no longer provide a mutually supporting pattern of influences upon the young, what are the likely consequences for the young child? What changes in the traditional processes of socialization may be expected if there are multiple sources of influences which are not consistent with one another in the values and behaviour they present?

Perhaps a useful way to consider this problem is to contrast the conditions presented by two extreme situations: a closed, cohesive society and a pluralistic society characterized by divisiveness and conflict. The Amish, a religious sect scattered in rural and small-town residential areas of the United States provide a contemporary example of the first; the more open and diffuse character of American society an illustration of the second.

Institutions and reference groups govern socialization through at least two learning transactions. They provide models of desired behaviour and they control rewards, exert sanctions and in other ways establish reinforcement schedules that shape the behaviour of young members. Perhaps more importantly, there is consensus as to what should be regarded and modelled and what should not. The norms are explicit or at least understood.

The effectiveness of a socializing agent thus depends upon the degree to which influences such as these can be exerted and the child kept from alternative sources of influence, or such inputs can be neutralized. The sociological and the psychological literature both offer some general principles which may provide estimates of the effectiveness of socializing agents (Bronfenbrenner, 1970; Dornbush, 1955). Some of the most salient of these are:

1. The control of reinforcement and models for behaviour is centralized.
2. The modelling persons are seen as having high status and competence.
3. Institutions provide multiple models displaying similar behaviour.
4. The socializing agents or institutions support one another in explicating values and sanctioning behaviour.
5. Compliance with norms of the group have been observed to have

positive effects and noncompliance seen to have been negatively rewarded.

6. The roles of the members in the group are well defined so that sanctions for inappropriate behaviour can be readily applied; status and duties rather than personal feelings are treated with regard.

7. There is an age–grade system of status which defers privileges and rewards and maximizes the importance of future roles and status.

As a socializing group, the Amish fulfil almost all of these conditions. The "closed" nature of the society is based not upon authoritarian sternness but upon the effectiveness of the system in establishing those conditions under which indoctrination of the young will take place (Hostetler and Huntington, 1971). The threat to this process in its initial form is not noncompliance but alliances with persons outside the group. The hazard of military service for their young men, then, was not only in its violation of religious beliefs. It presented an opportunity for members of the group to see alternatives they had not been aware of before. So long as the external (non-Amish) world could be defined in negative terms, the influence of news media and other impersonal sources was more readily controlled and neutralized. Personal friendships, however, and direct experience repeated over time, as in military service conditions, were a much more substantial breach of the cohesiveness of the group. This suggests that analysis of the impact of fractionation might be traced through personal friendship patterns and that models may be chosen on a sociometric basis.

The consequences of multiple non-congruent socializing groups follow in part from the diffusion of rewards and models that a pluralistic and conflictful society presents to the young. From the most simplistic point of view, a multiple and inconsistent set of reinforcing and modelling conditions will diminish the forcefulness of any given learning experience. The focus will be less intense, the learning experience less likely to be repeated and emphasized by redundancy. Predictions of negative consequences of non-compliance will be less certain and risk-taking to achieve short-term alternative gratifications likely to increase. The social control of internalized norms will be greatly diminished under fractionated conditions.

There is also a cognitive component that may be under-estimated. The child in an Amish-like society does not easily consider the possibility that there are alternative legitimate norms for many areas of behaviour. The child in a fractionated and fractious society becomes aware that alternatives exist and that reference groups are available to support and reward behaviour which for another group would be non-normative. This is a profound difference in perspective; evaluations of actions become relativistic and temporary. The experience of discarding one set of norms for another is always a possibility and the punitive consequences of non-normative behaviour are likely not to be seen as severe.

A basic research question that grows out of these socializing conditions has to do with the factors which determine which models and reference groups are selected in multiple choice situations. Little is known about the effects upon the child when faced with models of dissimilar and conflicting behaviour, all of which are rewarded.

There seems to be some tendency to imitate peers in preference to adults in non-conflict multiple model presentations (Grosser *et al.*, 1951) but data on this point are very scarce. The familiar criteria for selecting models—competence, status, credibility—do not easily explain why youth should turn to peers for models and rewards, unless there is a credibility of mutual experience and a shared disillusionment with the establishment that validates their own inner experiences.

It seems apparent that the authors of social studies textbooks in the United States have a nearly impossible task. Quite apart from the practical and political constraints from textbook adoption groups and local community organizations, there is astonishingly little in the psychological literature to assist them in designing a more suitable curriculum. In any case, the school cannot pursue a programme of politically relevant learning which the community does not accept; its effectiveness will be mitigated by competing sources of gratification and reward.

With so little evidence at hand, speculation is tempting. It is possible that the child needs to form attachments to institutions or a national political image in order to develop competence as a citizen even though these allegiances may be modified later? Does the development of a sense of nationalism or affiliation with a social institution serve identity needs? If so, the authors of the textbooks may be essentially on the right track.

It might be argued that even if the initial stage of the development of social competence is attachment to a national system and its institutions, there may be more effective ways to go about the process than to offer only images of a conflict-free and benign society. Certainly it seems sensible that in middle and secondary school years, it may be possible to bring the young into a better understanding of the problems which institutions face and the degree to which they need support from citizens. It would be reasonable, perhaps to present a picture of institutions as more dynamic, more adaptable to change and to emerging needs and as instruments to help solve social problems rather than portray them either as faultless or depict them as the origins of our national troubles.

Perhaps both processes need more careful attention. The development of an attachment to the society and its institutions through the non-conceptual routes in order to provide an affective base and more effective techniques to help the child comprehend the importance of institutions, the nature of their problem and the ways in which they can be helped to adapt usefully to deal with social transition and change.

REFERENCES

AMERICAN POLITICAL SCIENCE ASSOCIATION. 1971. Committee on Pre-Collegiate Education Report, *Political education in the public schools: the challenge for political science.* American Political Science Association, Washington, D.C.

BARRY, H., CHILD, I. L. and BACON, M. K. 1959. Relation of child training to subsistence economy. *American Anthropologist,* **61,** 51–63.

BRONFENBRENNER, U. 1970. *Two worlds of childhood: U.S. and U.S.S.R.* Russel Sage Foundation, New York.

BROWN, R. 1965. *Social psychology.* The Free Press, New York.

COUNTS, G. S. and LODGE, N. P. 1947. *I want to be like Stalin.* John Day, New York. Russian pedagogy by B. T. Yesipov and N. K. Goncharov.

DENNIS, J. 1968. Major problems of political socialisation research. *Midwest J. Polit. Sci.,* **12,** 85–114.

DORNBUSH, S. 1955. The military academy as an assimilating institution. *Social Forces,* **33,** 316–321.

EASTON, D. and DENNIS, J. 1969. *Children in the political system: origin of political legitimacy.* McGraw-Hill, New York.

GREENSTEIN, F. I. 1965. *Children and politics.* Yale University Press, New Haven.

GROSSER, D., POLANSKY, N. and LIPPITT, R. 1951. A laboratory study of behavioral contagion, Human Relations, IV. In U. Bronfenbrenner, *Two worlds of childhood: U.S. and U.S.S.R.* 1970. Russel Sage Foundation, New York.

HARVARD EDUCATIANAL REVIEW. 1968. **38,** No. 3, Summer 1968.

HAUSER, P. M. 1959. The chaotic society: product of the social morphological revolution. *Amer. Sociol. Rev.* **34,** 1–19.

HESS, R. D. and TORNEY, J. V. 1967. *The development of political attitudes in children.* Aldine, Chicago.

HOSTETLER, J. A. and HUNTINGTON, G. E. 1971. *Children in Amish society: socialization and community education.* Holt, Rinehart and Winston, New York.

McKINLEY, D. G. 1964. *Social class and family life.* The Free Press, New York.

OREGON STATE BAR. 1968. *The flag salute cases. Liberty and the law: case studies in the bill of rights.* Prentice-Hall, Englewood Cliffs.

RIDLEY, P., GODWIN, P. H. B. and DOOLIN, D. J. 1971. *The making of a model citizen in Communist China.* Hoover Institution Press, Stanford.

ROSZAK, T. 1969. *The making of a counter culture.* Doubleday, New York.

TAJFEL, H. 1969. The formation of national attitudes: a social psychological perspective. In M. Sherif and C. W. Sherif (Eds.), *Interdisciplinary relationships in the social sciences.* Aldine, Chicago.

VICKERS, G. 1970. *Freedom in a rocking boat.* Hazell, Watson and Viney, London.

WEILER, H. N. 1968. Education and political development. *Rev. Educ. Res.,* **37,** No. 3.

WEILER, H. N. 1972. Learning to tolerate dissent. In M. Kirst (Ed.), *State school and politics*. Heath, Lexington.

ZELLMAN, G. L. and SEARS, D. O. 1971. Childhood origins of tolerance for dissent. *J. Soc. Issues*, **27**, No. 2, 109–136.

Implications and Applications

Problems of Marrying Research with Clinical and Social Needs[1]

JOHN BOWLBY

Tavistock Centre

SOCIAL AND BEHAVIOURAL scientists working in academic settings are often dissatisfied with a role in which their research is divorced from application. On the one hand, they find themselves open to criticism— from outsiders, their own students and sometimes themselves—that their research is ivory tower. On the other, they find themselves frustrated both that they are not given access to problems they think should be studied and also that findings they believe of practical value are ignored. Since my colleagues and I at the Tavistock Clinic and Tavistock Institute of Human Relations have regarded these problems as central to our task, and not merely as peripheral irritants, we have given much thought as to how they can be solved.

The strategy we have adopted is modelled closely on one that has had considerable success in the medical field. It embraces two principles. The first is that research projects should spring from opportunities to collaborate in the solution of actual social problems. The second is that projects should be conducted by researchers committed in a professional role to assist those concerned. This strategy has a number of great advantages though it is bought at a price.

[1] The Tavistock Clinic and Tavistock Institute of Human Relations are sister organizations. The Clinic dates from 1920 and is concerned with the provision of psychotherapy and counselling for patients of all ages and their families, and also with related research and training. Since 1948 it has been part of the National Health Service. The Institute dates from 1946 and is incorporated (as a company limited by guarantee and not for profit) to study human relations in conditions of well-being, conflict or breakdown, in the family, the work group and the larger organization. It sets out to combine research in the social and psychological sciences with professional practice. Much of the present text is drawn from a policy document of the Institute which describes the principles of research that the Institute has adopted.

Amongst the advantages there are two principal ones. By enlisting the active cooperation of those studied, the method not only facilitates access to relevant data but makes more probable the further testing of findings and concepts that can only be achieved through application in real-life settings.

Human beings, whether individuals, families or larger groups, do not like to be intimately scrutinized. They tend to mistrust the purposes to which information about them may be put. Often, therefore, they are unwilling to provide a researcher with access to crucial data about themselves. When, however, they believe that we may be able to help them solve a problem that concerns them, and that he will certainly do so if he can, they are more willing to provide him with opportunities. There is a resemblance here to the understanding between clinician and patient which enters into medical research. Many investigations necessary to advance physiology and pathology are permitted by the individuals investigated only because, as medical patients, they are assured of treatment. In psychological and social research the need for the subject's active collaboration is greater, since many of the relevant data concern his feelings and motives and these are often in conflict and only partly conscious; they tend, in consequence, to be heavily guarded. Only in discussion with a researcher who is well known and trusted are such feelings and motives likely to become understood and communicated.

Because most individuals and groups are relatively set in their ways it must be expected that the findings of social research will frequently be disregarded. This may be irksome to the researcher, who is all too apt to react in a selfrighteous way with allegations of stupidity and blind conservatism. This is mistaken. First, none of us welcomes unasked for advice. Secondly, the practical man is often bombarded with findings which he does not fully understand and some of which are contradictory. He would be most unwise to act until he has had a chance to scrutinize and ensure for himself that the researcher has addressed himself to real problems and has solutions that can be applied in real life. The advantage of the research approach now recommended is that, when an inquiry is initiated wholly or in part by the individuals of the social groups concerned, they can insist that real problems are studied and relevant data gathered. They can also help both in finding solutions and in overcoming obstacles to their application. Within this context application of findings is made much more likely.

Furthermore, given this collaborative relationship, the researcher may become able to observe over a period of time how the functioning of a social group is affected after planned-for changes have been made in its structure and so discover whether the expected improvements actually occur. Although it is difficult to control the many relevant variables so that a project can fully meet the requirements of a rigorous scientific experiment, it is nevertheless, by proceeding in this way that the social scientist can come closest to exploiting methods which in the physical and biological sciences have proved a key to progress.

Among other advantages of the approach are that it encourages inter-disciplinary thinking, puts a premium on empirically based theory and promotes a responsible outlook in the researchers engaged.

Every academic discipline tends towards insularity. Not only is there the inevitable empire building but to bridge disciplines is hard work: assumptions, ways of thinking, theory and methods are all different. When, however, research is organized with a view to solving practical problems there is pressure to draw on the skills and concepts of any discipline that seems likely to be useful for the task in hand. In that way researchers of different backgrounds find themselves working on a single problem, mutual respect and friendships have a chance to grow and disciplinary barriers may be crossed.

For the same reasons a premium is placed on theory that is empirically based and of practical application; conversely, the construction of theoretical models remote from real life, always a temptation in the absence of practical pressures, is discouraged.

Once a social researcher undertakes a collaborative study aimed not only to solve a specific problem but to increase the capability of clients to recognize and solve their own problems, it is necessary for him to develop and maintain professional standards similar to those followed by all professional groups in preserving relationships with clients. These standards include constant regard for the client's interests and respect for any wishes he may have that information be kept confidential. Since this is a matter about which there is always a measure of conflict, and very often serious misunderstanding, it deserves discussion.

Scientific method requires that data be presented fully and accurately. Professional confidence often requires that data of great relevance be kept confidential. How is this dilemma to be resolved? Sometimes it is fairly easy, often it is difficult, and occasionally no resolution is possible.

There are two separate reasons why it may be necessary for data to remain unpublished. One is the client's fear that some of the information is to his discredit and that it will not be possible to disguise his identity. Sometimes disguise can be achieved without too much sacrifice of relevant data; but in the case of a large and well-known firm or institution, or the family of a behavioural scientist well known in his profession, this may be extremely difficult.

The second reason why publication may prove impossible is that the nature of the problems that come to light may be such that the organization and individuals in it may find themselves unwilling to accept the truth as the researchers find it, and may demand that the investigation be dropped and even that findings be destroyed. A situation of this sort is extremely painful for both parties. The researcher feels he has wasted his time and that science is not served; the client feels that the researcher has busied himself with issues that were none of his business and which, in any case, the client believes are irrelevant to the limited problem the researcher was asked to investigate. A dilemma of this kind is fairly common in medical practice. A patient consults his doctor about some apparently trivial symptom which turns out on investigation to be in all likelihood part of a serious condition. The doctor indicates his concern and advises further investigation of a kind that the patient regards as drastic and absurdly unnecessary. The patient then seeks other advice. Thus, what has promised to be a most interesting clinical enquiry is brought to a premature end.

Medical tradition had accepted that a patient has an absolute right to end an investigation, and a clinical researcher is trained, albeit reluctantly, to accept the limitations entailed. My colleagues and I at the Tavistock have tried to ensure that the same standards are applied in the field of social research—troublesome and exasperating though it may sometimes be. The reasons are simple. First, respect for other people demands it. Secondly, unless this respect is given, and given honestly, potential clients will not trust us and will not give us opportunity to carry out the investigations the progress of our science demands.

To adopt a research strategy of the kind outlined exacts a high price. First, the researcher is confined to those projects that clients are willing to collaborate in, which are unlikely to be exactly what he would specify if given the choice. Secondly, the variables influencing a real life situation are inconveniently numerous and difficult to measure or even to identify accurately. Thirdly, a very great deal of time, and above all, patience is required to obtain all the necessary permissions before starting, to achieve a mutually trusting partnership, to work through unwelcome findings, even to agree what the findings really amount to, and finally to agree to a form of publication which both respects confidentiality and is scientifically honest.

Further disadvantages are that projects of this kind are unlikely to conform to the neat lines usually required by research councils and foundations before they will give support, nor to give opportunity for young inexperienced graduates to undertake a limited project for purposes of a Ph.D.

Finally, there is a problem of scientific integrity. A scientist who has sought to influence policy, has taken part in public debate and has become identified with a particular point of view may find it especially difficult to step back from the heat of public controversy to consider the issues afresh in the light of new and perhaps uncongenial evidence.

In view of the difficulties inherent in adopting the strategy described it is evident that it could never be the only strategy to be pursued by social scientists. In both the physical sciences and the biological and medical sciences it has been found useful for research to be conducted at many levels, from that of pure science, which usually flourishes best in an academic setting, to applied research which requires a more task-orientated one. It is not for nothing that a very large fraction of all medical research is undertaken within the twin organization of medical school and teaching hospital, the one an academic and the other a service institution, nor that many of the scientists themselves undertake professional responsibility for the care of patients. It is a pattern of this kind, I believe, that should be aimed at by social and behavioural scientists who are eager that their research be directed towards meeting social needs.

Competence: the Growth of the Person[1]

JEROME BRUNER

University of Oxford

KEVIN CONNOLLY

University of Sheffield

To summarize adequately and succinctly all of the discussions and papers presented to the Study Group is not really possible. As a postscript therefore all that one can in effect do is to highlight and emphasize a few of the major points which emerged. Because of the inevitable selectivity of a postscript it must necessarily reflect the biased attention of the two chairmen and it should be treated as such. All of which is to say that what follows as the tailpiece is not so much a consensus as a rather more personal reaction.

What struck us first is that the study of early competence forces one to a renewed consideration of the functions of immaturity in the life cycle of the organism. This conclusion comes in an age of structuralist analysis, in which there have been many searching studies about the underlying structure of thought and logic and of perception, often in neglect of the kind of functional analysis that must be a part of any biologically based approach to understanding man. In various papers, the question arose of how one may best "manage" the period of immaturity, how shall it be used to equip the growing child with the where-withal in skills to get on in a complex culture. One is faced immediately not only with the task of analysing how in fact the period of immaturity is used in different species of the primate order, but (in the case of man) how one *should* use it. For it is characteristic of man that he in fact must create the patterns of behaviour that suit the very environmental conditions which he has also created. Man lives in a man-made world by

---

[1] Some of the points made in this final chapter are based on remarks made to the Group by Mrs. Barbara Finberg who kindly put her notes at our disposal.

shaping behaviour appropriate to it, or if not shaping it, predisposing it in certain ways.

In this important sense, the study of development involves what has been called "the sciences of the artificial"—constructing models and modes of operation. Once one takes this charge seriously, descriptive science very rapidly becomes normative or prescriptive. The study of development is then, perforce, a policy science, concerning itself with assessing the feasibility of goals in growth and the value of the various possible means for achieving such goals. It is in this sense that one comes eventually to the conclusion that there is really no clear division between the *study* of development *per se* and the *nurturing* of development. The developmental scientist by a slight change of perspective becomes the pedagogical theorist, then the experimental student of pedagogical strategies, and then moves back again to the description of what his strategies have wrought. But insofar as these strategies are in themselves as much part of the culture as any other, equally man-made traditional approach to pedagogy, the line between "studying" and "changing" a phenomenon is indeed obscure. And we rather sensed that most of the members of the study group felt that one might as well rest content with the inevitable mix of "policy" and "pure" science so characteristic of the study of competence.

This is not to say that it was the sense of the meeting that there were no biological constraints on the way in which human beings, in growing, could adapt to the environment, or that there were no constraints on the kinds of environments to which they could adjust. Plainly, there are needs and aptitudes and biological constraints on man adapting. Repeatedly, the dependence of the growing child on the social group intruded itself with the proper insistence of a biological theme. Repeatedly, we were reminded of the fact that in the deepest biological sense higher skills depend upon the acquisition and orchestrating of previously mastered constituent skills. And repeatedly, the crucial role of intention, idea, hope (or whatever the term), came up with the same biological urgency as crucial in the impulsion of intellectual effort in behalf of achieving skill. There are many invariant features in human growth, though the wide variety of means through which they achieve realization give ample room for the shaping of culture. Competence involves the development and empowering of functional systems—and if one takes this with due seriousness, the task is to find ways of increasing competence by using the intrinsic nature of the functional systems on which it is based. Just as with nutritional support of growth, there are many ways of assuring a balanced diet, each reflecting local conditions. But the underlying issue is how to assure that balance.

There was much discussion, as one might expect in these times, of the impact on growth of poverty, dispossession and the sense of powerlessness. Poverty does have significant effects on children and although less than 20% of the American people, for example, are reported to now have incomes below the poverty line, more than 25% of all children live in families with incomes below this level. Various of the contributions in the symposium shed new light on this technically difficult and politically tumultuous topic. No official "position" was taken. There probably is no single "position" that would serve to deal with the variety of the impact made by poverty and powerlessness on the life of growing children. But several things were clear in discussion and should be marked in our postscript. One was that it is plainly inaccurate and misleading as well as unprofitable to think of poverty and its impact as a form of impoverishment or deprivation, a kind of "avitaminosis" of culture. Rather, human beings in tough surroundings having to make do with a high chance of failure, adapt ways of covering themselves, trimming aspirations to a point where they protect against disappointment and further setback. Indeed, where poverty has been incorporated into a subculture for several generations, the very forms for protection against over-aspiring are built into the thought ways and transmitted. The experience of the last decades indicate that these adjustments do not change easily, but on the other hand there is nothing to support the view that the "culture of poverty" is irreversible or virtually so. It was plain in our own discussions, as in much informed contemporary public debate, that programmes of action in behalf of the young caught in the poverty cycle could not be simply "cognitive" or "skill orientated", much of the problem has to do with how one instills a feeling of being in control of one's own destiny, rather than feeling a victim. Further, we thought that the achievement of such a transformation would require not only psychological measures but also social, economic and political measures as well.

Could one conceivably stand clear of the great debates on these issues in our times? One of the members of the Study Group remarked that to stand clear was to take a stand—a stand for whatever was in process of being done. Social responsibility where the developmental scientist is concerned is not a choice. It is forced upon one. *How* one exercises this responsibility was a question which led to intense debate. In some of the sessions, the issue arose as to whether we were not trying to foist our technical conclusions about "optimizing competence" on to those whom we regarded as less competent than they "ought" to be. But by what right do we prescribe cures for whatever violates our definition of effectiveness? It became readily apparent that there is much which needs detailed examination and discussion in the realm of "strategies of social change", strategies which are compatible with the principles of a democratic society. Yet, as some members properly insisted, one cannot abide by a total voluntarism; Mills' reflections on the nature of liberty are just as valid a century and a half later as when first written. How can one prescribe a "minimum" competence below which no citizen can be permitted to fall lest it endanger the State, much as smallpox endangers the health of the community? These are issues which, in the light of the contemporary conditions of our technological society, are no longer "academic" or "philosophical" as they were (or were presumed to be) in the rhetoric of eighteenth century social philosophy. Worries concerning the extent and quality of our knowledge about the requirements for optimizing a child's growth and emergence as a whole and healthy person able to adapt to and develop his society were also aired. Without doubt much remains to be discovered and understood about the many faceted process of development, both biological and social. But we cannot sit back and wait until our knowledge is complete before offering our skills in the formulation of policy. For one thing our knowledge never will be complete since the burden of the concept of evolution is that the human species, like every other, exists in a fragile dynamic equilibrium. And what is more, if we withold our advice and research findings this will not stop policies being formulated, they will be made without whatever benefits our knowledge might contribute.

On the practical side of assuring the competence of the young, two matters intruded themselves persistently. One had to do with the changing structure of the family as the principal support system of the young. The feeling was widespread, though not universally shared in our group, that the crisis of the modern family—evidenced by increased working away from the home by the mother, by the economic pressures on the family, by the sheer ecology of the isolated urban family—that this crisis posed problems new to society. For example, in the United States, 50% of mothers with children below the age of 17 are now in the labour force, including 30% of those mothers who have children under the age of 5. Does one therefore attempt at this point in history to return to the classic (if indeed there is a classic) pattern for the family, assuring that mother is free enough either of social or economic pressures to give full attention to the growing young? Or had one best consider the signs of our times, readable in every social census, to indicate that there is something fundamentally in process of change, arguing for new inventiveness in providing support for the young. [Here too we must remember the changing role of women in developed societies. Gunnar Myrdal in 1944 pointed out that women suffer the social degradation of racial and religious minorities in some parts of the world but the signs for change though small are real and clear—women are about improving their lot.] There was not consensus in the Study Group, but there was a sense that it would be foolhardy to rule out the second possibility. We are possibly approaching, then, a new period in world history where we shall have to think how to give aid and support to the family, to the child through other supportive institutions as well, and in so doing, we shall have to think afresh what kind of human beings we want. How to use the years of growth for instilling the requisite forms of competence.

The second persistent matter was the school. It has become plain that it can no longer be taken as the major vehicle for solving the problem of how to instil skills and competence in the young. The school, rather, is itself part of the problem. Many of the most divisive and disrupting features of adult society are already to be found in the "informal" curriculum of schools as social institutions. Just as the family is in need of deep rethinking, so too is the school. How does it relate to the sense of vocation, a system of schooling that removes the child from contact with the economic structure of the "real world"? How can it bring to the child an understanding of what it takes to reshape and renew the society to meet the swift pace of change? These are only a few of the matters that must concern any close observer of schooling in the developed world as we approach the last quarter of the twentieth century.

The concluding chapter to a volume such as this should probably not end on a note of cautious pessimism. But in honesty we must. There is no reason to believe that at the present time research is organized appropriately to provide knowledge on these crucial matters. Nor indeed, even if it were, that there are the kinds of planning and action agencies that could use the knowledge to implement the necessary programmes for ensuring new generations of hopeful, competent, and assured human beings. Interdisciplinary cooperation and research are crucial and must be mounted in a more thoroughgoing way than before, for without this we are likely to continue to perceive the separate but unequal attributes of the elephant. Also the research scientist and the professional who implements policy must along with the policy maker consider the inter-relation and inter-dependence of their roles. What each of these levels in the scheme of things has to offer must be carefully orchestrated one with another. Finally let us remember that knowledge is not something which we acquire for its own sake but in the service of mankind.

Author Index

Numbers in *italics* refer to the pages on which references are listed at the end of each chapter

---

A

Aiello, J. R., 266, *280*
Ainsworth, M. D. S., 52, *70*, 104, 110, 111, 112, *115*, *116*, *117*, *118*, 119, *130*, 189, *192*
Altman, J., 21, *45*
American Political Science Association, 292, *298*
Annett, J., 138, *167*
Argyle, M., 265, *280*
Aronson, E., 122, *130*
Austin, G. A., 39, *45*

B

Bacon, M. K., 286, *298*
Barry, H., 286, *298*
Barsh, R., 27, *45*
Bartlett, F. C., 39, *45*
Bass, M. H., 266, *280*
Baxter, J. C., 266, *280*
Beach, F., 16, *45*
Bear, R. M., 218, *219*
Beckwith, L., 108, *117*
Bee, H. L., 184, *192*
Bell, S. M., 99, 102, 104, 105, 109, 110, 111, 112, *115*, *117*, 118, 124, *130*, 189, *192*
Bellugi, U., 78, 83, *93*, 198, 199, 200, 202, 214, *218*, *219*, *220*
Benchley, B., 67, *70*
Bennett, E. L., 21, *45*
Bentham, J., 42, 45
Bereiter, C., 201, *218*
Berger, P. L., 120, *130*
Berlin, I., 31, *45*

Bernal, J. F., 119, 122, 128, *130*, *131*
Bernstein, B. B., 228, *236*
Bernstein, I. S., 266, *280*
Bernstein, N. A., 20, *45*, 138, 139, 145, *167*, 169, 185, 192, *192*, 205, *219*
Bernuth, H. V., 121, *131*
Bever, T. G., 224, *226*
Birch, H. G., 26, *45*
Bishop, A., 20, *45*
Bishop, N., 15, 17, 18, 21, 22, 24, 33, *46*
Bissell, J. S., 215, *219*
Block, S. C., 35, *45*
Bloom, B., 14, *45*
Bloom, L. M., 77, *93*, 203, *219*
Blurton Jones, N., 127, *130*
Bodkin, P. T., 207, *219*
Booth, A. M., 51, *70*
Bosema, J. F., 135, *167*
Bower, T. G. R., 50, *70*
Bowlby, J., 38, *45*, 97, 108, *116*, 119, *130*
Braine, M. D. S., 61, *70*
Bronfenbrenner, U., 41, *45*, 287, 295, *298*
Brophy, J. E., 218, *219*
Brown, A. L., 61, *70*
Brown, R., 36, *45*, 78, *93*, 198, 199, 200, 205, 214, *219*, 294, *298*
Bronowski, J., 83, *93*
Bruner, J. S., 25, 28, 31, 34, 36, 39, *45*, *46*, 50, *70*, 136, 139, 145, 166, *167*, *168*, 169, 170, 185, *192*, 201, 205, *219*
Bryan, W. L., 144, *167*
Bryant, P. E., 182, *192*
Bühler, K., 36, *45*
Burridge, 29

315

H

Haggstrom, W., *193*
Hall, E. T., 265, *280*
Hall, K. R. L., 16, 28, 48, *46*
Hamburg, D., 17, 18, *46*
Hanson, N. R., 182, *193*
Harlow, H. F., 15, *46*, 54, 55, 60, 61, *71*
Harlow, M. K., 15, *46*, 55, 60, 61, *71*
Harsh, C. M., 18, *46*
Harter, N., 144, *167*
Harvard Educational Review, 292, *298*
Hauser, P. M., 284, *298*
Hayes, C., 17, 28, *46*, 53, 55, 60, *71*
Hayes, K. J., 17, 28, *46*, 61, 66, *71*
Hediger, H., 265, *280*
Heider, E. R., 207, *219*
Hein, A., 138, *167*
Held, R., 138, *167*
Herbert, M. J., 18, *46*
Hess, R. D., 5, *1*, 184, *193*, 218, *219*, 287, 293, 294, *298*
Hinde, R. A., 14, 28, 31, *46*, 54, 55, 59, 61, 62, 64, 66, *71*, *73*
Hockett, C. D., 34, *46*
Hogan, R., 104, *116*
Holst, E., von, 138, *167*
Holt, K. S., 143, *167*
Horner, V. N., 199, *219*
Hostetler, J. A., 296, *298*
Howell, F. C., 12, 35, *48*
Hull, C. L., 137, *167*
Humboldt, W., von, 37, *46*
Hunkeler, P., 60, *73*
Huntington, G. E., 296, *298*
Hutt, C., 121, *131*, 257, *264*
Hutt, S. J., 121, *131*
Hymes, D., 205, 206, *220*

I

Illingworth, 64
Inhelder, B., 124, 125, *131*
Ipsen, J., 123, *131*
Itani, J., 14, 18, 29, *46*, 51, *71*

J

James, J. W., 267, *280*
Jarvis, P. E., 207, *219*
Jensen, 64
John, V. P., 207, 211, 212, 213, *220*
Jolly, A., 14, *46*, 59, *71*

Jones, S. E., 266, *280*
Jooij, M., 25, *47*
Joseph, A., 199, 218, *221*, 229, *237*
Joslin, 24
Jusczyk, P., 121, *130*

K

Kagan, J., 50, *71*
Kaplan, B., 35, *48*
Kapune, T., 61, *71*
Kaufman, I. C., 266, *281*
Kawai, M., 274, *280*
Kawamura, S., 18, 28, 29, *46*, 51, *71*
Kay, H., 138, *167*
Keats, S., 143, *167*
Kellogg, L. A., 25, 55, *72*
Kellogg, W. N., 25, 55, *72*
Kennell, J. H., 121, *131*
Khroustov, G. F., 27, *47*
King, D. L., 32, *47*
King, M. G., 266, *280*
King, R. D., 228, *237*
Klaus, M. H., 121, *131*
Klaus, R., *193*
Klima, E. S., 202, *220*
Klopper, M. S., 56, *72*
Klopper, P. H., 56, *72*
Knobloch, H., 66, 67, 68, *72*
Koff, E., 200, 201, *220*
Kohlberg, L., 204, *220*
Köhler, W., 17, 18, 24, 25, 26, 27, *47*, 60, *72*
Kohts, N., 55, *72*
Konner, M. J., 127, *131*
Korner, A. F., 122, *131*
Kortland, A., 25, *47*
Koslowski, B., 25, *45*, 170, *192*
Kramer, P., 200, 201, *220*
Krauss, R. M., 207, 208, *220*
Krech, D., *45*
Kron, R. E., 123, *131*
Kummer, H., 91, *93*

L

Labor, U.S. Department of, 6, 7
Labov, W., 188, *193*
Laguna, G. A., de, 35, *47*
Lancaster, J. B., 21, 22, *47*
Landsmeer, J. M. F., 140, *167*

Subject Index

A

Action patterns, 247, 254, 258
  gestural, 301
Acts, 166, 170
  sequencing of, 137, 138, 139, 170
  voluntary, 137
Adaptation to environment, 3, 11, 12, 310
Adaptive complex of behaviour, 50–51
  in neonates,
Alienation, 41
Attachment, 50, 110, 112, 116, 119–120, 124, 246
  index of, 52
  infant-mother, 53, 99, 106, 109, 112
Attachment—exploration balance, 112
Attention, 36–39, 139
  of neonates, 121, 122
  span, 50
Attentional capacity and skill, 144
Attentional structure and primate bond, 15
Awareness,
  conscious, 225
  focal, 197
  subsidiary, 197

B

Baboons, 16, 20, 27, 54
  development of, 62–63
Behaviour,
  affiliative, 253
  agonistic, 253, 255, 263
  investigatory, 257
Bimanual co-ordination, development of, 144–164
Boiled egg problem, 139–140

Brain,
  size, 21
  volume, 12

C

Childhood, tasks of, 4
Chimpanzees, 15–30, 51, 54, 55, 60, 61
  communication in, 75–93
  curiosity, 91
  development of, 62–68
  dominance system, 91, 92
  exploration, 91
  language,
    Sarah, 85–89
    Washoe, 35, 60, 76–85
      combinations of signs, 77
      conceptual relations, 81
      errors in signing, 78
      questions, 83, 84
      redundancy, 82
      semantics, 85
      sentence structure, 83
  neonate, 57, 59
  play, 22–24, 91
  prehension, 65
  social interaction, 91
  tool use, 21, 22, 24, 60
Cognition, 97
  achievement and intelligence, 184
  competence, 169–192
  development, 204
  mother infant relationship, importance in relation to, 115, 123
  origins in infancy, 124
  play level of in relation to, 112
  preschool experience and growth, 191–192